HAWKE'S LAW
THE POLITICS OF MINING AND ABORIGINAL LAND RIGHTS IN AUSTRALIA

ALSO BY THE AUTHOR:
Toward an Africanized US Policy for Southern Africa
The Politics of Economic Power in Southern Africa

*To Kathy and Kathleen
who loved Australia*

Hawke's Law

THE POLITICS OF MINING AND ABORIGINAL LAND RIGHTS IN AUSTRALIA

by

RONALD T. LIBBY

The Pennsylvania State University Press
University Park, Pennsylvania

Copyright © 1989 by Ronald T. Libby

First published in 1989
by the University of Western Australia Press

Published in the United States of America
in 1992 by The Pennsylvania State University Press,
Suite C, 820 North University Drive, University Park, PA 16802

Library of Congress Cataloging-in-Publication Data

Libby, Ronald T.
  Hawke's law: the politics of mining and aboriginal land rights in
    Australia / by Ronald T. Libby.
    p.   cm.
  First published in 1989 by the University of Western Australia
    Press, Nedlands, Western Australia.
  Includes bibliographical references and index.
  ISBN 0-271-00835-0

  1. Australian aborigines—Land tenure. 2. Australian aborigines—
Mines and mining—Law and legislation. 3. Australian aborigines—
Politics and government. 4. Mineral industries—Australia.
5. Australia—Politics and government. I. Title.
GN666.L53 1992
333.2'0994—dc20   91-33979
                                                                                             CIP

Contents

Foreword   vii

Foreword to the American Edition   xi

Preface   xix

List of Abbreviations   xxii

Introduction   xxiii

CHAPTER ONE
Factional Politics and Land Rights Ideology   1

CHAPTER TWO
The Federal Initiative   19

CHAPTER THREE
The Breakdown in Initiative   37

CHAPTER FOUR
The Mining Industry Campaign in Western Australia   55

CHAPTER FIVE
The Liberal Party Challenge to Premier Brian Burke   85

CHAPTER SIX
AMIC's Offensive and the Aboriginal Counter-offensive   115

Conclusion   147

Epilogue   154

Notes   156

References   164

Index   171

LIST OF MAPS, FIGURES, AND TABLES

MAPS

1	Aboriginal Land and Mineral Deposits: Australia	xxiv
2	Aboriginal Land in Australia	xxvi
3	W. A. Land Tenure	68
4	Federal Land Rights Proposal: Australia	136
5	Federal Land Rights Proposal for Western Australia	137
6	Federal Land Rights Proposal for the Northern Territory	138

FIGURES

Chamber of Mines of Western Australia's newspaper and television advertisements used in the campaign against land rights legislation	70, 71, 77-79

TABLES

I	Issues to Consider in Land Rights Bill (National Aboriginal Conference State Papers)	25
II	Federal Principles for State and Territory Land Rights Legislation	44
III	Aboriginal Electoral Areas and Voting Swing	47
IV	Evaluating the Impact of the Western Australia Chamber of Mines Advertising Campaign	74
V	Evaluation of Public Attitudes on Aboriginal Land Rights in Western Australia	82
VI	Support for Granting Land Rights in Western Australia	83
VII	Distribution of Seats in the Legislative Assembly by Party Before and After the 1983 Election	89
VIII	Distribution of Labor Seats Gained in 1983 by Electoral Zone	90
IX	Comparative Advantage of the Labor and Liberal Parties in Western Australia between June and October 1985	91
X	Land Rights in Bunbury and Mitchell, Basic Attitudes and Why	93
XI	Land Rights in Mundaring, Joondalup, and Mitchell, Basic Attitudes and Why	93
XII	Reaction to the Defeat of the Land Rights Bill in the Legislative Council	94
XIII	Preferred Action for the State Government on Land Rights	94
XIV	Decline in Exploration Expenditure in the Northern Territory	119
XV	Mining Exploration in Australia	127
XVI	Private Exploration Expenditure: Australia	128
XVII	Northern Territory Shares of Expenditure on Exploration for Different Minerals and Groups of Minerals, 1982–1983 and 1983–1984	141

Foreword

On the surface, *Hawke's Law* deals with a subject primarily of interest to students of Australian politics, namely the politics of Aboriginal land rights, Yet in fact Ronald Libby's study has much broader implications. For a student of business-government relations in America such as myself, it demonstrates a number of striking similarities between the contemporary politics of business in both countries. Equally importantly, it suggests the emergence of a common intellectual framework for studying and analyzing the political activity and influence of business in advanced industrial societies.

Over the last two decades, most democratic industrialized nations have seen the emergence of a new political contituency. This constituency consists largely of relatively prosperous and well-educated middle-class individuals who are interested in 'social' issues such as environmentalism and the welfare of racial and ethnic minorities. These symbolic or idea-based interest groups have emerged as a major source of political opposition to business, supplementing, and to some extent competing with, the role historically played by the trade-union movement.

Indeed, one of the most fascinating elements of this study lies in its description of the tension between the ideology of socialism, which stressed the collective ownership of the nation's national resources, and the advocates of Aboriginal land rights, who contended that a major share of Australia's natural resources belonged to the continent's original inhabitants. Likewise in the United States, environmentalists and trade unions have often found themselves on opposite sides, with the latter frequently co-operating with business due to their common opposition to the 'green' agenda.

In both Australia and the United States, as well as in almost every other capitalist nation, the rapid emergence of this new constituency initially caught the business community off guard. Over the course of several decades, business managers had developed considerable experience in dealing with the political demands of organized labor, whose primary interest lay in assuring that its members received a larger share of the nation's wealth. But these new entrants to democratic politics had a very different objective. Many of the policies they advocated challenged not so much the distribution of wealth, as the ability of industry to create it in the first place.

Much of the importance of Libby's study lies in his detailed description and analysis of how the Australian mining industry attempted to cope with this new and unexpected political challenge. They began by recognizing that the public had come to take their contribution to the national economy for granted. Indeed, it was precisely the relative prosperity of much of the Australian mining industry that had made it so politically vulnerable: many citizens were simply unaware of the connection between their relatively high living standards and the mining industry's continued ability to open-up new areas for exploration and development.

More politically sophisticated mining industry leaders also understood that they could no longer rely on the 'insider' political strategies that had served them so well in the past. The emergence of this new issue onto the political agenda had transformed the political ground-rules. If the mining industry was to prevail on this issue, it needed to begin to play interest-group politics. Specifically, it had to actively mobilize public support. As a result, Australian mining firms, for the first time in their history, embarked on a major public-relations effort aimed at persuading the electorate of the merits of their stance on Aboriginal land rights. They assumed that if the public could be persuaded to support their position, so would a sufficient number of politicians.

Yet while the industry did manage to achieve many of its political objectives, Libby is a careful-enough student of politics not to attribute the industry's ultimate victory—partial though it was—simply, or even primarily, to the industry's own efforts. On the contrary, a central theme of this study is the critical role in the industry's victory played by divisions in the Australian Labor Party, at both the federal and regional levels. These divisions enabled the mining industry to play-off factions of the party against one another, which, in turn, increased the industry's political leverage.

This study thus makes it clear that public policy cannot be simply understood as the outcome of conflicts among interest-groups, however numerous or well organized they may be. Rather, political institutions, processes and even personalities also play an important role in determining political outcomes. For example, the fact that political power in Australia is divided between federal and state governments played a significant role in affecting the way the issue of Aboriginal land rights was addressed and resolved. Had Australia not had a federal system, or had important Labor Party politicians not felt politically vulnerable, the political outcome Libby documents might well have been rather different.

What does Libby's account tell us about the relative political influence of business in Australia? Is the political position of business a privileged or dominant one as Lindblom, along with most Marxist scholars, have argued? or is business, as the pluralists contend, simply another interest-group, competing with other political constituencies, such as the advocates of Aboriginal land rights, on a more-or-less-equal basis?

Hawke's Law does not provide a definitive answer to this question. No study will ever do so: the political and ideological divisions among scholars are too vast. Yet this book certainly suggests a line of inquiry that scholars who are serious about shedding additional light on this question might profitably pursue. There remains little point in debating the political power of business in the abstract. What we need are more case-studies like this one: careful and well-researched accounts that trace the way important issues emerge onto the political agenda and assess the extent to which efforts of business and various non-business constituencies were able to affect their resolution.

Will more such studies adequately enable us to capture the extent and scope of business political influence in capitalist societies? Or is there a danger that by confining our research to those issues that actually come to the attention of the public, we may be overlooking the 'second' or 'hidden' face of business power in capitalist societies? Fortunately, this problem has become less serious in recent years. For, as Libby's study illustrates, the number of issues whose resolution is potentially threatening to business prerogatives has expanded considerably in recent decades; the political agenda is much less dominated by business than was often true in the past. This, in turn, has required business to exercise its power and influence more overtly, thus making the task of measuring business power — though not the job of being a business manager — considerably easier.

At the same time, it is also important that we recognize the limits of generalizing from any particular case-study, however important or well researched. Libby's conclusions are valid for one industry, in one capitalist democracy, with respect to a particular issue, during a given historical period.

Nevertheless, I am struck by many of the similarities between his depiction of the politics of Aboriginal land rights in Australia and many of the issues whose emergence and resolution I examined in *Fluctuating Fortunes: The Political Power of Business in America*. This book traces the politics of business-government relations in the United States between 1960 and 1988. During the 1960s and 1970s, American business was caught off guard by the sudden political mobilization of middle-class reform groups and it suffered a number of important legislative defeats: this period witnessed a dramatic expansion of government controls over business decision-making in such areas as equal employment and environmental and consumer protection. Due to its sudden unpopularity, business found that it could no longer rely on a handful of well-placed senators and representatives to defend its interests in Washington. As a result, business firms were forced to increase significantly the money and personnel they devoted to politics — a political mobilization that has continued through to the present. The politization of the mining industry that Libby describes thus has clear parallels with the experience of many businesses in the United States during a roughly similar time period.

Hopefully, additional studies of the contemporary dynamics of business-government relations in other capitalist nations will help us arrive at a more sophisticated understanding of how, why and to what extent business exercises power in advanced capitalist societies.

DAVID VOGEL
School of Business Administration,
University of California, Berkeley.

efforts of business and various non-business constituencies were able to affect their resolution.

Will more such studies adequately enable us to capture the extent and scope of business political influence in capitalist societies? Or is there a danger that by confining our research to those issues that actually come to the attention of the public, we may be overlooking the 'second' or 'hidden' face of business power in capitalist societies? Fortunately, this problem has become less serious in recent years. For, as Libby's study illustrates, the number of issues whose resolution is potentially threatening to business prerogatives has expanded considerably in recent decades; the political agenda is much less dominated by business than was often true in the past. This, in turn, has required business to exercise its power and influence more overtly, thus making the task of measuring business power — though not the job of being a business manager — considerably easier.

At the same time, it is also important that we recognize the limits of generalizing from any particular case-study, however important or well researched. Libby's conclusions are valid for one industry, in one capitalist democracy, with respect to a particular issue, during a given historical period.

Nevertheless, I am struck by many of the similarities between his depiction of the politics of Aboriginal land rights in Australia and many of the issues whose emergence and resolution I examined in *Fluctuating Fortunes: The Political Power of Business in America*. This book traces the politics of business-government relations in the United States between 1960 and 1988. During the 1960s and 1970s, American business was caught off guard by the sudden political mobilization of middle-class reform groups and it suffered a number of important legislative defeats: this period witnessed a dramatic expansion of government controls over business decision-making in such areas as equal employment and environmental and consumer protection. Due to its sudden unpopularity, business found that it could no longer rely on a handful of well-placed senators and representatives to defend its interests in Washington. As a result, business firms were forced to increase significantly the money and personnel they devoted to politics — a political mobilization that has continued through to the present. The politization of the mining industry that Libby describes thus has clear parallels with the experience of many businesses in the United States during a roughly similar time period.

Hopefully, additional studies of the contemporary dynamics of business-government relations in other capitalist nations will help us arrive at a more sophisticated understanding of how, why and to what extent business exercises power in advanced capitalist societies.

DAVID VOGEL
School of Business Administration,
University of California, Berkeley.

Foreword to the American Edition

Hawke's Law is a classic political science study of the politics of a democratic nation in addressing justice and land needs of its indigenous population. The study concerns Australian efforts to pass national legislation protecting Aboriginal land rights and the mining interest-group lobbying campaign against that effort. This study is important for readers in the United States because of the many striking political parallels in relationships between indigenous and nonindigenous people within both nations.

Hawke's Law examines political strategies of the mining industry on national indigenous issues from the point of view of the industry itself; it is the first major study of its kind based upon unrestricted access to industry sources and documents. My task is to supply an appropriate historical and international backdrop for the study. I am honored to do this for the American edition of *Hawke's Law* and, as an American Indian, will develop my comments largely from an indigenous perspective so that the mining industry effort to influence public policy on an indigenous issue can be viewed in a broader context.

To what extent, if any, should indigenous native people—whether they are American Indians or Australian Aborigines—be secure in their land, cultural integrity, and basic human rights under the law and social policy of contemporary pluralistic democratic nations with colonial origins? Why should such nations address long-standing domestic indigenous issues? And what political processes should be followed when addressing sensitive indigenous issues?

International and Domestic Importance of *Hawke's Law*

The above are far-reaching international questions in the world today. The way in which nations answer them tells much about their national character, values, honor, basic principles, and their place in the world. In fact, domestic treatment of indigenous peoples and cultures tells the international community far more about a nation than its claimed principles or diplomatic policies advanced in international forums.

National honor is an important ingredient in international relations that can drive the foreign policy of nation-states in certain areas of national self-interest. Issues of indigenous justice are, at bottom, moral issues involving national honor. Therefore, the political process followed in addressing them is just as important, perhaps, as the end solution itself. The politics and social processes that define the place of indigenous people in the larger society, as studied in *Hawke's Law*, reveal much about that larger society and its commitment to stated principles. For those countries that have inherited indigenous cultures from colonial origins, the disposition of long-standing issues of justice is a clear barometer of the overall moral direction that those nations will take in the years to come.

Politically and socially, the United States and Australia are complex contemporary nations subject to many major influences, including democracy, capitalism, and pluralism, to name a few. At the risk of oversimplifying the political and social systems of these modern democracies, I think that "settlerism" as described by the American leftist David Stock may supply a useful analytical construct for considering indigenous issues in each of these nations.

Internationally, the concept of the "settler state" is familiar in the Western Hemisphere and in Australia. For several hundred years, Western European nations engaged in a competitive rush to colonize as much of the New World as possible. Some nations later broke colonial ties and retained their indigenous character. In these nations, the settlers or colonists either left after independence was achieved, adapted or merged with host populations, or cast their lot with the natives. Many independent African and Asian nations provide examples of such states. By contrast, "settler states" are nations—some considered legitimate in the world community and others not—where the colonists also revolted against the colonial homeland yet maintained colonial patterns and relationships with indigenous populations.

In "settler states," the colonists or settlers sought freedom and a better life for themselves—but rarely, if ever, applied those high ideals to original inhabitants. The "Founding Fathers" simply replaced colonial patterns of domination or exploitation. Culturally, the colonists in "settler states"—such as the United States, Canada, Australia, South Africa, and several South American nations—continued to maintain strong cultural ties and identity with their homelands after independence was achieved. Their descendants *never* adopted values or outlooks from the host indigenous cultures, nor adapted to the land as "native" in the way that the indigenous people had done. This interesting phenomenon left most of those descendants, culturally, as little more than "visitors" and "strangers" to the lands where they live, even though they found themselves ensconced as the dominant society and as stewards of the land.

The goal of "settler state" societies to retain a strong cultural identity with colonial homelands while, at the same time, ignoring, oppressing, or rejecting indigenous cultures in their own lands engenders much injustice and harm to natives and prompts much of the cultural and political conflict between indigenous and nonindigenous people seen today. A Sioux chief, Luther Standing Bear, observed that even several hundred years after Columbus's arrival in the New World:

> The white man does not understand America. He is too far removed from its formative processes. The man from Europe is still a foreigner and an alien. And he still hates the man who questioned his path across the continent. But in the Indian the spirit of the land is still vested; and it will be until other men are able to divine and meet its rhythm. Men must be born and reborn to belong. Their bodies must be formed of the dust of their forefathers' bones.

For indigenous people of the United States and Australia, the legacy of settlerism is an overarching reality in their lives. Its implanted cultures and political institutions not only furnish the political and social systems in which vastly different tribes, indigenous nations, and traditional people must live and survive as distinct cultural entities, but often makes natives "strangers" or "outsiders" in their own land. Settlerism also impacts nonindigenous citizens and institutions in fundamental ways. Although European colonialism went into eclipse long ago, its lapse left lasting social, cultural, and political marks in its settler-state progeny. Those marks are seen in domestic administrative systems, judicial decisions, political and economic patterns, and social attitudes employed for dealing with indigenous populations and their rights.

In sum, settlerism is a widespread international characteristic. It was implanted throughout the New World by Old World powers. As seen in *Hawke's Law*, settlerism struggles to this very day to find a proper balance between indigenous and nonindigenous rights and responsibilities.

Domestically, that political struggle to find a just and proper balance will affect the complexion of the settler state in fundamental ways. Government treatment of indigenous people—more so than treatment of other citizens, aliens, and voluntary immigrants—provides a social and political barometer for democratic settler states that value diversity, plurality, equality, and individual liberties. Felix S. Cohen, the founding father of "federal Indian law" in the United States—a pluralistic democracy that prides itself on such values and rightfully urges them upon the rest of the world—observed in 1953:

> The Indian plays much the same role in our American society that the Jews played in Germany. Like the miner's canary, the Indian marks the shift from fresh air to poison gas in our political atmosphere; and our treatment of Indians, even more than our treatment of other minorities, marks the rise and fall of our democratic faith.[1]

Indeed, if legal and governmental institutions cannot effectively protect basic rights of even the smallest, weakest, most different, and often despised or unpopular segment of society, these institutions must often lack sufficient vitality to protect the rest of society. Moreover, when a settler state oppresses natives in its backyard, does it not forfeit standing in the international community to advocate morality, human rights, and high ideals that is so often needed as an important tool of foreign policy?

These domestic and international considerations are not lost on the nations that have inherited the settler-state legacy, as they continue the search for just solutions through their respective political processes—even though that lofty search sadly seems to elude most settler states, even democratic ones. In the United States, for example, when upholding American Indian treaty obligations, land and property rights, or Native human rights, judicial decisions and congressional declarations often speak of the "national honor." Similarly, in *Hawke's Law*, even though the political effort to pass national Aboriginal land rights legislation failed, one government leader advocated the legislation in order to remove "a stain from our national honor" and bring back "justice and equality to the Aboriginal people."

Comparative Historical Backdrop for *Hawke's Law:*
Settler-State Relations with Indigenous People in America and Australia

In the United States and Australia, many historical parallels exist that can familiarize the American reader with the Australian case study. A brief compara-

---

1. *Handbook of Federal Indian Law* (Michie: Bobbs-Merrill, 1982), p. v.

tive examination of those parallels provides a backdrop for the in-depth political treatment provided in *Hawke's Law*, even though much of the backdrop is regrettable when viewed through contemporary eyes and would understandably much sooner rather be forgotten or ignored by many people and policymakers in settler states.

Both nations were inhabited by tribal peoples for thousands of years before Europeans arrived. Aborgines and Native Americans were highly adapted to their lands, as reflected through their rich and diverse cultural and religious heritages and the pristine environmental integrity of these continents before European contact. Anthropologically, the Indian and the Aborigine represent wholly distinct and separate races within the small and finite human family with unique and irreplaceable cultures. As such, without question they contributed, and continue to contribute, valuable and irreplaceable diversity to the human family. Today, most contemporary Americans appreciate human and cultural diversity and want indigenous cultures preserved, even though such preservation may require new laws in certain areas, such as a law to protect Native American religious freedom.

However, as a historical matter, Europeans "discovered," conquered, colonized, and christianized America and Australia without regard for indigenous rights, sensibilities, or cultural integrity. As contemporary nations, both the United States and Australia began as British colonies.

America was colonized to enrich Europe, and that it did. Mountains of gold, silver, other precious medals, furs, fish, new food crops, medicines, and other resources poured out of the Americas to fill Old World coffers and to sustain the monarchies, aristocracies, theocracies, oligarchies, and other nondemocratic Old World governments of the emergent nations of that period.[2] Much of the enormous colonial impact upon the Western Hemisphere since 1942 is graphically described by historian Kirkpatrick Sale in environmental terms:

> Rainforest area in the Western Hemisphere, originally 3.4 billion acres, is down to 1.6 billion, and going fast, at the rate of 25 million acres a year, or 166 square miles a day; U. S. forestland, originally more that a billion acres, is down to 500 million commercially designated acres, some 260 million having gone for beef production alone.
>
> Topsoil depletion and runoff in the United States reaches a rate of 80 million feet per day, nearly 30 billion tons a year.
>
> Twenty-five years after the U.S. Endangered Species Act went into effect, listing 500 of the several thousand threatened species in the country, twelve of the protected species have become extinct and 150 more are losing population at a rate that will lead to extinction within a decade. Two hundred threatened plants native to the United States have become extinct in the last five years. At least 140 major animals and bird species have become extinct since 1943. . . . Wilderness areas, officially designated at 90 million protected and 50 million unprotected acres, have been reduced from about 2.2 billion acres in pre-Columbian times—a decrease of roughly 96 percent.
>
> The population of the native people of North America is about 20 million, only 1.5 million outside of Mesoamerica.[3]

---

2. See, generally, Jack Weatherford, *Indian Givers: How the Indians of the Americas Transformed the World* (New York: Fawcett Columbine, 1988).

3. Kirkpatrick Sale, *The Conquest of Paradise: Christopher Columbus and the Columbus Legacy* (New York: Alfred A. Knopf, 1990), pp. 363–364.

Foreword to the American Edition xv

Australia was colonized as a British "prison colony" in a bizarre penological experiment to permanently rid England of unwanted criminals. For the first hundred years of its colonial existence, England transported more than 160,000 convicts in chains to Australia for exile in a harsh prison society complete with all the trappings.[4]

Both nations, since their inceptions, have a long and deplorable history of mistreatment and exploitation of their native peoples. However, that relationship extends further back to Old World attitudes brought to the New World long before these two nations were created and reflect, in a larger sense, basic cultural conflicts between the Old World and the indigenous peoples of the New World. On his very first day in the New World, Christopher Columbus introduced Europe's long heritage of religious intolerance and cultural insensitivity into the Western Hemisphere, stating this about the first people he saw on October 12, 1492:

> They ought to be good servants and of good intelligence.... I believe that they would easily be made Christians because it seemed to me that they had no religion. Our Lord pleasing, I will carry off six of them at my departure to your Highnesses, in order that they may learn to speak.[5]

Although Columbus did not tarry too long ("I do not wish to delay but to discover and go to many Islands to find gold"[6]), his legacy of conquest, colonialization, and christianization continues today. It is a cornerstone in many of his descendants' attitudes and relations with indigenous peoples of the Western Hemisphere.

Spain, it may bluntly be said, raped South America and competed with Britain and France to loot North America. American Indian tribes suffered a long and unrelenting 500-year history of disease, starvation, loss of land/culture/ identity, war, poverty, and forcible assimilation. Tribes were confined onto small American reservations where Indians were stripped of their language, religion, and culture by government-sponsored missionaries as a prerequisite to citizenship, ultimately granted in 1924.

Although surprising to many, religious liberty for American Indian, Native Alaskan, and Native Hawaiian citizens remains a serious human rights problem in the United States today. For example, two recent Supreme Court decisions deny First Amendment protection against government infringement upon tribal religious practices that predate the founding of the United States.[7]

These decisions place Indian religion in a wholly unprotected class under American law and social policy. As a result, tribal leaders are gathering to ask Congress to pass legislation to protect sacred sites and the endangered religions of America's native people. Many assume that passage should be quick and easy in a society that prides itself on protecting individual liberties, especially since

---

4. See, generally, Robert Hughes, *The Fatal Shore: The Epic of Australia's Founding* (New York, Alfred A. Knopf, 1987).

5. Quoted in *The Conquest of Paradise*, pp. 96–97.

6. Ibid., pp. 104–105.

7. *Employment Div., Dept. of Human Resources of Oregon v. Smith*, U.S., 108 L.Ed.2d 876 (1990), denying constitutional protection for the Indian Peyote religion, which ranks among the oldest, largest, most continuously practiced religions in the Western Hemisphere; *Lyng v. Northwest Indian Cemetery Assn.*, 485 U.S. 439 (1988), denying constitutional protection for an ancient Indian Holy Place located on a mountaintop on public lands from destruction by the Forest Service.

most people value the rich Native American cultures and want them preserved. However, powerful mining and timber interests have blocked Indian legislative efforts to protect Native sacred sites to date by lobbying against the Indians in collaboration with the Forest Service and other federal land agencies.

Australia may be more liberal in its human rights treatment of the religious liberty of its native people, as noted in *Hawke's Law*, by the existence of statutory protection for Aboriginal sacred sites. However, the general history of indigenous relations in Australia is similar to the record in the United States.

In 1688, Englishman William Dampier, an early discoverer of the Australian Continent, described in "one of the minor classics of racism" the Aboriginals that he observed in these terms:

> The inhabitants of this country are the miserablest people in the World.... they differ little from Brutes. They are tall, strait bodied, and thin, with long limbs. They have great Heads, round Foreheads, and great Brows. Their Eye-lids are always half-closed, to keep the Flies out of their Eyes .... therefore they cannot see very far. ...
>
> They are long-visaged, and of a very unpleasing aspect; having no one graceful feature in their faces. ... I did not perceive that they did worship anything.[8]

The English immediately pronounced that Aboriginals were "landless" and "propertyless"—a fiction that continues to this day in that country.

With such attitudes, it is hardly surprising that early relations did not go well. The convict colonists, who furnished slave labor for the colony, needed scapegoats for their miserable exile under harsh penal conditions in a land far from their homes; and, being at the very bottom of the rigid prison-class society, the prisoners needed a group that they could look down upon. In documenting white settlement in the penal colony, historian Hughes concluded that "the coming of the whites was an unmitigated disaster for everyone with black skin."[9] That history is beyond the scope of *Hawke's Law* and is referenced only for historical context. Suffice it is to say that, sadly, that history is similar to what happened to Indians in the United States.

However, neither Indians nor Aborigines have disappeared, and their survival testimony is to the vitality of these peoples and their ways of life. Both groups are alive and well today as distinct cultural communities. The political challenge of our generation is to find just solutions so that these irreplaceable cultures can survive and prosper within their homelands.

Conclusion: Legal and Political Status of American Indian Tribes

In closing, it is useful to summarize the legal and political status of Native Americans under United States law, so that the Australian efforts described in *Hawke's Law* can be viewed in relation to our Indian policies.

There are five sources of law that make up the bundle of legal rights and responsibilities in American Indian affairs: international law, the United States Constitution, treaties, federal statutes, and Supreme Court decisions.[10]

---

8. Quoted in *The Fatal Shore*, p. 48.
9. Ibid., p. 273.
10. The classical legal treatise that describes this large body of law is Felix S. Cohen, *Handbook of Federal Indian Law*. See note 1 above.

The Constitution refers to four governments that make up our political system: the federal government, states, Indian tribes, and foreign governments. Originally considering them like foreign nations under international law principles, the United States entered into several hundred treaties with Indian tribes that were ratified by the Senate and signed by the President. These treaties are the supreme law of the land under the Constitution. These contracts between sovereign entities typically secured land from Indian tribes for white settlement, reserved certain preexisting Indian land and usufructuary rights (such as hunting, fishing, gathering), and set forth other rights and responsibilities between Indian tribes and the United States government.

In the 1820s and 1830s, Chief Justice John Marshall defined the contours of our constitutional framework. His decisions described Indian tribes as "domestic dependent nations" with sovereignty over their lands and people. The Marshall Court also established the principle of federal guardianship over Indian tribes, under which the United States assumed a trust responsibility for Indian tribes. The sovereignty and trust principles are cornerstones of federal Indian law that have been continuously upheld by Supreme Court decisions, all Presidents, and by the Congress in exercising its plenary power to legislate as trustee in Indian affairs.

Today, there are about five hundred Indian tribes and Native groups in the United States with a population of 1.7 million people who speak approximately two hundred languages. About half of these Native citizens live on Indian reservations established in rural areas by the United States through treaties, executive orders, and statutes.

Indian reservations are governed by Indian tribal governments; and there are 308 of these governments that are federally recognized within our constitutional system of federalism. These 308 Native tribal governments lawfully exercise civil and criminal jurisdiction over their territory and members, including civil jurisdiction over nonmembers within their jurisdictions, that is duly exercised through executive, legislative, and judicial branches of tribal government. In addition, many tribal governments have reserved off-reservation treaty rights to hunt, fish, and gather within aboriginal lands ceded to the United States.

Title to Indian reservation land and lands allotted to individual Indians from such land, including all appurtenant natural resources (such as water, minerals, and timber), is held by the United States government in trust for the tribal or individual Indian owners, with restrictions against alienation. There are substantial natural resources located on Indian and tribal lands within the United States, such as oil, gas, uranium, coal, timber, and grazing lands. With respect to non-Indian exploitation of these Indian resources, Indian consent to lease their lands for mining, agriculture, or other purposes is required. Lease-income royalties are collected by the federal government and placed in trust accounts for the Indian owners. Because the power to tax is a basic attribute of any government, the Supreme Court has upheld the power of tribal governments to tax non-Indian lesees, including the mining industry, and others doing business within Indian country.

Tribal governments in the United States typically defend Indian political, property, and human rights through litigation and legislative struggles. In the United States, unlike Australia, questions of basic tribal sovereignty and land-rights principles have long been well settled, although the courts and Congress continually refine the meaning and extent of indigenous rights. However, because of an increasingly conservative Supreme Court, which has embarked upon a disturbing trend in recent years to trim long-standing Indian rights, Native Americans more often find themselves cast into the political arena in order to protect basic rights. Increasingly, Congress is looked on as the principal institution to safeguard fundamental rights of indigenous people and to fulfill constitutional responsibilities toward Indian people in ways that the courts used to do. Unfortunately, because legislative success usually depends upon power, wealth, and influence, Native Americans are seriously handicapped in life-and-death struggles over vital interests, because they are the smallest and poorest minority group in the United States.

The fate of America's native people, like that of the Aborigines in *Hawke's Law*, may be decided in the political processes of our democratic "settler state" in ways that will fundamentally affect Indian and non-Indian people and the basic character of our nation.

September 1991
Walter Echo-Hawk, Staff Attorney
Native American Rights Fund

Preface

It may be useful to the reader of these pages to indicate what the book is about. The unifying thread of the study is the mining industry's efforts to influence public policy toward national Aboriginal land rights under the federal Australian Labor Party government of Bob Hawke. The focus is upon the political tactics and strategy of the miners' campaigns, first in Western Australia and then nationally. The first campaign was conducted by the C.M.W.A. (Chamber of Mines of Western Australia) and the second campaign by A.M.I.C (Australian Mining Industry Council). The book attempts to evaluate the impact of the miners' efforts to influence government policy on national Aboriginal land rights.

For this reason, the focus of the analysis begins with the election of the Western Australian Labor government of Brian Burke in February 1983, until May of 1987 when the federal government introduced amendments to the Northern Territory Land Rights Act (1976) into the Senate. The significance of this period is that C.M.W.A. designed its political campaign against the Burke Government in 1983 with a view to defeating uniform national land rights legislation which it feared the federal Australian Labor Party government was committed to implementing. The study ends in 1987 with the amendment to the Northern Territory Land Rights Act, because this was the final action in the federal government's decision to abandon national land rights legislation.

While the industry did attempt to influence Aboriginal land rights policy before 1983, this is peripheral to the study. It is only discussed insofar as it influenced the industry's campaign against national land rights legislation during the period under examination. Therefore, Aboriginal policies toward land rights, the role of the Northern Territory government, the conservation movement and, indeed, the diversity of views within the mining industry itself regarding land rights, are not examined in any detail.

The work necessarily over-simplifies the mining industry's position on Aboriginal land rights by focusing upon the Chamber of Mines of Western Australia and the Australian Mining Industry Council's campaigns against land rights legislation. For example, it could be argued that the Aboriginal Affairs Committee of the Australian Mining Industry Council does not represent its employer companies and, therefore, does not necessarily represent industry views on Aboriginal mining issues. However, while strictly speaking this is true, it is also true that, of the roughly 125 member companies in the Australian Mining Industry Council, all but four contributed financial support to the Australian Mining Industry Council's campaign against uniform national land rights legislation in 1985. The companies which did not contribute to the campaign were relatively small, and the reasons they gave for declining to participate were financial and not differences over policy. Therefore, the assumption that on the whole the industry supported the campaigns conducted by the Chamber of Mines of Western Australia and the Australian Mining Industry Council is defensible.

Likewise, the study tends to over-simplify the Northern Territory Aboriginal land councils' lobbying campaign in 1986 and early 1987 to retain the veto provisions in the Northern Territory Land Rights Act. For example, the environmental lobby played a key role in persuading the Australian Labor Party Federal Caucus to retain the veto in order to restrict mining operations in the Kakadu National Park in the Northern Territory. A measure of the success of the so-called 'green-black' alliance during this period was the fact that the Australian Labor Party federal sub-committees on the environment and Aboriginal affairs held joint meetings to consider the mining veto provisions of the Northern Territory Land Rights Act.

However, the role of the conservation lobby in persuading the federal government to retain the mining veto in the Northern Territory Act is secondary to the focus of the study. The book is primarily concerned with the mining industry's campaigns against national land rights legislation. While the Aboriginals did ultimately wage a successful campaign to retain the mining veto (albeit modified), and while the mining industry opposed the veto, this was simply the culmination of the miners' campaign against national legislation. Therefore, while the Aboriginal campaign (with the support of environmentalists) to retain the veto in the Northern Territory Act is important, it is not central to the book's thesis.

I should like to acknowledge the contributions of the many institutions and individuals who generously assisted in the research. Most of the research was carried out during a ten-month period from 1986 to 1987 while I was a Senior Research Fellow at the NARU (North Australia Research Unit) of the Australian National University based in Darwin. The generous funding and support I received there made it possible for me to carry out the research. It also enabled me to travel throughout Australia to collect data and conduct interviews essential for the project.

In particular, I wish to express my appreciation for the marvelous efficiency and assistance provided by Janet Sincock at NARU. She was far more than an executive secretary. Her tireless work in arranging and co-ordinating interviews, composing letters, typing drafts and removing any obstacles to my work substantially contributed to the completion of the project. Colleen Pyne, NARU's excellent librarian, made it possible to overcome the problems of distance in securing materials and documents necessary for the research. I should also like to thank Jim Toner, Jann King and Helen Blair for their efficiency, hard work and friendship in making my family and I welcome and comfortable during our stay in Darwin. Finally, I would like to thank Professor Gerry Ward, Dean of the Research School of Pacific Studies of the Australian National University, of which the North Australia Research Unit is a constituent. Professor Ward gave me the necessary encouragement and support to complete a difficult project.

Mining industry representatives provided unique assistance in the project. I was given unrestricted access by the Assistant Director, Murray Hohnen, to the archives of the Australian Mining Industry Council, and by the Executive Officer, Michael Gamble, to the archives of the Northern

Preface

Territory Chamber of Mines. David Fardon, the Executive Officer of the Chamber of Mines of Western Australia, provided copies of the chamber's newspaper advertisements, gave me access to its television advertisements, and generally explained how the campaign in Western Australia was implemented. Special thanks are due to Murray Hohnen, whose faith in the objectivity of social science research sustained the project throughout. Without the mining industry's co-operation, the research would never have been completed.

Kingsley Palmer, the Director of Research of the Australian Institute of Aboriginal Studies, gave me permission to examine the institute's archival holdings of the National Aboriginal Conference documents. This gave me access to correspondence between Aboriginal organizations and the Minister for Aboriginal Affairs, Clyde Holding, on the issue of national land rights. It also gave me access to the minutes of meetings of Aboriginal groups concerned with land rights, including the minutes of their meetings with Minister Holding and other government officials.

I am grateful for comments and suggestions for revising draft chapters. Jon Altman read the entire manuscript and made important suggestions for revision. Louis T. Wells Jr, Theodore H. Moran and David Vogel also read the entire work and made helpful comments. Special thanks to David Vogel for his generous Foreword. John Warhurst and Kosmas Tsokhas made recommendations for improving the Introduction. Bob Gregory made useful suggestions on the Introduction, Chapter One and the Conclusion. The observations made by Ken Turner on Labor Party factionalism (in Chapter One) were invaluable. Special thanks to Lois Anderson for her detailed comments and suggestions for improving sections on the Labor Party throughout the book. Jamie Gallagher, the Director of Research of the Northern Land Council, and Martin Mowbray, the Senior Project Officer of the Central Land Council, read and commented on Chapters Two, Three, and Six. I appreciate the comments of Brian Burke on Chapter Five and the suggestions of Graham McDonald on Chapters Four and Five. Duncan Bell made detailed comments on Chapter Four, and Bill Hassell read and commented on Chapter Five.

I am grateful for the skillful work of my cartographer, Robin Mita, who prepared the maps and graphic reproductions, and I appreciate the work of Jeremy Bennett, the graphic artist who drew the television 'wall' advertisement. I am indebted to the Internal Research Committee of Victoria University which generously funded the art work and covered the expenses incurred in completing the book.

I am also grateful for assistance from Geoffrey Gallop, Elizabeth Harmon, John Hicks, Rob Riley, Phillip Toyne, George Savell, H. C. 'Nugget' Coombs, Tim Duncan, Senator Ted Robertson and Senator Michael Beahan. Cabinet ministers in the Western Australian, Northern Territory and the federal governments generously gave their time to discuss the project. Opposition politicians Fred Chaney and Michael Macklin also provided helpful insights.

I alone, however, am responsible for any errors of fact and interpretation that remain in the book.

RONALD T. LIBBY
Wellington, New Zealand
December 1988

LIST OF ABBREVIATIONS

ACTU	Australian Council of Trade Unions
ALP	Australian Labor Party
AMIC	Australian Mining Industry Council
ANOP	Australian National Opinion Polls
CLC	Central Land Council of the Northern Territory
CL	Centre left faction of the Labor Party
CMWA	(Chamber of Mines of Western Australia)
CU	Centre Unity faction of the Labor Party
DAA	Federal Department of Aboriginal Affairs
EL	exploration mining license
NAC	National Aboriginal Conference
NARU	North Australian Research Unit
NFF	National Farmers Federation
NLC	Northern Land Council of the Northern Territory
PGA	Pastoralists and Graziers Association of Western Australia
PIA	Primary Industry Association of Western Australia
SL	Socialist Left faction of the Victorian Labor Party
TO	Traditional Aboriginal owner of land
WMC	Western Mining Corporation

Introduction

Writers have tended to assume that because of the importance of the mining industry to the Australian economy, the industry exercises great influence in national politics.[1] For example, Corrighan (1984: 28) argues that because of the attractiveness of mining as an international investment outlet, the Australian government has placed emphasis upon the mining sector and, by implication, this has given the industry political leverage over the federal government. Thompson (1983: 99) asserts that the political influence of the mining industry in Australia is immense, and Crough and Wheelwright (1982: 99) go so far as to claim that Australia is losing its political independence to foreign mining interests.

A major weakness of this literature is that it fails to explain the mechanism by which miners exercise influence in Australian politics. The tendency is to infer the industry's political influence over the government on the basis of public policies which appear to serve the interests of the industry. However, this begs the question of whether the industry seeks the adoption of particular policies and beyond that if, in fact, it plays a role in persuading the government to accept those policies.

This ignores entirely the question of whether the mining industry has a political agenda and whether it has strategies to implement its agenda. Contrary to dependency arguments, we cannot assume that the industry's economic importance is automatically translated into political influence. In other words, we cannot simply assume that mining executives are part of a 'ruling class', are rational political actors, important actors, or, indeed, that at any given time they are even active in the political arena. In order to address these questions it is necessary to examine concrete attempts by the mining industry to influence government policy. It is necessary to evaluate the political strategies it employs, and to assess the outcome of their efforts.

The purpose of the present study is to undertake such a project. I will evaluate the political strategies of the mining industry in relation to one particular issue of major importance to it: national Aboriginal land rights under the ALP (Australian Labor Party) government of Bob Hawke. This was the industry's first major political campaign. It was initially mounted in the state of Western Australia in 1984 and then shifted to a national campaign in 1985. The nature of the campaign, including the reaction to it and its impact upon Western Australian and federal policies will be examined.

The Dependency Framework

The scholarly literature on the relationship between mining and politics in Australia tends to fall within the dependency framework of analysis. Representatives of this approach are Crough and Wheelwright (1981, 1982), Wheelwright and Buckley (1983), Thompson (1983), Corrighan (1984), and Bryan (1984). This approach assumes tht Australia is a 'client state' within the Pacific region and that it is dominated by 'core' or leading capitalist states (especially the United States and Japan). In this analogy, the semi-pheripheral states of Australia, Canada, and New Zealand provide core states with minerals, metals, and primary agricultural produce. In return, core states supply them with capital and technology. Because of the unequal terms of trade between the core and semi-periphery in the world capitalist system, Australia and other semi-peripheral states are said to be dependent upon the core states.

According to Wheelwright, Australia's 'dependent economy' has given rise to a dependent ruling class which is dominated by an international *bourgeoisie* under the control of foreign corporations. This condition has transformed Australia into a dependent state under the control of a 'transnationalized élite' comprised of corporate executives, representatives of the mass media and top government officials. This line of argument is not unlike the work of C. W. Mills (1957) applied to Australia.[2]

The literature on the politics of mining and Aboriginal land rights in Australia is strongly influenced by the dependency thesis. The usual interpretation of the political relationship between the mining industry and Aboriginal land rights begins with the assumption that the miners have commanding political influence in national politics. In contrast, Aboriginals are described as not only occupying the lowest socio-economic position in society, but also as being exploited by trans-national corporations, repressed by governments (state and federal), and ostracized in the wider community. Examples of this literature are Jennett (1983, 1985), Drakakis-Smith (1983), and Nettheim (1986).

Interest-Group Politics

The literature on the politics of industry groups in Australia is dominated by the Anglo-American interest-group, or pluralist model of democracy which was popular in the United States after World War II (see Almond and Powell, 1966). Brian Galligan (1985: 25) notes, for example, that the orthodoxy of Australian political science is responsible party government 'complemented by pluralist interest-group activity'. He explains that Australian writers have been preoccupied with institutional studies of interest-group activity in the parliament, the cabinet and bureaucracy, and in political parties.

The essence of this approach is the free market of competing interest-groups. In this analysis, it is assumed that a competitive political market place ensures that all organized private interests receive a share of the government's attention and resources, and that no single group dominates.[3] However, consistent with Dahl and Lindblom (1976) and Lindblom's (1977) revision of democratic pluralism, corporations are assumed to have a 'privileged position' within the political economy. Business firms and their lobbying representatives are assumed to have disproportionate access to political resources and government officials are said to defer to their wishes. In this conceptualization, primary producer 'pressure groups' such as the National Farmers Federation and the Australian Mining Industry Council have 'inside influence' over government policy. In contrast, 'outsiders' such as the unemployed, homeless and minorities, including Aborigines, tend to be relatively neglected by public policies (Davis et al., 1988: 101-13; and Matthews, 1980: 462).

This characterization of the unequal distribution of political influence, which is based upon differences in the organizational strength and resources of interest-groups, tends to ignore what Lunch (1987: 214-23) calls symbolic or 'idea-based groups' which have recently come into prominence in the United States. These new interest-groups tend to be ideologically oriented, single-issue groups based upon national causes, movements and ideas in social and political life. According to Lunch, the new interest-groups rely upon three major strategies to influence public policy: expertise, publicity, and litigation.

In the Australian context, the conservation movement, anti-uranium mining, and pro-Aboriginal groups, among others, would appear to fit this new type of interest-group politics. For example, Davis et al. (1988: 93) acknowledge that, despite being 'outsiders', the Women's Electoral Lobby, the Australian Conservation Foundation and Aborigines now have formal recognition within the Australian federal government. In other words, they are now 'insiders'. However, traditional interest group theory which stresses organizational resources cannot account for the political influence of these new interest-groups.

Indeed, Lunch argues that the 'old system' of interest-group politics in Washington has tended to decline and the traditional economically motivated interest-groups such as major corporations have been placed on the defensive by the new idea-oriented public-interest-groups. Traditional economic interests can no longer rely upon making policy by government consultation. They now must compete with the idea-oriented, often single-issue interests for public attention in order to influence public policy.

In order to understand the political interplay between the traditional economically oriented interest-groups and the new idea-based interests in Australian politics, it is necessary to critically examine the political strategies and tactics of the various groups competing for influence over public policy. It is also important to examine the political context or environment in which this competition occurs.

Davis. et al. (1988: 102) note that because some interest-groups are associated with opposition parties they may not be able to influence policy through their insider status. Therefore, they may resort to protest tactics, a strategy usually employed by outsiders. Farmers' rallies at Parliament House against the Hawke Government are mentioned in this regard.

The mining industry's campaign against national Aboriginal land rights legislation from 1984 to 1986 is a graphic example of an inside interest-group relying upon the tactics usually employed by outside interest-groups in order to gain political influence. The mining industry was associated with the Liberal Party and, therefore, had difficulty influencing the ALP government's land rights policy. In the circumstances, the miners sought to mobilize public opinion against the Western Australian and federal Labor governments in order to influence national land rights policy.

Political Context

The study places the mining industry's efforts to influence national Aboriginal land rights policy into a political context. I will argue that the political influence of the industry was largely determined by that context. As major changes occurred in the political arena, the industry's political influence changed. During the period under discussion, from 1983 to 1987, the political arena or context of national land rights policy was dominated by internal factional conflict within the governing Australian Labor Party.

Davis *et al.* (1988: 89) argue that the Labor Party's policies are guided and circumscribed by party principles and by the 'balance of factions' within the organization. I will argue that when the Labor Party is in power, not only is party policy influenced by factional alignments, but government policy is also influenced by factional politics. In the case of national land rights policy, the influence of the mining industry as well as other groups upon the government's land rights policy was subordinated to ALP factional politics.

When the Australian Labor Party was in a consensus mode on land rights, the miners appeared to have minimal influence upon policy. However, during periods of heightened factional division over the question of Aboriginal land rights, the industry enjoyed its greatest influence over policy. In fact, there is evidence to suggest that industry representatives designed their campaigns to influence public policy in the light of strategic opportunities to exploit factional divisions within the ALP. Therefore, they made their greatest efforts to influence policy during periods of attenuated factional party conflict, and they reduced their efforts to influence land rights policy when factional divisions within the ALP diminished.

The mining industry's political influence will be evaluated in terms of the stages or phases of Labor Party factional conflict over Aboriginal land rights. There were at least three distinct phases of internal ALP conflict. The first period was from the ALP's assumption of office in 1983 to mid-1984. During this time, consensus within the ALP on the party's land rights policy was high. The party had yet to implement its land rights policy and, therefore, resistence or opposition to the policy had not yet emerged. The mining industry's influence on the government's land rights policy during this period was negligible.

The second phase of Australian Labor Party factionalism on the issue of Aboriginal land rights occurred from late 1984 when the Western Australian ALP challenged the Party's national policy, until early 1986 when the party worked out a compromise position on land rights policy. During this period, the mining industry exercised its greatest influence over policy. However, this was not simply due to the political power or influence of the industry *per se*. Rather it was due to the fact that the miners did not have to change an agreed policy position within the party on an important issue. The miners only had to support a factional position on the issue within the party against other factions. In other words, the mining industry's influence on national land rights policy was magnified by virtue of the fact that a major faction of the ALP had aligned itself with the position taken by the mining industry.

The third phase of ALP factionalism on the land rights issue began in early 1986. At this time, the party restored much of its former consensus on the land rights issue. The mining industry's influence on government policy correspondingly declined during this period.

Mining and Land Rights in Australia

In order to understand the political context in which the mining industry mounted its campaign against land rights legislation, it is necessary to describe the Aboriginal population and its legal rights to control mining in Australia. According to the 1986 census, there were 227,638 Aborigines (including Torres Strait Islanders) in Australia, or 1.42 per cent of a total population of about 15.9 million. In 1986, the Indian population of Canada (i.e. registered under the Indian Act) was estimated to be about 400,000, which was 1.5 per cent of the total population of just over 25 million. This compares with an American Indian population in the United States in 1980 (latest census) of about 1.4 million, representing 0.6 per cent of the total population.

Aborigines in Australia owned (i.e. had freehold title) 643,079 km^2 of land in November of 1985. This compared with 373,614 km^2 of tribal trust and other land controlled by American Indians, and 187,850 km^2 reserved for the exclusive use of Indians in Canada.

Under the Australian Constitution, all mineral (or sub-surface) ownership rights are vested in the Crown (i.e. the state). With a few exceptions such as New South Wales (excluding gold, silver, oil or coal), mineral rights are vested in the Crown. Therefore, as owners of mineral rights, the state, territorial, and federal governments are the recipients of royalties and other payments derived from mining activities on land in their respective jurisdictions. In major mining states such as Western Australia and Queensland these revenues constitute up to 20 per cent or more of total budgetary revenue. The governments of these states, at least, would not willingly jeopardize such a major source of revenue by placing it under Aboriginal control (see Map 1).

In Australia, as well as in most other countries, private citizens, including Aborigines, do not possess ownership rights to minerals. This contrasts with the United States where private individuals do possess ownership rights to sub-surface as well as surface land, including title to minerals. The usual explanation for the differing legal systems is the historical background in the United States and Canada, on the one hand, and Australia on the other. In the United States and Canada, Indian governments and their customary laws are recognized. For example, in the United States, tribal governments have been classified by the courts as 'domestic dependent nations' with full internal sovereignty subject only to express congressional oversight. By contrast, the legal doctrine of *terra nullius* applies in Australia. This assumes that at the time of colonial settlement, Australia was regarded as unoccupied or belonging to no one. Not only have Aboriginal claims of sovereignty been rejected in Australia, but their customary laws have not been accepted by the courts.

The significance of this difference in legal systems is obvious. American Indians not only possess an absolute right to consent to mining on their land, but they also have the power to tax mineral development. This extends to the imposition of property tax, value-added taxes, severance taxes and

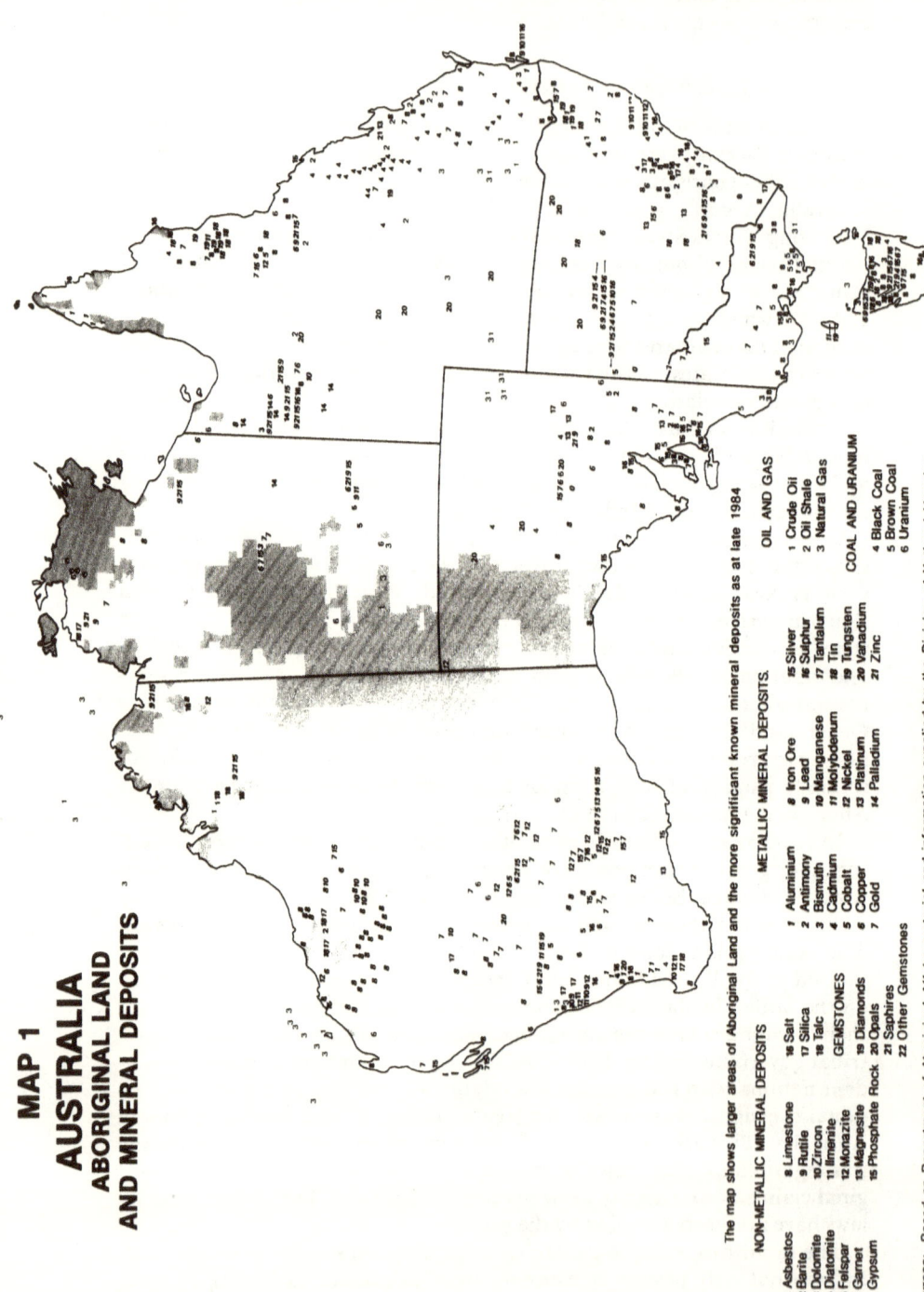

special excise taxes (see Redhorse and Reynolds-Smith, 1982). Canadian Indians are also able to secure access to financial benefits from mineral development on their lands primarily through royalties that can be as high as between 50 and 65 per cent of the total value of production (McGill and Grough, 1986: 31).

Since Australian Aboriginals, on the whole, do not have the statutory powers to extract the economic benefits of mineral development on their land, the only recourse open to them to achieve that end is to resort to non-statutory methods. One way they can raise resource revenues from mining development on their land is to use their powers to deny miners access to the land (a *de facto* veto) as a way of exercizing bargaining power with the mining companies for commercial advantage.

The Australian mining industry's campaign against national land rights legislation was directed largely at the Aborigines' right to deny resource developers access to their land for the purpose of exploration and mining. The mining industry took the position that, since the state owns the minerals, any tax levied on mining activity should be paid to the government and not to Aborigines. They argued that what the government did with mining revenues was its business. However, if the government wished to improve the welfare status of any particular group in society, such as Aborigines, then the revenues for that purpose should come from general budgetary funding and not primarily from the mining industry. They argued that the industry should not be expected to carry the burden of providing for the welfare of Aborigines.

In contrast, the Aboriginal position toward the industry was that obtaining revenues from mining activity on Aboriginal land was one of the few ways they could raise capital. The reason for this was that most Aboriginal land was inalienable (i.e. ownership was non-transferable) and, therefore, it could not be mortgaged or sold. Hence, their land had limited commercial value.

The literature on the politics of mining and Aboriginal land rights in Australia, on the whole, fails to recognize this crucial area of conflict between the mining industry and the proponents of Aboriginal land rights. The reason for this undoubtedly relates to the dependency framework that writers bring to this issue. Hence the mining industry is assumed to exercise an overpowering political influence in disputes involving Aboriginal land rights.[4]

Most frequently mentioned in this regard is the so-called Noonkanbah affair involving an American company, Amax Petroleum, and an Aboriginal protest against drilling on sacred Aboriginal land in Western Australia. However, examination of the circumstances surrounding the controversy does not support that interpretation. Instead, it shows a highly embarrassed oil company that, if anything, was guilty only of buckling under pressure from a strong-willed, and single-minded state Premier — Sir Charles Court (see Kolig, 1988; Vincent, 1983; and Reece, 1980).

Equally, Aborigines are characterized as being weak, disorganized, and incapable of putting forth demands for their own land rights. This was evident in the criticism by pro-land rights groups of the Hawke Government and particularly the Minister for Aboriginal Affairs, Clyde Holding, for misleading Aborigines by creating false expectations and then betraying them. This interpretation reduces Aborigines and their representatives to

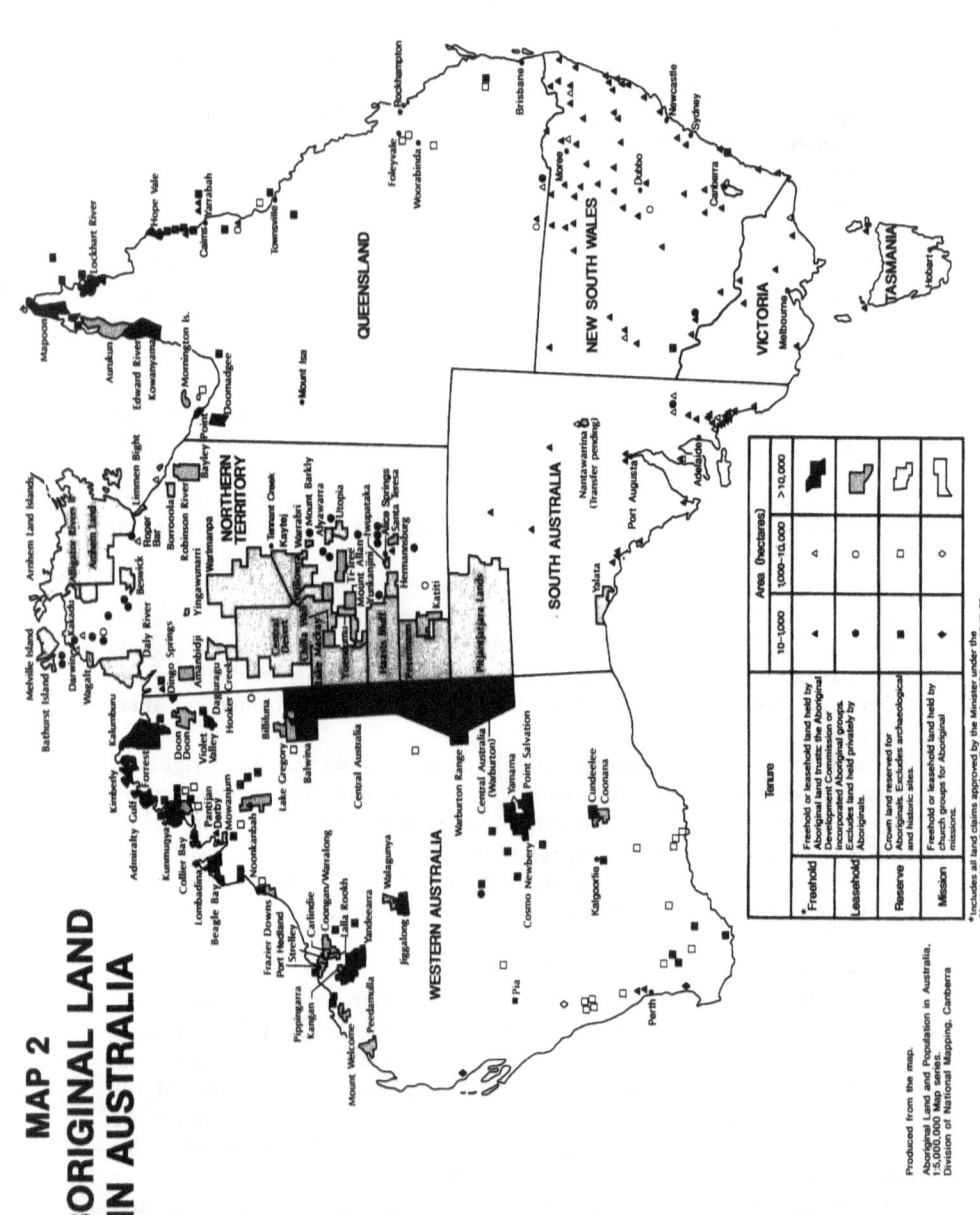

veritable wards incapable of determining what is in their own best interest and acting upon it.

Neither of these characterizations reflects the political realities of the situation. The mining industry is not always, nor even usually, a dominant political force, nor are the proponents of Aboriginal land rights invariably powerless. The relative political influence of these groups depends very much upon the country's political climate or context and the interplay of strategies and tactics employed by these groups. For example, before the mining industry conducted its first major political campaign against national Aboriginal land rights in 1984, land rights legislation was already in force in two states (South Australia—1981 and 1984, and New South Wales—1983), and in the Northern Territory—1976. The fact that the industry publically opposed land rights legislation at least as early as 1973 (AMIC, 1973), suggests that, in general, they have not been successful in blocking or preventing land rights legislation.

Likewise, the adoption of this legislation as well as the transfer of huge areas of Crown land (i.e. federally owned land) to Aborigines suggests that proponents of land rights in Australia are not as powerless as they are often portrayed. For example, in 1985, about 8 per cent of Australia's total land area was owned by Aborigines. In addition, another 284,785 km^2 was either leased by Aborigines or occupied as Aboriginal reserves or missions. In the Northern Territory, Aborigines owned about 32 per cent of the total land. In South Australia, the state government handed over about 10 per cent of its entire land area, about 102,000 km^2, to the Pitjantjatara people in 1981. A further area of about 76,000 km^2 (the Maralinga land) was also granted to South Australian Aborigines in 1984 (see Map 2).

In order to gain insight into the political influence of the various groups involved in the land rights controversy it is necessary to examine the political environment and the strategies of the major parties to the conflict. In the pages that follow I will focus upon the political context in which the land rights drama was played out from 1983 to 1987. While the proposed national legislation was ultimately defeated, this does not permit us to conclude, as many have, that it demonstrates the political dominance of the mining industry. Nor does it demonstrate the impotence of Aboriginal groups and their supporters. What it does show, however, is the overriding importance of the political context of the state of play among the parties to the conflict. It also shows the importance of the political strategies adopted by the mining industry and by pro-land rights groups.

While the miners clearly had important political victories in the aftermath of the conflict, they did not get everything they wanted. In fact, the industry was unable to remove or vitiate any of the existing land rights legislation. Likewise, while pro-land rights groups made major political concessions in their demand for national land rights, they did not lose any major legal rights and powers they had when going into the conflict. Furthermore, it is arguable that they have, in fact, even made advances in terms of land rights as an outcome of the controversy.

CHAPTER ONE

Factional Politics and Land Rights Ideology

FACTIONAL POLITICS

In order to understand the political context of the controversy over national Aboriginal land rights legislation, it is necessary to appreciate the highly factionalized nature of the Australian Labor Party. The ALP is the oldest party in Australia and yet it has had the least electoral success at the national level of the major parties.[1] The Labor Party is a federation of six autonomous state and two territory parties (i.e. the Northern Territory and the Australian Capital Territory).

The decentralized nature of the party and its trade-union origins[2] has contributed to the evolution of a highly factionalized national party. Each state and territory party branch has its own platform, organization and leadership which is based upon idiosyncratic local factors such as religion, ideology, patronage, and personal networks of friendship. Factional divisions generally occur when a group of parliamentarians sides with one faction against parliamentarians who side with another faction. A constant source of factional conflict within the ALP has been union rivalries.

Factional divisions also arise between the 'parliamentary parties' and the so-called 'party machines' or branch organizations (see Parkin and Warhurst, 1983: 21). All members of the ALP sign a pledge to support the party platform. While there are several internal forums for debating issues, a decision of the state or territory party conference is binding on all members of the party in public. This has tended to produce tension and divisions within the party when MPs (members of parliament) have not voted in Parliament according to non-parliamentary labor members' interpretations of the party platform.

The Labor Party has a history of internecine political warfare over contentious issues. Crisp (1955: 132–41) notes, for example, at various times branches of state party 'machines' have challenged the federal Parliamentary Labor Party. Major factional conflict threatened to break out within the ALP over the issue of national land rights legislation. The principal antagonists in the conflict were the Western Australian ALP, led by the Premier of the state, Brian Burke, and the Victorian ALP, led by Gerry Hand, president of the state party and convenor of the largest faction of his state Labor Party, the SL (Socialist Left).

The source of the dispute was the differing mining and land rights situations in Western Australia and Victoria and their assessment of the political costs of supporting national Aboriginal land rights legislation. In

1

Western Australia, the importance of the mining industry to the state economy, the large areas of Crown land that could be claimed by Aboriginals, and the relatively large Aboriginal population, led the state ALP to conclude that their support for national legislation would not only cost them political office, but could also produce a voting swing away from the ALP nationally, threatening the federal government.

By contrast, the relatively insignificant mining industry in Victoria, the absence of large areas of land claimable by Aborigines, and the small rural Aboriginal population, led the Victorian ALP to minimize the political risks to them of supporting national land rights legislation. Therefore, the Victorian Socialist Left and its supporters within the ALP took the position that the Burke Government and his supports (principally the Prime Minister Hawke and the New South Wales 'right wing') were exaggerating the electoral threat posed by land rights legislation. Furthermore, the SL argued that the Burke Government had sabotaged the ALP's national party platform on Aboriginal land rights.

They asserted that the party had an over-riding moral commitment to fulfil the ALP's National Party platform on Aboriginal land rights. This commitment had been in force at the national level since 1982 (1978 in Western Australia). Burke's actions were condemned by the Victorian SL for subverting the ALP's national land rights policy without consulting national party colleagues or, indeed, without even raising the issue at the party's annual national conference in 1984.

The factional dispute over the land rights issue was mirrored in the unique leadership and organizational characteristics of the Western Australian and Victorian ALP party branches. These state parties represented sharply contrasting styles of political leadership and organization. The Western Australian ALP was united under the leadership of Brian Burke. He stressed a 'pragmatic and businesslike' approach to politics and emphasized the importance of having a close working relationship with the business community.

By contrast, the Victorian ALP was riddled with factions and lacked effective political leadership. Until coming to state office in 1982, the party had been in power for less than nine years despite being the second-oldest Labor Party in Australia. It has been described as a militant industrial party and its dominant faction, the Socialist left, was characterized by strong left-wing ideologies which made the Victorian branch of the ALP skeptical of any political alliance with business interests. While it is beyond the scope of the present study to examine ALP factional politics in any detail, it is necessary to briefly contrast the political style and leadership of both state branches in order to appreciate the political context of the controversy over national Aboriginal land rights.

Western Australia: a Pragmatic Party

The Western Australian Labor Party represents a sharp contrast to the Victorian ALP. This is because the Premier of the state, Brian Burke, had the support of all major factions within the state ALP.[3] He was firmly in control of the state party. Burke took control after a so-called political coup by the 'Young Turks' in 1981 against the leader of the party, Ron Davies. Burke formed a political alliance with his long-time and left-leaning rival Mal Bryce, who became the deputy Premier.

According to Gallop (1983: 5-9), the coup represented a victory for a younger generation of party leaders who had entered parliament during the 1970s. A key figure in the coup was Michael Beahan, who was elected secretary of the state ALP just before the coup. It is important to note in passing that Beahan (now Senator Beahan) replaced Bob McMullan, who moved to Canberra to become the national secretary of the ALP.

Gallop points out that the change in leadership had the support of the state ALP as a whole. While the traditional left was suspicious of Burke and his 'pragmatic and businesslike' approach to politics, the by-election victories by the party in March and July of 1982 under Burke's leadership, strengthened his position in the party. Labor's new image under Burke was reflected in the ALP's campaign slogan for the 1983 election: 'Brian Burke, best new leader in Australia'.

An important part of Burke's new style of party leadership involved the cultivation of an image of professionalism and moderation. To this end, Burke and his parliamentary supporters established a close working relationship with the business community in Western Australia. One measure of Burke's success in this strategy was the large campaign contributions the business community made to the ALP during the lead-up to the 1983 elections.

The significance of Burke's new leadership image for the Western Australian ALP was the fact that resource development was the key economic strategy of the Liberal-National Country Party coalition which governed Western Australia under the dominant leadership of Sir Charles Court from 1974 to 1981. During that period, the coalition parties were able to capitalize upon their campaign strategy emphasizing the transformation of Western Australia from a 'Cinderella state' to a 'state of excitement' in which mining investment led the way.

In order for the Labor Party to make a decisive breakthrough in the electorate, Burke and his colleagues reasoned that they had to present a credible alternative to the Liberal Party's economic policy which capitalized upon the state's rapid economic growth (based largely on mining development) during the 1960s and 1970s. The first step in stealing the Liberal Party's thunder on economic policy was to win the backing of the business community for the Labor Party's policies. Burke reasoned that one way to win business support was to emphasize political leadership based upon professional managerial competence.

In taking over the leadership of the ALP, Burke's major concern was winning political office. Before World War II, the state ALP had held power for almost the entire period between 1924 and 1947. However, after the war, the party's fortunes were reversed. Between 1947 and 1983, the ALP was in office in Western Australia for only nine years (1953-9 and 1971-4) while the conservative parties won nine out of the fourteen elections.

Burke placed the blame for this dismal showing at the polls upon the left wing of the party led by the Western Australian branch secretary, Joe Chamberlain. Burke's suspicion and hostility toward the left wing of the ALP also had a personal side to it. Burke not only blamed the left wing for the ALP's long periods out of office, but he blamed it for what he regarded as the unjust expulsion in 1955 of his father, Tom Burke, a former member of the federal parliament representing Perth. As a result of this experience, Brian Burke acquired a deep suspicion bordering on hostility toward federal ALP politics. In fact, he vowed that he would never go into federal politics. Indeed, Burke declared that if he won a second term as Labor Premier he would resign from political office at the end of that term, in 1988; a promise he fulfilled.

Burke was a social conservative and a traditional populist Labor politician. He was primarily concerned about the efficient economic management of the state's economy and about securing the votes of the working and middle classes, who comprised the bulk of the electorate. The Premier was highly critical of left-wing elements of the party for diverting attention away from 'bread and butter' issues and toward trendy issues such as the environment, nuclear disarmament, and Aboriginal land rights. While he regarded these issues as important, they were not as important as the standard of living for every Australian. Burke supported Prime Minister Bob Hawke's emphasis upon the importance of economic issues over these social issues.

The Premier took the position that the left wing of the ALP, in effect, functioned as the opposition, while the official opposition tended to be ignored. Like Hawke, Burke courted business with a view toward achieving sound economic management of the economy. And he emphasized consensus between management and labor. Also like Hawke, Burke effectively used a consensus-building strategy to isolate and defeat his political enemies. He did this by characterizing them as representing extreme positions on vital issues. In this regard, both Burke and Hawke had a keen sense of the limits of public support for their policies.

Victorian Labor Party: in Perennial Opposition

In contrast to the relative absence of major factional conflict within Western Australia's Labor Party after Joe Chamberlain, the Labor Party in Victoria was riddled with self-destructive factional divisions. There were at least three major factions within the Victorian ALP. There was not only intense competition and tension among the factions, but there was also conflict between the dominant faction of the state ALP, the Socialist Left, and the state ALP government of Premier John Cain and the federal ALP government of Bob Hawke.

In 1985, the largest faction of the Victorian ALP was its Socialist Left comprising 45 per cent of the vote at state conference. This compared with the Centre Unity faction (formerly Labor Unity) or 'right wing' which had a voting strength of about 38 per cent, and the Independents who had approximately 11 per cent of the vote.[4] Roughly six per cent of the Victorian ALP was non-aligned.

Despite being the largest faction, however, the SL was badly divided between a so-called 'old left' or 'crazy left' led by Bill Hartley and George Crawford, who controlled the Victorian branch before the national ALP executive intervened in Victoria in 1970 against them, and a 'smart left' or moderate left led by Gerry Hand and Peter Batchelor, president and secretary, respectively, of the Victorian ALP. The basis of the division within the SL related to the historic or traditional role of the state branch as an opposition party. After the party won political office in February 1982, the factions were faced with the necessity of making a transition from opposing to supporting the government in power. While the Hand element of the SL was prepared to make that transition in the party's new role, the Hartley supporters were less prepared to make this change.

The Hartley and Hand factions both professed to be the keepers of the party's socialist principles.[5] However, the Hand faction (which was in the majority) recognized that, since they were now the government, they must be prepared to compromise in order to achieve at least some of their socialist goals. But this placed Hand in the difficult position of trying to fashion practical compromises on doctrinaire issues such as the banning of uranium mining, stopping US nuclear ship visits, nuclear disarmanent, conservation, opposition to the entry of foreign banks to Australia, and national Aboriginal land rights. Attempts by the pragmatic SL to compromise on any of these issues was regarded by the Hartley faction as an abandonment of the ALP's socialists principles.

One indication of the vehemence of the traditional left wing's opposition to the ALP's 'pragmatic' policies was the controversy surrounding Bill Hartley himself. For example, Hartley said publicly that his faction would 'fight the [ALP] government', that there was a 'huge wave of opposition' within the state ALP building up against the Victorian ALP Government of John Cain and that, because of the ALP's disappointment with the Labor government, the party would probably lose office in Victoria and Canberra (*The Bulletin*, 17 December 1985: 30). From the point of view of the old or traditional Victorian left wing, therefore, there is reason to believe that many of them would have preferred to remain in political opposition than support an ALP government which compromised their socialist principles.

This placed the leadership of the pragmatic Socialist Left in a highly vulnerable position. According to Duncan (*The Bulletin*, 10 September 1985: 39), the fatal weakness of the pragmatic SL was that, unlike the traditional left, the pragmatic faction had something to lose in almost every situation. The traditional left, on the other hand, had nothing to lose and could place its sub-faction above the Victorian left-wing faction, the Victorian ALP, and, indeed, above the national ALP itself. What was particularly worrying from the point of view of federal ALP politicians was that, while the Socialist Left did not have the numbers to determine the outcome of federal parliamentary caucus, concerted left-wing opposition to the remainder of caucus and cabinet would severely embarrass the federal government.

The second major faction in the Victorian ALP was the CU (Centre Unity) or right wing. This faction was led by Senators Gareth Evans and Robert Ray, Minister for Aboriginal Affairs, Clyde Holding, and included the Prime Minister, Bob Hawke. Like the SL, the Centre Unity faction was tightly disciplined and active in the selection of ALP candidates for parliament. However, this faction was primarily oriented toward winning and retaining political office. For example, one of the principal criticisms against Clyde Holding, former leader of the ALP opposition in the Victorian parliament for a number of years, was his failure to lead the state ALP to an election victory.

The Victorian Centre Unity faction also identified with the ALP's socialist doctrine. However, it stressed the importance of staying within the limits of broad public support for their policies. It is important to note the fact that while Bob Hawke was a member of this faction he was also able to capitalize upon his ACTU (Australian Council of Trade Union) and other union connections, and the fact that he was President of the ALP gave him the broad appeal, connections and support within the labor movement necessary to lead the party. In this regard, Hawke had the support of some members of the Centre Left faction.[6] Nevertheless, Hawke's factional base of power within the national ALP was the Labor Unity faction or 'right wing' (Centre Unity in Victoria). Since the Labor Unity faction in New South Wales dominated this key state branch of the national ALP, Hawke tended to rely upon them for support on major policy issues. For example, whenever Hawke got into political trouble within the national ALP, the New South Wales Labor Unity and their leaders, Paul Keating and Graham Richardson, closed ranks behind him.

Hawke regarded the Victorian Socialist Left as his political enemy.[7] He and the New South Wales Labor Unity (plus right-wing factions in other states and his supporters in the Centre Left faction) waged a successful battle to partially dilute the power of the Victorian SL which was the powerhouse of the left wing in the national ALP. Hawke did this by securing control of the federal executive of the ALP and using its power to intervene in the affairs of the Victorian ALP to weaken the position of the left wing. However, the anti-Hawke faction of the Victorian ALP (i.e. Socialist Left) countered Hawke's efforts to reduce the power of the Socialist Left. For example, the SL refused to endorse pro-Hawke candidates for parliament. Senator Gareth Evans, a Hawke supporter, was denied pre-selection (i.e. party nomination) for the Victorian seat of Jagajaga in 1984 because of his factional identification with Hawke. The significance of this for Gareth Evans was that it ruled-out his succession to the Prime Ministership since only a member of the House of Representatives can be elevated to that position.

On the issue of national Aboriginal land rights, the pragmatic Socialist Left, led by Gerry Hand, took a strong stance in favor of it. One reason for Hand's high profile position in support of land rights was the fact that the issue had cross-factional support within the ALP. That is to say, it was not only an issue which the Victorian SL had traditionally supported, but it also had the backing of other factions. Hence it provided an ideal issue upon which to unite a badly divided Victorian SL. It also had the advantage of involving relatively low political costs in terms of factional conflict within the party. However, when Brian Burke and the Western Australian ALP came out in public opposition to national land rights legislation in 1984, it brought the Western Australian branch of the ALP into direct conflict with the Victorian ALP which was dominated on the land rights issue by the SL.

In order to prevent what Hawke saw as the very real possibility of Labor losing government in Western Australia in February 1986, and risking losing federal seats in Western Australia in the next national election, Hawke intervened in support of Burke's position on land rights. It is important to note in this regard that the ALP held nine out of thirteen federal seats in Western Australia and, prior to the July 1987 federal election, the loss of these seats would have defeated the ALP government nationally. However, this placed the Prime Minister and his government in a vulnerable position.

The reason for this was that initially, at least, Hawke's own Centre Unity faction was divided on the issue and, therefore, not united in supporting him. Furthermore, the Centre Left faction was divided, and at least two Centre Left cabinet Ministers, John Dawkins and Susan Ryan, continued to support uniform national land rights legislation despite Burke's opposition to it and despite Hawke's support for Burke. In effect, this meant that the Prime Minister only had the support of the New South Wales Labor Unity faction, plus Burke and some members of the Centre Left faction (several of whom were from Western Australia), to sustain his position within the national ALP on the land rights issue.

In response to Burke's challenge to the national Labor Party platform on Aboriginal land rights, the Hand faction of the Victorian SL plus the left wing of the national ALP and Aboriginal and pro-Aboriginal groups, waged a counter-offensive against the Prime Minister's position. They did this by lobbying within the ALP parliamentary caucus against the stance taken by the Burke and Hawke Governments.

Context of Factional Politics

In order to evaluate the political influence of the mining industry on the issue of national land rights, it is necessary to place it in the context of ALP factional politics. That is to say, the miners had more influence on the government's land rights policy at certain times. This was determined in large measure by the changing status of intra-party factional politics.

Hence, before Premier Burke openly opposed national land rights legislation in 1984, the mining industry's input into federal land rights policy was relatively insignificant. However, after Burke challenged the federal ALP initiative on land rights legislation, the industry's influence on government policy increased. The reason for this was that the mining industry's opposition to national land rights legislation had the support of the Western Australian branch of the ALP. By contrast, in March 1986, when the Western Australian and federal ALP negotiated a compromise agreement on the land rights issue, party consensus on land rights was restored. After this date the miners' influence on land rights legislation correspondingly declined. The reason for this was that cross-factional support for counteracting the influence of the mining industry on land rights legislation had emerged within the ALP.

After March 1986, the Prime Minister's concession to the miners to remove the Aboriginal mining veto from land rights legislation was reversed. The federal government's decision to remove the mining veto from the Northern Territory Land Rights Act was rescinded; although restrictions were placed upon its use. The reason for the reversal of Hawke's position on the mining veto was the increased influence of Gerry Hand, the convenor of the left wing of the ALP parliamentary caucus, upon the government's land rights policy. However, Hand's influence was not due to any new initiatives or efforts by his faction. Rather it was due to the emergence of cross-factional support within the ALP for Hand's position on the land rights issue.

The 1986 Hawke-Burke agreement to abandon national land rights legislation produced a strong cross-factional reaction within the ALP caucus. In this changed factional situation, Hand was able to mobilize the

ALP caucus to oppose the government's decision to remove the mining veto from the Northern Territory Land Rights Act. Factional realignment within the ALP had therefore made it possible for the left wing of the party to effectively challenge the Prime Minister's position on land rights policy. In other words, it was no longer simply a left-wing challenge to the government.

After March 1986, the land rights issue was not only a matter of socialist commitment within the ALP, but it was also seen by many as an assault upon the basic democratic character of the Labor Party. The feeling among some ALP backbenchers and lay members of the party was that, unless they took a stand on land rights, not only would there be no further gains for Aborigines, but their existing rights would be sacrificed to the mining industry and others in the interest of political expediency. Hence many in the party felt it was necessary to take a stand on the issue lest the Hawke Government completely disregard the party platform on Aborigines and perhaps ignore the party's other major policy positions.

After the March 1986 decision to abandon national land rights legislation, the influence of the mining industry was negligible. The efforts of the miners to weaken existing land rights legislation was effectively blocked by the party in the interest of re-establishing ALP unity. The so-called compromise amendment to the Northern Territory Act was largely a compromise between warring factions of the ALP. It was not a compromise between the mining industry and Aboriginal groups as was widely reported.

The political campaign by the mining industry to defeat national Aboriginal land rights legislation, and the efforts of pro-land-rights groups including the Aborigines themselves, must be evaluated, therefore, primarily within the context of factional conflict within the ALP. It is essential to separate conceptually the campaign of the mining industry from that of the Burke Government's opposition to national land rights legislation. Likewise, it is necessary to distinguish the Victorian SL and the national left wing's influence upon government policy from the pressures exerted by Aboriginal organizations such as the Northern Territory land councils.

AUSTRALIAN LABOR PARTY LAND RIGHTS IDEOLOGY

The political controversy over national land rights was accompanied by shifts in the ALP's Aboriginal land rights ideology.[8] At the time that the federal ALP came to power in March 1983, there was a high degree of ideological consensus within the party on Aboriginal land rights. This was due largely to the fact that the party's national land rights policy had yet to be implemented and, therefore, no major political faction or group had been threatened by it. The function of the ideology during this period was one of symbolic unification. It was a highly emotive doctrine that not only articulated the party's equalitarian goals, but was used in election campaigns by party leaders to differentiate the ALP from the other major Australian parties.

This situation changed, however, in 1984 after the federal ALP government sought to implement the party's land rights policy. Sharp conflict concerning Aboriginal land rights emerged within the party. Competing factions sought to interpret the ideology in the light of their own political interests. Land rights ideology during this period changed from being symbolic to performing an instrumental function on behalf of sectional interests of the party.

In early 1986, however, the competing factions of the party reached a compromise agreement on land rights policy in order to avert a major conflict. During this period, ideological disagreements on the land rights issue were played down and the doctrine returned to its former role of fostering symbolic unity within the party.

Ideological Consensus

The Australian Labor Party's position on the question of Aboriginal land rights prior to their election victory in March 1983 set the stage for the political controversy over land rights. The Labor Party had a history of support for Aboriginals prior to coming to office in 1983. The Labor government of Gough Whitlam, from 1972 to 1975, elaborated the party's first comprehensive Aboriginal policy. Whitlam also articulated a political doctrine to legitimate that policy. Moreover, Whitlam's Aboriginal land rights policy received bipartisan support. It was not challenged by the succeeding Liberal-National Party coalition government of Malcolm Fraser, from 1976 to 1983. It was only after the ALP came to power in 1983 that the opposition parties challenged the ALP's land rights policy.

The ALP's Aboriginal doctrine as elaborated by Whitlam and others was characterized by lofty goals, a strong moral tone, and a linkage with Australia's standing in the world. Speaking soon after the ALP's election victory in November 1972, Whitlam articulated this doctrine. He said that Australia's 'true test' in the international community was how it treated its Aboriginal people. According to Whitlam, history would judge Australia on that basis. Addressing Aborigines in Canberra in February 1973, for example, Whitlam expanded upon this theme:

> If there is one ambition my Government places above all others, if there is one achievement for which I hope we shall be remembered, if there is one cause for which future historians will salute us, it is this: that the Government I lead removed a stain from our national honour and brought back justice and equality to the Aboriginal people. (Whitlam, 1985: 468)

Whitlam sought to give expression to these grandiose sentiments by introducing innovative policy in the area of Aboriginal affairs. For example, he set up the first separate Ministry for Aboriginal Affairs, and created an independent DAA (Department of Aboriginal Affairs). His government provided free legal services for Aborigines in court cases, and substantially increased federal appropriations for the improvement of Aboriginal welfare in areas such as health, education and housing. Government expenditure for Aborigines increased from $61.44 million in 1973 to $185.79 million in 1976. This represents an increase in real terms of about 105 per cent. The government also established the first national Aboriginal advisory body, called the National Aboriginal Consultative Council (incorporated later as an elected body and renamed the NAC [National Aboriginal Conference] in 1978).

In 1973, the Whitlam Government established the first Aboriginal Land Rights Commission for the Northern Territory, headed by Mr Justice Woodward. The Woodward Commission issued a report in 1974 which was subsequently endorsed by the Whitlam Government and the ALP as the basis for national legislation for the granting of land rights to Aborigines. This report remains the centerpiece of the ALP's model for Aboriginal land rights. It also became the center of controversy during the height of the ALP conflict over Aboriginal land rights.

As early as 1972, Whitlam promised to pass Aboriginal land rights legislation. In fact, within a week of assuming office, Whitlam announced the formation of a Royal Commission to study the most appropriate method of granting land to Aboriginals in the Northern Territory. The Northern Territory was selected for this legislation because, unlike the states, the federal parliament had exclusive jurisdiction over the territory. Therefore, while the commission was instructed to recommend the most appropriate method for transferring land to Aborigines in the Northern Territory, this was regarded as the first step in designing comparable legislation for Australia as a whole.

There was never any doubt about the government's intention. The only question was the most suitable way to go about it. Whitlam's government and the ALP subsequently endorsed Woodward's report virtually *in toto*. For this reason, it is essential to identify the major proposals in the report. It contained eight major recommendations:

1. Federal legislation was required to grant land rights to T.O.'s (traditional Aboriginal owners) with Title to the land held by an Aboriginal Lands Trust which was directed by regional land councils;
2. Minerals and petroleum on Aboriginal lands should remain the property of the Crown;
3. However, Aborigines should have the right to prevent exploration for them on their traditional lands;
4. This Aboriginal power of veto should only be overridden if, in the opinion of the government, the national interest required it;
5. Any such decision of the government should be subject to disallowance by both Houses of the Parliament;
6. Royalties from mining on Aboriginal land should be paid into a trust managed by and used for the benefit of Aboriginal peoples;
7. An Aboriginal Land Commission should be established to expedite the acquisition and transfer of pastoral leases to traditional Aboriginal communities;
8. Where traditional lands are unavailable for claim, compensation should be negotiated with the Aboriginal community.

In 1974 the Whitlam Government created an Aboriginal Land Fund with an annual budget of $5 million for ten years for the purpose of purchasing land for Aboriginal communities. The government also introduced the Northern Territory Land Rights Bill in 1975. Both initiatives were closely patterned after Woodward's recommendations.

The Northern Territory Land Rights Bill, however, was rejected by parliament. The reason was that the Senate (i.e. the upper house of the parliament) was controlled by the opposition parties which were against all reform legislation initiated by the ALP. Therefore, the Act lapsed in November 1975, the same month that the Whitlam Government was dismissed by the Governor-General, ostensibly for its failure to secure Senate approval of the 1975 federal budget. Nevertheless, the Liberal-National Country Party coalition government of Malcolm Fraser, which succeeded Whitlam, did not kill the Northern Territory Land Rights Bill. To the contrary, and in the spirit of bipartisanship, the Fraser Government passed an amended version of the ALP government's Aboriginal Land (Northern Territory) Bill in December 1976.[9]

This Act became the center of political controversy concerning Aboriginal land rights, particularly after the ALP next won federal office in 1983 and sought to carry out its land rights policy. For example, the government which gave birth to the Act, the Liberal-National Country Party coalition, took the position that it did not foresee the full implications of the bill. The administration of the Act subverted their original intentions for it with the result that the development of the mineral-rich Northern Territory had been frustrated.

The ALP, on the other hand, took the position that, by amending the Labor government's bill, the Fraser Government unjustly limited Aborigines' rights to veto mining on their traditional land. A frequently mentioned example of this is the Ranger uranium mining agreement. Despite the fact that there was substantial opposition by Aboriginal traditional owners to the proposed mining of uranium in the Northern Territory, the Fraser Government forced the regional land council representing the traditional owners, the NLC (Northern Land Council), to agree to the mining project. The NLC was forced to accept the federal government's terms of agreement under the threat of modifying the Northern Territory Land Rights Act (1976) so as to remove Aborigines' powers of consent (see High Court of Australia, 1985: 9).

The Labor Party argued that only an Act that was faithful to the Woodward Commission recommendations would meet these requirements. In effect, it argued that the only legitimate grounds for limiting Aborigines' rights to veto mining on their traditional land was 'National Interest', and that should not be determined by the Minister for Aboriginal Affairs but by the parliament.

The debate concerning the Northern Territory was extended to the issue of national Aboriginal land rights. Hence the ALP argued for a national land rights bill patterned after the Woodward recommendations. And the Liberal-National Party coalition argued that if a bill based upon a modified version of the Woodward recommendations thwarted mineral development in the Northern Territory, then a similar bill for the country as a whole would be an economic disaster. Therefore, the Liberal-National Party coalition argued that each state and territory should decide for itself the most appropriate way to redress the historic injustice to Australian Aborigines. In response, the ALP argued that this was a prescription for abandoning its commitment to justice for Aboriginals, since the 'conservative states' of Queensland, Western Australia and Tasmania, were insensitive to Aborigines' demands for land rights justice.

The ALP's position on Aboriginal land rights was unchallenged within the party until mid-1984. For example, the party's federal Aboriginal platform was passed unanimously at the 36th biennial national conference in July 1984 (ALP, 1984: 733).

Ideological Conflict

Soon after the federal Labor government came to power in 1983, it initiated efforts to implement the party's Aboriginal policy. Foremost was an undertaking to 'grant land rights to Aboriginal and Islander communities, using the principles and recommendations of the Aboriginal Land Rights Commission (Woodward Report) as a basis for legislation.' In practice, this was interpreted to mean that Aboriginal groups were to receive inalienable freehold title to their traditional land. The ALP's platform included the important proviso that Aboriginal people 'shall have the right to refuse permission for mining on their lands or to impose conditions under which mining may proceed'. This power could only be set aside by an Act of Parliament, and only if the 'national interest' required it (West, 1980: 68; ALP, 1982: 334; ALP, 1983: 6).

However, within a year of taking office, a major ideological dispute arose within the ALP. Factions within the ALP interpreted the party's federal Aboriginal land rights platform in the light of differing political interests, and they responded to the federal government's initiative on national land rights in the light of those interests.

There were two major positions taken on the issue. One position was forcefully expressed by Gerry Hand, the leader of the Victorian Socialist Left, and the other position was articulated by Graeme Campbell, Member of the House of Representatives for Kalgoorlie, in Western Australia.

Both politicians claimed to be giving a correct interpretation of the ALP platform, and both claimed to be speaking on behalf of Aboriginal people. Hand co-ordinated his efforts closely with the regional Aboriginal council for the Northern Territory — the CLC (Central Land Council) in advancing his interpretation. Campbell claimed to represent the views of Aborigines in his electorate, who were more numerous than in any other electorate in Australia (with the exception of the Northern Territory and Leichardt, in northern Queensland). These politicians and others argued their positions on the land rights issue within the parliamentary caucus of the ALP, as well as at biennial national conferences and elsewhere. I shall examine each position in order to understand the nature of the ideological conflict within the ALP.

The Doctrine of Moral Responsibility

Consistent with the Victorian Socialist Left's style of political leadership, Gerry Hand presented a highly principled stance on the question of the federal Labor Party's land rights policy.[10] He argued that the ALP government had a moral responsibility to adhere strictly to the party's Aboriginal platform. If the ALP did not live up to its responsibilities, then Aboriginal and Islander people would suffer further oppression at the hands of white Australians. According to Hand, Aborigines had suffered from almost 200 years of colonial oppression, and it was up to the federal caucus and the

ALP to correct this injustice by recognizing their rights as the 'prior owners' of Australia. He argued that these rights had to be enshrined in federal legislation.

In making his case, Hand relied heavily upon Justice Woodward's 1974 Report. Citing sections 3 and 4 from the Report, for example, he stressed the linkage between land rights and the ALP's duty to provide justice and compensation to Aborigines for the dispossession of their land and for the oppression they endured (Woodward, 1974). Hand re-stated Woodward's rationale for granting Aboriginal land rights. For example, Woodward argued that Aborigines' spiritual linkage with their land gave them a sense of identity. Justice Woodward stated that it was a matter of 'simple justice' that Aboriginal people be given title to land that was taken from them without their consent and without compensation. Quoting Woodward, Hand argued that this would achieve three of the ALP's major goals: promote social harmony within Australia by removing a major, legitimate grievance of a minority group; enable Aboriginal people to improve their depressed socio-economic status in society; and improve Australia's standing in the world by demonstrating its fair treatment of an ethnic minority.

Hand argued that the ALP's Aboriginal and islanders section of the party platform (especially clauses 1-6), which were based upon the Woodward Report, made it clear that the federal government had a 'moral and philosophical responsibility' to provide land rights for Aboriginals throughout Australia (Hand, 1985: 6). He pointed out that the federal government had already acknowledged its moral responsibilities in this regard. The Minister for Aboriginal Affairs, Clyde Holding, had expressed this commitment, for example, in 1983 to the Parliament (Holding, 1983: 5) and in an address to the United Nations Working Group on Indigenous Populations in Geneva in July 1984 (Holding, 1984: 11).

Holding stated in these addresses that the Australian government recognized Aborigines' rights to land according to the following five principles:

1. Aboriginal land was to be held under inalienable freehold title;
2. Aboriginal (*sacred*) sites were to be protected;
3. Aborigines were to have control of mining on their land;
4. They were to have access to mining royalty equivalents; and
5. Compensation for lost land to be negotiated between the federal government and Aboriginals.

Hand also pointed out that Minister Holding committed the federal government to carrying out a 'consistent national approach to land rights' according to the five principles. This ruled-out a state-by-state and territory solution to the land rights problem on the grounds that, individually, state or territorial governments would 'cave-in' to pressures from 'vested interests' and abandon the federal ALP's Aboriginal platform. He pointed out that if land rights were solely a state responsibility it would enable them to deny Aboriginal people control over their land as envisaged in the ALP platform (Hand, 1986: 7).

Hand declared that the 'integrity and future' of the ALP and of the federal Labor government depended upon fulfilling its moral responsibility to carry out the party's platform commitment to Aborigines. Failure to do so would not only deprive Aboriginal people of justice, but it would also disappoint those who 'were led to believe that they could finally expect to be granted some justice by non-Aboriginals.' Hand claimed that if the Parliament did not grant Aborigines freehold title to their land it would be destroying Aboriginals and killing their culture' (Hand, 1986: 15).

Given the emotive nature of Hand's argument, it is not surprising that he launched a vituperative personal attack against those presenting opposing interpretations of the ALP's Aboriginal land rights policy. For example, he attacked miners and pastoralists for 'greed' and he attacked those 'vested interests', plus the government of the Northern Territory, for launching a campaign against the ALP platform based upon 'misinformation, ignorance and [*racial*] prejudice'.

Hand also attacked Western Australian Premier Brian Burke personally, accusing him of weakness by giving-in to the demands of miners and pastoralists. Hand said that there was no justification for Burke's public threat to resign his premiership if the federal government instituted land rights legislation in Western Australia based upon the ALP's land rights platform. In Hand's view, Burke had abandoned the party's principles of 'justice and social reform' because he was intimidated by 'vested interests'. Hand accused Burke of being one of the 'main instigators' in 'torpedoing' the ALP's land rights policy (ALP, 1986: 91-2). He even accused Burke and, by implication, Prime Minister Bob Hawke, of a 'potential double-cross' of the ALP in making a joint press statement in Western Australia on 19 October 1984 during a federal election campaign. The statement read in part as follows:

> There is no intention on the part of the National Government to introduce federal legislation that would override Western Australia's decisions: not to permit any veto over mining or exploration; and to ensure that any mechanism to resolve access disputes would not contribute to a de facto veto. (Hand, 1986: 3)

Hand argued that this joint statement was in direct conflict with the party platform and was issued without consultation with the Aboriginal people of Western Australia, the ALP caucus, the ALP rank and file and, indeed, the federal cabinet. At the federal Labor Party's Biennial National Conference in Hobart in July 1986, Hand continued his attack against Brian Burke.

Hand's remarks were in response to a statement made by Burke at the Hobart conference. Burke pointed to a paradox that, after four years of ALP government in Victoria, they had yet to implement land rights legislation. However, they were the 'most vocal' critics of Western Australia's efforts to secure land rights for its Aborigines. Hand responded by saying that his remarks were a message from the Victorian ALP to the Western Australian ALP. He accused Burke of getting 'into bed with the miners' by allowing them to influence his land rights legislation for Western Australia. Hand said that he rejected Burke's attitude toward land rights, and he rejected the people who support Burke's attitudes to Aboriginal land rights' (ALP, 1986: 92).

Another important element of the land rights doctrine as expressed by Gerry Hand relates to the 1976 Northern Territory Land Rights Act. He argued that that legislation was fundamental to the party's social reform policy. Therefore, it should be strengthened, not weakened, as critics have argued. Its principles should constitute the basis of national land rights legislation for Aboriginal people throughout Australia.

The Party's Socialist Doctrine

In a letter to the ALP parliamentary caucus preceding the party's 1984 Biennial National Conference, Graeme Campbell argued an opposing interpretation of the party's Aboriginal land rights platform (Campbell, 1984). Campbell said that 'one issue zealots' had managed to write into the party's platform an Aboriginal land rights commitment that was at odds with the party's 'socialist philosophy'. If this continued, it would inevitably lead the ALP into a political land-mine. He attributed this ill-conceived land rights commitment to the 'ultra democratic nature of the ALP structure' which a group of one issue zealots could exploit during the 'dying days of conferences' when general interest was waning.

Campbell argued that the notion of land rights in the party's Aboriginal affairs platform was misconceived. It was essentially an 'emotive white term' that, in fact, conflicted with the ALP's 'socialist policy'. He indicated in this regard that it was primarily the 'tribal' Aboriginal who required access to land and not the 'urban part-Aboriginal' who had lost traditional cultural identification with the land.[11]

Furthermore, he said that tribal Aborigines in his electorate did not demand ownership rights to minerals on their land. They merely wanted access to land, and this could easily be satisfied by granting them title to unalienated Crown land (i.e. land not being used by anyone else and which could not be sold, borrowed upon nor deeded). Hence their land use needs could be met by simply granting them pastoral leases or similar title to land.

Campbell argued further that, since tribal Aborigines in his electorate had not demanded the ownership of minerals on their land, they also had not argued for the right to royalties that derived from the exploitation of minerals. Furthermore, even in cases where such demands have been made (i.e. usually at the instigation of 'white zealots' or 'part-Aboriginals'), that would violate a fundamental principle of the party. He pointed out, in this regard, that article 3 of the federal Labor Party's platform, constitution, and rules, states unequivocally that the party believes in the democratic control and strategic social ownership of Australian natural resources for the benefit of all Australians' (ALP, 1984a: x).

Campbell asserted that this can only mean one thing. The Labor Party is committed to the 'socialist principle' that minerals and royalties derived from mining belong to all Australians, regardless of race and the type of land ownership (i.e. leasehold, freehold or any other land tenure). He pointed out that if the ALP contradicted its own socialist doctrine by giving Aborigines privileged rights to mineral ownership, it would produce a backlash against Aborigines and against the ALP.

According to Campbell, the source of the backlash was the working class throughout Australia. Unlike the proponents of Aboriginal land rights, who claim that this backlash was restricted primarily to country or rural electorates, Campbell argued that the Aboriginal land rights issue was likely to affect all working-class areas of Australia. In fact, he argued that it was already 'on the agenda' in working-class areas. It was not an issue that was limited to Western Australia and Queensland alone. He said that if lower socio-economic groups, one of the ALP's major constituencies, perceived that a minority was given economic advantages denied to them, it was certain to engender a hostile reaction in them to Aborigines. He pointed out that this was likely to happen even if working-class perceptions of threats to them were unfounded. To ignore this potential backlash would present a very real threat to the party.

Campbell pointed to Ayers Rock as an example of 'extreme tokenism' in the granting of land rights that was counter-productive to the overall advancement of Aboriginal interests. He said that Ayers Rock (the Ayers Rock-Mt Olga National Park in Central Australia) was granted to a small Aboriginal community ('the former traditional owners of the region'), while two years later neighboring Aboriginal communities still did not have potable water or power available to them. He argued that the recipients of Ayers Rock received little in the way of tangible benefits, that the transfer of land unnecessarily incurred the hostility of the great majority of the Australian population.

In relation to the Northern Territory Land Rights Act (1976), Campbell said that this was an example of the counter-productive effects of Aboriginal land rights. He quoted Sir Joh Bjelke-Petersen's (Premier of Queensland) over-dramatized statement regarding the effects of the Northern Territory Act to illustrate the point. Bjelke-Petersen said that Aboriginal mineral rights in the Northern Territory created a 'class of black sheiks'. Campbell added to this the 'many mediocre White lawyers who have grown fat on land rights'. He said that Aboriginal mineral rights in the Northern Territory have no relevance for urban Aboriginals, that they have done nothing for Aborigines who do not have minerals on their land, and they are anathema to the ALP's socialist philosophy. He concluded by saying that mineral rights will have to be 'clawed back' from Aborigines in the Northern Territory.

Campbell also stressed the politically damaging effects that Aboriginal land rights could have upon the ALP's electoral prospects. This theme was developed primarily by ALP politicians from Western Australia. For example, speaking at the 37th Biennial National Conference at Hobart in 1986, Bill Thomas made the point that the opponents of Aboriginal land rights have been given a powerful argument to use against the ALP. He said that the notion of Aboriginal land rights, as interpreted by a certain section of the party, gave the opposition a strong campaign issue. For example, they could argue quite effectively that ALP policy is to give Aboriginals an absolute or inherent veto over mining on their land which can be used as a *de facto* means of raising royalties. He said that this was a highly divisive issue which could be potentially damaging to the party.

Thomas concluded that he had no doubt that if 'uniform national land rights' legislation modeled after the ALP Aboriginal land rights platform were imposed upon Western Australia, the ALP would lose every federal seat in the state. He added that, if the state government were seen to be a party to this legislation, the ALP state government would be voted out of office (ALP, 1986: 86). Campbell and others recommended that the party follow a path of low key 'consolidation' and address the 'real' problems of Aborigines without stimulating white backlash against them and the ALP.

Return to Ideological Consensus

In early 1986 the competing factions of the Australian Labor Party reached a compromise agreement on the Aboriginal land rights issue. The party's land rights ideology returned to a consensus position reflecting the resolution of factional conflict over land rights. All major factions within the ALP once again professed to identify with the party's land rights doctrine.

The ALP's re-affirmation of the new consensus on the ideology was expressed by Kim Beazley, federal Minister for Defence. He was a key conciliator in resolving the factional dispute. This was because he was a senior federal cabinet minister, and a senior Western Australian politician who was close to Burke personally and ideologically. This gave him direct access to both Burke and Hawke, and the federal cabinet.

At the party conference in Hobart in 1986, Beazley summed-up the party's new-found consensus regarding Aboriginal land rights. He pointed out that all factions of the party recognized the importance of land ownership for Aboriginal people. He said that this was necessary for their economic survival and for their dignity. Everyone in the party agreed with that. The only question, therefore, was how best to achieve that objective. On that point, Beazley said that even Aboriginal people disagreed on the best way to achieve their land rights objectives.

Beazley said that the only differences in the party were over how that goal could be achieved within the framework of both the federal Constitution and what is politically feasible. The Minister said that the agreement reached between Western Australia and the Minister for Aboriginal Affairs, Clyde Holding, on land rights was the best way to realize Aborigines' land use requirements in that state. He pointed out in this regard that the package agreement between Brian Burke and Clyde Holding was a solution to the Aboriginal land rights problem within the framework of the ALP platform.

The agreement granted title to substantial areas of land under a 99-year leasehold (an area of land equal to the entire state of Victoria), and Aboriginal sacred sites and mineral rights were also protected. He pointed out that if Victoria wished to implement land rights in a somewhat different way, that was their privilege. All Western Australians expected was the right to implement land rights in a way that could be sustained politically, and be protected by future Labor governments.

Beazley emphasized the hallowed principle of states' rights, with particular stress upon the potential electoral consequences of imposing national land rights upon the states. He argued that survey research had shown quite clearly that there was massive public opposition to Aboriginal land rights. For example, he said that surveys conducted in Western Australia indicated that about nine per cent of the electorate was prepared to change its vote to the opposition if national land rights legislation was introduced in that state. This meant that the ALP would lose all but one federal seat in Western Australia. If this were to be repeated throughout the country in a federal election, it would mean that the Hawke Government would be voted out of office.

Given this reality, Beazley asked what was to be gained by introducing legislation which would defeat the ALP. The political opposition could easily campaign on that issue and, once securing office, would simply revoke the legislation, thus leaving Aboriginal people with little or no gains in the area of land rights. He said that it took little courage for Gerry Hand and the Victorians to say that they will not be intimidated by miners because there was practically no mining industry to speak of in Victoria. By implication, it was a very different matter to confront the powerful mining constituency of Western Australia which was crucial to the state's economy.

Beazley also pointed out that, even if the ALP did decide to press for national land rights legislation, it could not be achieved by 1988 (the 200th anniversary of the 'invasion of Australia' by the British). The reason for this was that state governments would take the federal government to court arguing for compensation for the granting of unalienated Crown land to Aborigines in their state.

For example, he noted one study of a Queensland Aboriginal reservation. If it were compulsorily transferred from state ownership to Aboriginal ownership the federal government would be faced with compensation to the Queensland government of $450 million. If this were multiplied by the areas of Crown land claimed by Aborigines throughout Australia, the cost to the federal government would be staggering. He said that there was no way the federal government would sacrifice its defense or social welfare budget in order to compensate states for the Crown land granted to Aborigines. He also warned that there was no doubt that the Premier of Queensland, Joh Bjelke-Petersen, or somebody else (implying Brian Burke), would take such legal action if the federal government sought to impose national land rights legislation upon the states.

Beazley concluded that everyone in the ALP supported Aboriginal land rights. However, each state must be given the freedom to achieve that objective in a way that is politically feasible. He also appealed for understanding from critics of Western Australia. The government in Western Australia deserved credit for confronting 'massive public opinion' against Aboriginal land rights and for succeeding in handing over to Aborigines a huge area of their state.

The Minister for Aboriginal Affairs, Clyde Holding, affirmed the federal government's support for the consensus position expressed by Kim Beazley. He said that there was no point in adopting the 'high moral ground' on the question of national land rights because he had tried to achieve that for two and a half years and it had failed. Holding offered two reasons for this. First, Aborigines themselves had opposed his 'preferred national land rights' model. Secondly, the system of land holding in Australia varied so widely that no single piece of legislation would serve the interests of Aboriginal people as a whole. He noted, for example, that, since most Aboriginals live off reserve land, there is very little unalienated Crown land which they could claim.

Holding concluded that since the state governments were making 'substantial efforts' to meet the land rights needs of Aborigines, and since Aboriginal people themselves are satisfied by this effort, the federal government was also encouraged with this development. He stressed that rather than engage in 'disjointed debates' about past promises and efforts, the party should concentrate upon finding solutions which benefit Aboriginal people.

CHAPTER TWO

The Federal Initiative

Soon after the federal Australian Labor Party won office in March 1983, it embarked upon an initiative to formulate national Aboriginal land rights legislation. The source of the initiative was Clyde Holding, the newly appointed Minister for Aboriginal Affairs.

Political Strategy

In order to formulate the legislation, Holding established an Aboriginal land rights steering committee and a panel of lawyers to advise him. The steering committee was comprised of representatives of Aboriginal organizations. It consisted of the national chairman and deputy chairman of the NAC (National Aboriginal Conference) the six state and territory chairpersons of the NAC, representatives of the Aboriginal land councils including the Northern Land Council, the Central Land Council (both from the Northern Territory), the Kimberley Land Council (from Western Australia), the Northern Queensland Land Council, plus the federal Minister for Aboriginal affairs, and the Chairman of the Aboriginal Development Commission, Charles Perkins (the first Aboriginal appointee).

The panel of lawyers was comprised of nine.[1] Three were appointed by the NAC (including one from the National Aboriginal and Islander Legal Services), two were appointed by the National Federation of Aboriginal Land Councils (led by Pat Dodson, the Director of the Central Land Council), one from the Northern Land Council, one from the DAA (Department of Aboriginal Affairs) (under Holding's portfolio), one representing Minister Holding, and one appointed by the Minister to assist the panel.

Holding's initial strategy was to spell out the federal government's principles for national Aboriginal land rights in the form of draft federal legislation. This legislation was to be developed in consultation with Aboriginal groups.

The Minister's plan was to put pressure upon the state and territorial governments to legislate Aboriginal land rights up to the position of the draft federal legislation. Holding sought to do this by taking a high-profile position insisting upon uniform national Aboriginal land rights. In one scenario, states would be given a deadline for adopting legislation commensurate with the federal position. After that deadline, the federal government would adopt over-riding legislation in order to 'top up' or bring all states up to the federal position.

In this approach, Aboriginal land rights would be spelled-out under both state and federal legislation. Hence each piece of state legislation would be followed up with federal legislation in order to fill in the gap and bring all states up to a uniform standard of Aboriginal land rights. Initially, Holding considered the Aboriginal Land Rights (Northern Territory) Act of 1976, and the proposed Victorian Aboriginal Land Rights Bill, as models for his national land rights legislation.

Holding examined each state and territory with a view towards assessing the extent to which they would adopt legislation that would meet his uniform national standard. For example, in Western Australia, there was a Labor government committed to granting land rights to Aborigines based upon the principles of the Woodward Report (the basis of the Northern Territory Act). He felt that, as an important first step, the Western Australian government could simply hand over its Aboriginal reserves, but he would have to wait for the outcome of the Seaman inquiry (commissioned in March 1983) before acting. In South Australia the Labor government was having difficulty getting legislation (i.e. the Maralinga Bill) passed by the upper house of the state parliament which was controlled by the opposition. The Minister said that the federal government could pass the necessary over-riding legislation but, instead, would wait to be asked by the state government to act on its behalf.

In Victoria there was a land rights bill under consideration, but he did not think the legislation was going to go very far because of political opposition in the upper house, implying the necessity for action by the federal government. In the Northern Territory, Holding felt that the existing land rights legislation of 1976 met the basic needs and principles which the federal government sought for Aborigines throughout Australia. However, he felt that there were some aspects of its operation which needed 'upgrading.' In addition to a lack of provisions for the protection of sacred sites (other than buying the land itself), there was particular concern for the necessity of granting excisions of land on pastoral leases (i.e. privately owned land). The Northern Territory government had strict requirements limiting the potential for Aboriginal people to excise small parcels of land from leaseholds. Holding felt that this had to be overcome in order to give Aborigines land rights justice there. Holding appointed Justice Toohey in June 1983 to head a review of the Aboriginal Land Rights (Northern Territory) Act 1976 for this purpose.

In Queensland, Holding felt that the state Minister for Aboriginal Affairs was moving toward implementing Aboriginal deeds of grant in trust legislation. However, he planned to see the Queensland Minister in the near future to assess progress there. And, in the case of Tasmania, Holding noted that it was obvious that the state government had refused to act on land rights.

The irony of Holding's assessment is that the major challenge to national land rights legislation came from an unexpected source—Western Australia. It was a state with a Labor government committed in principle, at least, to state land rights legislation based upon federal principles. While Holding described Western Australia as being 'racist' (along with Queensland, Tasmania and the Northern Territory) he apparently did not expect major opposition to national land rights legislation from Western Australia.

Aboriginal Consultation

In a December 1983 speech by Clyde Holding to Parliament (which was never ratified), the Minister outlined the pivotal role which he envisioned for the NAC in the development of national Aboriginal land rights legislation. He said that his ministry gave the National Aboriginal Conference enlarged resources (doubling its annual budget for 1983 to $7 million) to enable it to 'speak to the Government as the national voice of Aboriginal interests' (Holding, 1983: 4). In this new role, the NAC was described by some as a democratically elected 'black parliament'.

Holding said that, unlike preceeding governments that overlooked or disregarded the NAC, his government would be guided by the NAC's advice. Holding went beyond this to state that on an issue of primary importance to Aborigines, land rights, he would not bring national legislation to the parliament without the approval of the NAC (Holding, 1983: 5). Holding later modified this to also give the Federation of Aboriginal Land Councils and the Northern Land Council (Northern Territory) veto powers over any proposed national land rights legislation. To underscore the close working relationship he envisioned with the NAC, Holding said that they would have a representative attached to his office to act as liaison officer. This representative would have access to all relevant documents in the Minister's office.

In the same speech to Parliament Holding said that national land rights legislation would be guided by his previously declared five principles. The NAC regarded the Minister's promise not to introduce land rights legislation without the prior approval of the NAC with such importance that they referred to it as the federal governmment's 'sixth principle' for national land rights legislation.

The steering committee and the panel of lawyers were expected to perform the function of formulating the federal government's land rights policy and translating that policy into national law. The function of the steering committee was to make political policy by deciding what was to go into the land rights legislation after nation-wide consultation with Aboriginal people. The NAC, in particular, was charged with the responsibility for determining the land rights needs of Aborigines throughout the country.

After determining the policy, the panel of lawyers was supposed to draft land rights legislation in the light of the steering committee's instructions, and the principles of Australian law. The panel had the additional assignment of accompanying the Minister for Aboriginal Affairs in his negotiations with state ministers of Aboriginal affairs to ensure that state land rights legislation was consistent with the federal government's five basic principles (Neate, 1983 and Jacka, 1983: 3). Holding's position was later modified to allow two NAC, and Federation of Aboriginal Land Council delegates from the steering committee, to be present and to take part in negotiations between Minister Holding and state governments (Malezer, 1983: 6).

However, the Minister's plans for the steering committee and the panel of lawyers did not come to fruition. In fact, the Aboriginal organizations did not advise the Minister for Aboriginal Affairs on land rights legislation. Instead, Holding tended to disregard the advice he was given by the steering committee. He imposed rigid deadlines upon the steering committee (comprised of the NAC and the land councils) for endorsement of policy decisions he, and others, had already made.

Holding reversed the roles of the advisory groups he created, giving the panel of lawyers drafting instructions, and only later informing the steering committee of his decisions after the policy had been made. When the Aboriginal groups on the steering committee opposed the Minister's proposed land rights legislation, the formalities of consultation ceased altogether and Holding dismantled the NAC, claiming that the organization did not represent the views of Aboriginal people.

Ironically, when Holding finally produced his 'preferred model' for national land rights in February 1985, and it was almost universally condemned by Aboriginal groups, he used their opposition to justify the federal government's decision to abandon national Aboriginal land rights legislation. He offered the spurious argument that they did not want national land rights legislation.

From the point of view of the Aboriginal groups represented on the steering committee, Holding's actions were tantamount to a betrayal of the Labor Party's solemn commitment to the Aboriginal people. They accused the Minister for Aboriginal Affairs and the Prime Minister of deceit, of betraying the Labor Party's principles on land rights, and of selling out Aboriginal people to powerful sectional interests — particularly the mining industry in the interest of political expediency (see, for example, *Land Rights News*, 1985).

However, while Aborigines' sense of betrayal by the ALP was understandable, it begs an important question. It assumes that the party's initial symbolic land rights ideology constituted an unqualified commitment to national Aboriginal land rights by all factions of the party. Clearly, this was not the case. However, the Minister for Aboriginal Affairs encouraged Aboriginals in this belief. He promised them that they could determine the nature of national land rights legislation and, indeed, even said they had a veto power over it. They were also encouraged in this belief by the Minister's failure to clearly set out the political limits of land rights legislation — i.e. legislation that the ALP felt could be sustained in the larger Australian community.

Confronted by the threat of major factional conflict over land rights legislation, the Prime Minister forced Holding to revise his previous undertakings with Aboriginal groups without consultation. This action undermined Aborigines' trust in the Minister and led to a falling out between him and the steering committee. It led to Aboriginal protests and demonstrations against the federal government. The government's response to this action was to disband the NAC and discontinue altogether its consultation process with Aboriginal people outside of the government bureaucracy. However, Northern Territory land councils responded to this situation by waging a highly effective lobbying campaign with the support of the Victorian SL, the left wing of the national ALP, and the Australian Democrats, to protect existing federal land rights legislation in the Northern Territory.

THE BREAK-DOWN IN ABORIGINAL CONSULTATION

The reversal of policy-making roles between the Minister and the Aboriginal steering committee was partly due to the absence of consensus among Aboriginal groups. However, it was largely due to the political pressures under which the Minister was operating—emanating primarily from the Western Australian ALP. I shall examine each factor in order to understand the collapse in the federal government's land rights initiative.

Absence of Aboriginal Consensus

Soon after the Minister announced the formation of an Aboriginal steering committee on land rights, disputes arose among Aboriginal groups concerning their status on the committee. One dispute was over the powers of the National Aboriginal Conference relative to the land councils. Pat Dodson, Director of the Central Land Council, and co-ordinator of the National Federation of Land Councils, objected to the land councils' initial exclusion from the steering committee on the grounds that the NAC did not represent their interests. He also demanded a right of veto comparable with the NAC's power to accept or reject land rights legislation.

Dodson challenged the Minister's decisison to give the NAC exclusive power to approve national land rights legislation (Dodson, 1983). He expressed dismay at Holding's support for an organization that 'lacks credibility with the Aboriginal people of this country and represents no point of view but its own.'[2] Dodson accused the NAC of publically reaching agreement, then reneging at will, and of failing to reach any clear position on issues involved in the proposed land rights legislation.

Dodson also criticized the NAC for failing to even propose how it would seek the views of Aboriginal people on whose behalf it was supposed to negotiate. He was concerned that the Minister would use the NAC to back land rights legislation that was against the interest of the land councils. He also insisted on the right to disassociate the national Federation of Land Councils from the entire federal initiative.

Holding acceded to Dodson's request that the Federation have veto powers over the proposed legislation comparable with that of the NAC. The NAC responded to this by passing a resolution of its own stating that it reserved the right to break off the relationship with the Federation. In order to resolve the dispute between the NAC and the National Federation of Land Councils, the Minister created a joint steering committee on national land rights legislation. The NAC and the Federation were given equal representation on the committee.

However, in a perceptive observation at a steering committee meeting in 1984 held to discuss national land rights legislation, Bryan Keon-Cohen, one of the lawyers representing the NAC, expressed his concern at the haphazard nature of the Minister's support for the steering committee and the potential for disaster due to insufficient resources, no terms of reference, no judicial standing, and no Department of Aboriginal Affairs support (Steering Committee Meeting, 1984: 26). As it turned out, these were prophetic remarks.

Another dispute arose concerning the representativeness of the Federation of Land Councils. The NLC (Northern Land Council) refused to affiliate with the Federation of Land Councils led by Dodson and the CLC (Central Land Council of the Northern Territory). The official reason given for this was that the Federation, unlike the NLC, was not a government-sanctioned body. However, a more likely reason for their objection was the fact that the NLC was the largest and best-funded Aboriginal organization in Australia, and their interests did not necessarily coincide with that of the CLC and other Aboriginal organizations. For example, the NLC strongly favored federal permission to proceed with the development of new uranium mines in the Northern Territory, whereas the CLC, the NAC (as well as the Victorian left and the left wing of the ALP) did not support that position. In order to resolve the conflict between the Federation and the NLC, the Minister granted the NLC a special position on the steering committee (implying veto powers), as well as having a legal representative on the panel of lawyers.

In addition to the internecine conflict over status on the Minister's land rights steering committee, there was no consensus among Aboriginal groups about what should or should not be included in a national land rights bill. This was clear, for example, at the meeting of NAC state chairmen in Melbourne from 14 to 16 September 1983, called to discuss the development of national land rights legislation. A document assessing NAC state papers on the issues to be considered in a national land rights bill was circulated. Table I indicates the range of interests in land rights legislation expressed by Aboriginal representatives from the various states and territory. The responses to the NAC survey clearly indicate the wide-ranging concerns that Aborigines throughout Australia had in relation to land rights legislation.

This divergence of interests among Aborigines in relation to land rights can be explained in terms of the differences in state and territory laws, the type of land available for Aboriginal claim, and the tribal (rural or country) versus urban character of the Aboriginal population. For example, states such as Western Australia had large areas of Crown land available for Aboriginal claim, whereas eastern states such as New South Wales and Victoria as well as Tasmania had virtually none. And almost all Crown land in the Northern Territory had already been granted to or was under claim by Aborigines.

The tribal/urban dichotomy of the Aboriginal population also explains their differences regarding a national land rights bill. For example, the procedures for making an Aboriginal claim to land in the Northern Territory (where most Aboriginal people retained their traditional tribal ties), would not be appropriate for making claims to land in Victoria, New South Wales or Tasmania, where they no longer had those ties. In the Northern Territory, in order to successfully make a claim for Aboriginal land it is necessary to demonstrate to a judicial tribunal a traditional Aboriginal attachment and occupation of land, including a knowledge of sacred sites. However, since urban Aborigines have for the most part been dispossessed of their land for almost 200 years, they could not meet the Northern Territory's criteria for making claim to land.

For this reason, tribal Aborigines tended to be content with having inalienable title to their traditional land, whereas urban Aborigines demanded private ownership rights (i.e. ownership in fee simple) to land which they regarded as 'reparation' for the dispossession of their land under

TABLE I
ISSUES TO CONSIDER IN LAND RIGHTS BILL (NAC STATE PAPERS)

Issues	NSW	Vic.	Qld	SA	WA	NT
Aboriginal Sovereignty	X	X	X			
Bill of Rights			X			
Control of Lands held by National Parks & Wildlife Service	X					
Registration of Land Claims/Claims Tribunal National Register	X	X	X			
Land for City & Town Dwellers	X			X		
Land for Fringe Dwellers				X		
Land for Traditional Purposes	X					
Land for Economic Purposes						
Various Titles for Categories of Aboriginal Land	X		X			
Just Compensation	X	X	X	X	X	X
Needs Claims			X			
Control of Forest Lands	X					
Control/Access (according to tradition) Aboriginal Land Pastoral Properties, Forests, all Crown Land	X		X			
Excisions on Pastoral Properties				X	X	X
Aboriginal Land & Development Trust	X		X			
Control of Cultural Heritage/Sacred Sites Protection	X		X		X	X
Aboriginal Environment Control	X		X			
Control over Minerals/Mining	X		X		X	X
Hunting and Fishing Rights	X		X			
Water Rights	X					
Arbitrator to Decide on Conflict			X			
Aboriginal Title:						
a. Aboriginal Occupied Houses and Land		X				
b. Vacant Blocks of Land		X				
c. Crown Land		X		X		
d. Reserve Lands					X	
e. Church Lands used by Aborigines					X	
f. Aboriginal Pastoral Land					X	
Royalties		X	X			X
Specific Functions for Land Councils/Enterprise Councils/Trusts		X	X			
National Legislation not to be Detrimental to Existing Land Rights Legislation				X		X
Aboriginal Land to be given Inalienable Freehold Title			X			
Title/Funds Community Controlled			X		X	
Use of International Covenants						X
Legislation to Reflect Perpetuity of Aboriginal Culture/unextinguished Traditional Title			X			
Self-Reliant/Determination Economic Development						X
Definition National Interest			X			X
Moratorium on Alienation of Indigenous Lands			X			
Closure of Seas			X			

Source: National Aboriginal Conference Report of the Meeting of State Chairmen on 14-16 September 1983 in Melbourne.

colonial repression. Likewise, there were differences between Aboriginal groups that had mineral-rich land and those which did not. Aborigines with economically viable mineral-bearing land (and the land councils that represented them in negotiations with the mining companies) insisted upon access to royalties derived from mining operations on their land, while those who did not have mineral-rich land were naturally less concerned with royalties.

This absence of consensus on national land rights legislation was evident in the steering committee's reaction to the Minister's first initiative in late February 1984. In fact, the absence of consensus on land right legislation was one of the factors that led to the Minister's decision to reverse the consultation process he had originally proposed for the development of the legislation.

Subversion of the Consultation Process

The Minister's original scenario in the formulation of national land rights legislation was five-fold. The first step was for the National Aboriginal Conference and Federation of Land Councils to consult with their constituencies and determine an Aboriginal position on land rights. Secondly, the NAC, Federation, and the Minister were to agree upon the principles and terms of land rights legislation. Thirdly, the Minister and Aboriginal representatives were to negotiate on a state-by-state basis, with state/territory governments to determine suitable complementary state legislation. Fourthly, instructions were to be given to the panel of lawyers to prepare a land rights bill. Fifthly, the draft of the bill was to be approved by the federal cabinet and enacted into law by Parliament. The original deadline for this was set by the Minister for August 1984 during the budget hearings of Parliament.

This process, however, was short-circuited by the Minister and, in fact, reversed in order of procedure. For example, instead of the NAC and Federation of Land Councils determining the Aboriginal position on land rights, and allowing time for consultation, the Minister instructed the panel of lawyers to prepare a list of questions relating to land rights legislation for consideration by the steering committee (NAC, 1984). The resulting thirty-eight questions dealt with issues which the lawyers thought any land rights legislation should cover.

This prompted debate among the lawyers themselves as to whether they should be raising the questions with the steering committee or whether the questions should be raised first by the steering committee and then directed to the panel of lawyers, as the Minister's consultative process had outlined. The concern was expressed that, by asking specific questions about what form the land rights legislation should take, the lawyers had in effect pre-determined the form that the legislation would take.

Furthermore, members of the steering committee only received the thirty-eight questions a few days in advance of the meeting in Melbourne held during 20-23 February, 1984. And when members of the steering committee arrived at the meeting, they were presented with answers to those questions suggested by the Department of Aboriginal Affairs. In addition, at the meeting, the Minister insisted upon on-the-spot responses from committee members to the questions. He ignored members' requests to undertake consultation with their constituents prior to taking positions on the questions.

To Aborigines' requests for more time and additional funds to consult their communities on the questions, Holding responded by saying that when the legislation was completed it would be given to the NAC for its approval. At that point they would have three options: to say yes, the legislation is satisfactory; no, it is unsatisfactory; or more time is needed for consultation before the legislation is endorsed.

The Minister explained that it was necessary to proceed this way for two reasons. The first reason was that opinion surveys were starting to show that people thought that enough was already being done for Aborigines. The second reason was that he did not want to have legislation 'hanging around in public' where it could be torn to pieces while he waited for Aborigines to endorse it. Holding said that this was what was happening at present to the land rights legislation in Victoria.

For the same reason Holding thought it was ill-advised for the Burke Government to conduct the Seaman inquiry. Not only did he think that it was presumptuous for a state to have an inquiry and expect the federal government to pay for it (Western Australia requested $300,000 to finance the inquiry), but Holding feared that the inquiry would get bogged-down and would divert Western Australia from the principles for land rights legislation that the federal government had laid down. For this reason, Holding had advised Burke not to conduct such an inquiry.

Holding told the steering committee that he preferred to rely upon the Aboriginal leadership assembled there to guide him in developing national land rights legislation. The Minister also reiterated his promise that he would not proceed on land rights legislation without their approval. However, despite the Minister's attempts to crystallize Aboriginal consensus on a land rights bill to meet his August 1984 deadline, Holding's efforts failed. This was evident at the steering committee meeting in Melbourne in February 1984. Major areas of contention between the Minister and Aboriginal representatives centred upon the kind of land available for Aboriginal land claims and the procedures for making those claims.

Several Aboriginal representatives, including Pat Dodson of the Central Land Council of the Northern Territory, Michael Mansell (an uninvited representative, since Tasmania did not have a National Aboriginal Conference branch), and Les Collins (Northern Queensland Land Council), argued that private land should be available for Aboriginal claim. Collins said that his constituents in Queensland wanted 'reparation' for being denied the use of their land. Mansell supported Collin's view that Aborigines should be compensated for the denial of their land over the last 195 years. Dodson also supported this argument, pointing out the fact that, in some areas of Australia (including the Northern Territory), private land was all that was available to claim.

The Minister disagreed with them. He explained that the whole basis of the land rights argument (presumably the Labor Party's position) was that land provided a spiritual and cultural base for Aborigines, and that part of land rights includes compensation to those who have lost that base. He said that in the Northern Territory at the moment, Aboriginals could claim land under the Land Rights Act by demonstrating their traditional linkage with the land. However, in some southern states, Aborigines were so dispossessed of their land and alienated from their culture that they could not substantiate such claims. In cases like this, the federal government, through the Aboriginal Development Commission, would be able to assist Aborigines. This was to be addressed, for example, through the Commission's Bicentennial Program which would give $800 million ($100 million over eight years) in loans to Aborigines for the purpose of financing the purchase of homes.

Holding said that, as far as he was concerned, this compensation (along with educational scholarships and health services) was reparation to the current generation of Aborigines to enable them and their children to take their rightful place in Australian society. When pressed on the question of compensation, Holding stated that receiving it would not preclude Aboriginals from making future claims to land.

Holding rejected the Aborigines' argument that they had a right to claim private land on the grounds that it was not 'politically feasible' at present. The Minister warned that this line of argumentation was precisely the one being used effectively in the 'anti-land-rights' campaign. The Minister said that meetings were being held in Victorian communities, for example, where opponents of land rights were telling gullible whites that Aborigines wanted to claim 'their back yards and their houses'. Therefore, if Aboriginals took this line they were, in effect, provoking the hostility of the larger community towards the Aboriginal land rights cause rather than winning its sympathy. He also pointed out that this raised the whole question of Aboriginal sovereignty—the proposed 'Makarrata' or treaty between Aborigines and the federal government.[3] Holding said that he could not support Aboriginal sovereignty at present.

Another major difference between the Minister and Aboriginal representatives on the steering committee concerned the procedure for making land claims. Mansell and Ray Robinson (NAC, Queensland) argued that there should be no claims procedure or tribunal for making Aboriginal land claims. Mansell said this involved Aborigines justifying what they felt was their land. Instead, it was white people who should justify their claim for continued occupation of Aboriginal land. Robinson questioned why Aborigines should have to prove their prior ownership. He pointed out that they used to own all of Australia.

Holding responded to this argument by saying that the land claims process in the Northern Territory was acceptable to Aborigines there and, therefore, should be acceptable to Aborigines elsewhere. The Minister said that, as in the case of the Northern Territory, he preferred to have a land-claims tribunal consisting of one judge. The tribunal would hear Aboriginal claims, would comment on the detrimental effects upon non-Aborigines arising from a successful claim, and would make a recommendation to the Minister for final decision on the claim. He argued that, politically, the Northern Territory land-claims procedure would itself be difficult to sell in national legislation. The Minister also responded to the argument that Aborigines once owned all of Australia by pointing out that, while Aborigines may have occupied all of Australia, individual clan groups were only associated with particular parts of Australia. It was this type of clan association that he felt should form the basis of traditional claims to land ownership.

National Aboriginal Conference Position on Land Rights Legislation

Despite the absence of consensus on specific points to be included in national legislation, the NAC had prepared its own tentative policy position on land rights legislation (NAC, 1984a). By April 1984, the land rights sub-committee of the NAC had developed five general principles for national legislation:

1. All land in Australia should be available for claim by Aboriginal people;
2. Land to be returned to Aboriginal ownership under the legislation and without going through the claims procedure should include all existing reserves and other lands identified as being of particular significance to Aborigines in each state;
3. The definition of 'land' under the legislation should include areas of sea and inland waterways adjacent to the land under claim;
4. Aboriginal groups should be able to claim land on any one or more of the bases of traditional ownership; historical association; economic, social, or cultural need; and compensation;
5. In principle, all land returned to Aboriginal ownership under the legislation should be held under inalienable freehold title. However, there should be further discussion of the notion of restricted fee simple.

The NAC land rights sub-committee was scheduled to meet again after the Easter break in April to do further work on its specific land rights policy. The next step was to meet with the land council representatives and other members of the steering committee in order to reach a common position on land rights legislation. After the steering committee members completed consultations with their constituencies they planned to give preliminary instructions to the panel of lawyers so that they could put their policies into the form of a land rights bill.

However, their specific policy recommendations for national land rights legislation never went beyond the NAC's five stated positions. The reason for this was that the political pressures upon Holding to abandon national Aboriginal land rights legislation began to mount after April 1984. This forced the Minister to retreat from his initial undertakings with Aboriginal groups. From this point on, he lost control of the federal initiative.

MOUNTING POLITICAL PRESSURES

Political pressure upon Holding's strategy for enacting national Aboriginal land rights legislation ultimately undermined the federal initiative. This pressure increased in four stages. The first stage took place during Holding's efforts to enact interim cultural heritage legislation to protect Aboriginal sacred sites and objects under threat. The second period of increasing political pressure occurred during the Labor Party's 36th Biennial National Conference at Canberra in July 1984. The third stage of mounting political pressure occurred in August 1984 when the Minister, in consultation with the Department of Aboriginal Affairs, drafted a steering committee discussion paper on national Aboriginal land rights. The fourth stage occurred in October 1984 after the Prime Minister and cabinet decided to remove the Aboriginal right to veto mining from land rights legislation (discussed in Chapter 4). The political pressure generated by these four events combined to undermine Holding's undertaking with Aboriginal representatives to formulate national land rights legislation.

Interim Cultural Heritage Legislation

At a meeting of the steering committee on 21 February 1984 in Melbourne, Holding gave the first indication of political trouble on the horizon. Aboriginal representatives at the meeting asked Holding to give his views on reports in the media of an imminent federal election. Specifically, they wanted to know how the Minister thought it would affect his August 1984 timetable for parliamentary consideration of a national land rights bill. Holding said that there was early election talk in the air and there may well be an early election in March 1985. He said that it was an attempt by the Hawke Government to secure control of the Senate.

Ominously, he followed this comment by saying that the passage of the cultural heritage legislation they had been discussing would presage the kind of political problems they would encounter in introducing the land rights legislation (Steering Committee Meeting, 1984a: 2). Indeed, that is precisely what happened.

Background

At a meeting between the panel of lawyers, the NAC and Aboriginal land councils, on 23 and 25 November 1983, it was decided that there should be immediate emergency legislation to protect Aboriginal sacred sites that were under imminent threat (Panel of Lawyers Meeting, 1983). It was agreed that this legislation should be followed up by a more in-depth and detailed legislation designed to protect Aboriginal heritage, folklore, relics, objects, and deal with matters of compensation for desecration.

The process of drafting this legislation was to follow the proposed pattern for drafting a national land rights bill. The panel of lawyers, in consultation with the NAC and land councils, were to draft the interim heritage legislation. After the final draft of the legislation was complete, it was to be presented to Aboriginal people for comments and endorsement or revision. The principal objective of the Act was to quickly bring in interim legislation in order to give the federal government powers to make declarations to protect significant sites that were in immediate danger. Aboriginal groups on the steering committee felt that such interim legislation would give them time to consider the more difficult issues involving the registration of sacred sites, and to determine which Aboriginal bodies should administer the legislation.

However, at the steering committee meeting of 19 and 20 December, Holding informed them that the federal cabinet and Parliament would not accept such interim legislation without long and drawn-out negotiations. This would defeat the very purpose of the legislation.

Holding said that there had been more departmental objections to his proposed legislation than had ever been received for such legislation. While some Aborigines criticized the draft for not going far enough in protecting Aboriginal sites and objects, government departments and ministers felt it went too far. Their feeling was that the draft instructions for the proposed legislation did not provide adequate guidelines for ministerial action. For example, there were no definitions of what was 'significant' in terms of Aboriginal objects and sites. This was to be determined solely by the Minister.

It was feared that this would place the Minister under immense political pressure. It would also give him enormous powers. For example, he would have the power to stop highly controversial mining projects such as the Roxby Downs uranium mine or the Argyle diamond project. Likewise, he would have the authority to force mining companies and Aborigines to continue negotiating mining projects against their wishes.

Holding said that the draft legislation was not politically feasible (in terms of it being passed in the current session of Parliament), because there was too much opposition to giving the Minister such broad powers. He told the steering committee that the bill would not be passed by the House of Representatives without intensive lobbying and, even if it were passed by the lower house, it would most likely be defeated in the Senate.

At the 4 April 1984 meeting of the steering committee, Holding proposed that a new draft of the Aboriginal and Torres Strait Islander (Heritage Protection) Bill be accepted. This draft of the bill, however, was not only not produced by the panel of lawyers, but they and the steering committee members had not even seen the document prior to the meeting. The draft had, in fact, been produced by the Attorney-General's Department under the supervision of the Attorney-General, Senator Gareth Evans.

Aboriginal members of the committee objected to the fact that the Attorney-General's bill, unlike the panel of lawyers' draft, did not provide protection for significant sites and objects unless the Minister gazetted a declaration protecting specified sites or objects, and that this delayed action. Also the draft did not protect restricted information on sacred sites (in traditional culture only adult men in the clan concerned were allowed this knowledge). And federal protection was extended only to human remains, not to objects such as those in museums and private collections.

Significantly, the Act would only apply to sites and objects under threat. It would not apply to those things that were under state jurisdiction or 'protection'. This was a matter of particular concern to Aboriginal groups, since one of the objectives of the interim federal legislation was to counter state legislation which allowed human remains and objects to be handled contrary to the wishes of Aboriginal people.

Nevertheless, the Attorney-General's bill had some advantages for Aborigines. For example, it would over-ride the Tasmanian government's proposed legislation providing for the disposal of Aboriginal human remains contrary to Aboriginal tradition.

Holding responded to the criticism of the Attorney-General's bill by simply saying that it was not satisfactory to Aborigines nor to himself. However, it was 'the best we can expect to get through cabinet and Parliament quickly' (Steering Committee Meeting, 1984*b*: 4). He added that if he thought he could get other things through, he would have included them. Holding also said that he had to exercise his political judgement as to whether to support the Attorney-General's draft, or to have nothing now and wait for the land rights legislation.

NAC lawyer Heather Sculthorpe asked Holding whether they could have more time to comment on the document, since neither the steering committee nor its legal advisers had seen it before the meeting. The Minister responded by saying that he had to take the proposals to a party subcommittee meeting that afternoon, so there was no more time for consideration of the draft. Aboriginal members asked for assurances, which Holding gave, that the draft could be amended in the future. The committee reluctantly approved the draft. However, CLC's Pat Dodson dissented, then relented and withdrew his dissent.

The expectation was that Parliament would pass interim cultural heritage legislation by June 1984 and, because of the imminent prospect of federal elections, national land rights and permanent cultural heritage legislation would be enacted next year, probably by March 1985. However, growing political pressure on the federal government not only altered his timetable but changed the outcome itself.

The 1984 Australian Labor Party National Conference

The outcome of Aborigines' efforts to amend the ALP's Aboriginal land rights platform at the Labor Party's national policy conference in Canberra in July 1984, was a major source of disillusionment. Although the party platform did not change in any substantive way (except for the inclusion of children's rights), Holding rejected the National Aboriginal Conference's proposed amendments to the platform.

The Aboriginal groups on the steering committee took the position that, although remaining the same in real terms, the ALP's proposed platform on Aboriginal land rights policy represented a 'complete departure' from the position of the steering committee (NAC, 1984b: 2).

They argued that the ALP's proposed platform (as well as the existing one) was based upon the Woodward Commission recommendations that were designed for the Northern Territory during the 1974-75 period. They pointed out the fact that the recommendations formed the basis of the Aboriginal Land Rights (Northern Territory) Act of 1976. This Act had, in turn, been reviewed by Judge Toohey in the light of Minister Holding's five principles for national Aboriginal land rights legislation. Therefore, the proposed platform was not only out of date, but did not address the problems facing the implementation of national land rights. Furthermore, even in the case of the Northern Territory, the platform did not address the recommendations of the Toohey Report concerning excisions of Aboriginal land on pastoral leases.

Representatives of Aboriginal groups pointed to the fact that the proposed platform emphasized the welfare needs of Aborigines. It did not promise Aboriginal land rights and economic development. Essentially, they said that the platform turned social welfare funding into a form of compensation for the dispossession of Aboriginal land. And it turned the promise of national Aboriginal land rights into the unsatisfactory Northern Territory legislation which was formulated and reviewed by non-Aborigines. The National Aboriginal Conference pointedly asked why there was no mention in the proposed platform of the 'sixth principle' of national land rights legislation agreed to by the Minister—that the NAC must approve land rights legislation?

They argued that the Minister was also back-tracking on his promise to 'upgrade' the Northern Territory Act by warning the Central Land Council that it would not get all it hoped for from the Toohey Report. For example, it was suggested that Aborigines pay compensation to pastoralists for excisions on pastoral properties. Aboriginal representatives wanted to know the source of this funding. Was it to come from existing Aboriginal welfare revenues, or from mining royalties derived from Aboriginal land?

Steering committee members accused the ALP of 'buckling under to anti-land right pressure' against national land rights legislation. For example, they noted the fact that the ALP proposal called for land grants to be held under *secure title* instead of *inalienable title* as set forth in the Minister's five principles for Aboriginal land rights. Furthermore, the proposed platform emphasized the importance of seeking complementary state or territory legislation. In this formulation, the federal government would only use its powers if all else failed rather than providing the impetus for state legislation.

The steering committee regarded this as a complete about-face by the Minister. The chairman of the NAC's sub-committee on land rights, Ossie Cruse, approached Holding prior to the party conference and requested a change in the wording of the proposed platform from 'secure title' to 'inalienable title' (NAC, 1984d). However, the Minister refused to make this change on the grounds that he did not want to 'hamstring the states and the people who wanted different titles.' He argued that the platform already mentioned the Woodward Commission recommendations which referred to inalienable title as the major title that would be issued to Aboriginal communities.[4] When pressed on this issue, Holding mentioned the Coombs Report as another reason for refusing to agree to their request.[5]

In fact, during Aboriginal lobbying efforts at the ALP conference, the party's major factions agreed to a compromise to avoid an open split on the Aboriginal land rights issue. According to Ossie Cruse, the right wing of the ALP (including the Western Australian delegation) countered the left-wing's support for amending the proposed ALP land rights platform to bring it into alignment with Holding's five principles for land rights. The right wing did this by threatening to introduce its own amendments to the land rights platform if the left wing introduced any major amendments to it. The countervailing amendment most widely mentioned by the right wing was to remove the Aboriginal right of veto over mining on Aboriginal land.

As a result of this factional truce at the ALP conference, the Aboriginal representatives found that their lobbying efforts had little success. For example, Cruse informed the committee that the Labor Party built a 'bloc vote' at the conference so that voting on ALP land rights policy was largely a matter of procedure. He said that it was difficult to even get the Centre Left to look at their proposed amendments (NAC, 1984d: 3).

In the aftermath of the ALP's 1984 conference, the NAC made two decisions. The first was to launch a major national publicity campaign to highlight their dissatisfaction with the ALP land rights platform and to combat the anti-land-rights campaign in the media. It noted a newspaper report indicating that the Leader of the Opposition federal Liberal Party, Andrew Peacock, felt that Aboriginal land rights would be an issue at the next federal election in Western Australia, Queensland, and the Northern Territory.

The Aboriginal land rights sub-committee of the NAC recommended that a Western Australian public awareness program on land rights that they had been planning, be endorsed as the basis of a national strategy. They also argued that the campaign should be independent of the Department of Aboriginal Affairs and the Aboriginal Development Commission. It was argued that an independent campaign would better enable the NAC to put across its point of view, plus, it would be likely to persuade the Minister to take more notice of them. They recommended an overall budget for the campaign of $300,000 to be obtained from the DAA public awareness campaign funding, from a special allocation from the Minister, from the NAC budget, and from corporate funding. The second decision taken by the NAC was that, if they failed to convince the ALP to accept their policy, they should stop negotiating with Holding on the steering committee.

Steering Committee Discussion Paper on Land Rights

In August 1984 the Minister virtually discontinued consulting the steering committee in his effort to enact some form of national land rights legislation. This occurred in August when the Minister presented the steering committee with a so-called 'steering committee discussion paper' which had been prepared by the DAA.[6] The paper was presented to the steering committee on 24 August just prior to a scheduled meeting. Neither the steering committee nor the panel of lawyers had seen the document before the meeting.

In the discussion paper the Minister argued that he had to set forth the parameters for federal land rights legislation. He pointed out that this was necessary to defuse growing anti-land rights pressure. He said that the federal government had already come under attack for the Aboriginal and Torres Strait Islander Heritage (Interim Protection) Act of 1984.

Opponents of land rights were able to mobilize public fears of the detrimental impact of land rights legislation upon them. For this reason, it was necessary to clearly specify the limitations of the proposed federal legislation. Holding emphasized the fact that it was important that the parameters of land rights be 'responsible' and 'embody an equitable balance of interests'. Without that, he said, it would be impossible to counter the growing resistance to land rights legislation. He emphasized that this was essential to ensure its acceptability by the federal government, and to form the basis for consultations with the states, miners, rural and other concerned interests.

The Minister pointed out that the outcome of the Seaman Report on the Western Australian Aboriginal land inquiry, as well as the Western Australian government's response to it, would significantly affect the federal government's land rights legislation. Since the Seaman Report was scheduled for public release during September 1984, the timing of the Minister's discussion paper in late August must, in part, have been an effort by Holding to prevent the Western Australian government from taking the initiative from him on the land rights issue.

The steering committee's reaction to the discussion paper was predictably hostile. It stated that the federal government had not taken the advice of the land councils or the NAC, and seemed to be moving toward its own form of land rights legislation. The steering committee expressed three objections to the discussion paper: the categories of land eligible for claim; the land claims procedures; control of Aboriginal land (Steering Committee Meeting, 1984c).

On the question of land eligible for Aboriginal claim, the steering committee rejected the Minister's proposal to exclude public purpose land, private land, and land within town boundaries. On the issue of land claim procedures, the steering committee rejected the proposal to set up state tribunals to settle land claim disputes. The Minister's proposal was that tribunals (comprised of a single judge) only had the power to recommend to the state ministers (the federal minister in the case of the Northern Territory). The committee also objected to a ten-year time limit for lodging Aboriginal land claims.

In relation to control of Aboriginal land, steering committee members argued that if Aboriginal communities agreed to mineral explorations, that in itself did not constitute a *de facto* acceptance of mining on their land. And if Aborigines and a mining company did not agree to the proposed mining operation, they should not be forced to submit to arbitration, especially not by state tribunals.

The land councils also objected to the proposal that mining royalty equivalent funds should be linked to the delivery of services to Aboriginal communities affected by mining activity. They argued that this was contrary to the principles of self-development for Aboriginal people. They should be free to use these funds as they wished. Of course, another reason for land council opposition to this proposal was that it would place restraints upon the use of the land councils' principal source of revenue (especially in the Northern Territory).

Holding told the steering committee that the discussion paper was not a final document. Nevertheless, it had to serve as the basis for discussion. He said that the parameters could vary somewhat, that if members of the steering committee disagreed with the proposals then he would be willing to put forward their proposals to the cabinet.

Aboriginal members said that they would prepare position papers on areas of disagreement with the discussion paper for presentation at the next scheduled meeting of the steering committee in early October 1984. However, before members of the steering committee could prepare these papers, political events intervened to make it extraneous.

The political events involved Premier Burke's two-day meeting in Canberra on 24 and 25 September with the Prime Minister and members of the cabinet. Burke went to Canberra to discuss the Seaman Report, along with the Western Australian government's statement of its position on land rights which was scheduled for official release on 27 September, 1984.

According to news reports, Burke expressed at the meeting his opposition to major elements of the Seaman Report. This also put him at odds with Holding's five principles for Aboriginal land rights legislation. (See, for example, *The Age*, 25 September 1984, and *Sydney Morning Herald*, 25 September 1984.)

Before going to Canberra, Burke had already warned the federal government not to interfere with state land rights. At the federal cabinet meeting he reportedly warned them that ALP polls conducted in Western Australia showed that sixty-eight per cent of the state's population opposed land rights. He pointed out that this was a politically explosive issue, especially since Western Australia was faced with three November by-elections, not to mention the federal election which was expected later in the year.

The media reported that the Prime Minister and cabinet also considered Holding's discussion paper but, despite their earlier support for them, backed away from the principles it set out. According to press accounts, Prime Minister Hawke and Minister for Resources and Energy Peter Walsh wanted to water-down Aboriginal control over mining. Instead of giving Aborigines the automatic right to refuse mining on their land, as in the Aboriginal Land Rights (Northern Territory) Act of 1976, they argued for an arbitration procedure.

They proposed the adoption of legislative principles along the lines of the South Australian land rights legislation (i.e. the Pitjantjatjara Land Rights Act of 1981) in which Aborigines can oppose mining on their land but, if there is a dispute between them and mining companies, then the dispute must go to arbitration. According to the press, cabinet thought that this was necessary to balance Aboriginal land rights with the rights of a major economic interest — the mining industry. Specifically mentioned in this regard was the argument by miners that the Northern Territory Land Rights Act had discouraged mineral exploration in the Northern Territory. By implication, if the mining provisions in the Northern Territory Land Rights Act were adopted in national legislation, then future growth in this vital industry would be discouraged throughout Australia.

Aboriginal members of the steering committee reacted violently to these press reports (Scutton, 1984 and Riley, 1984). For example, Stan Scrutton, Chairman of the Central Land Council, sent a telex to Minister Holding informing him of its refusal to attend the next steering committee meeting scheduled for 4 October unless the Minister provided full disclosure of meetings held between Premier Burke and federal cabinet. Scrutton insisted upon having copies of any proposals initiated by Holding, or any other Minister, which were considered by the cabinet and had the potential to affect land rights in the Northern Territory.

Scutton also demanded to have the proposed agenda, plus papers for discussion, prior to the next steering committee meeting. This telex to Holding was followed by another telex from Rob Riley, National Chairman of the NAC, Margaret Mallard, NAC state chairman for Western Australia, and Darryl Kickett of the Kimberley Land Council. The second telex expressed support for Scutton's telex to the Minister, and said that they did not intend to be used as 'scapegoats' by the federal government in any attempt to enact land rights legislation that was unacceptable to Aboriginal people.

CHAPTER THREE

Breakdown in Initiative

The breakdown in the federal initiative on Aboriginal land rights legislation occurred after an October 1984 meeting of the steering committee in Canberra, the national capital. The meeting was hastily called by Clyde Holding to discuss extraordinary developments during the previous month which affected the federal land rights initiative. In calling the meeting, Holding was responding in part to demands by Aboriginal leaders for a disclosure of information regarding Burke's meeting with the Prime Minister and the cabinet in late September.

The extraordinary developments about which the Minister spoke to the steering committee were the consequences of a unilateral decision by Prime Minister Bob Hawke to remove Aborigines' power to veto exploration and mining on their land. This decision, which Aborigines later referred to as 'Hawke's law', was made without consultation with federal cabinet, ALP caucus and, indeed, without prior discussion with his own Minister for Aboriginal Affairs.

Hawke's decision caught everyone by surprise. Cabinet colleagues tended to react to this development by either accommodating or opposing the decision. Ministers Beazley, Evans, Walsh and Keating backed Hawke's decision on the grounds that mineral development was necessary for Australia's national defense and continued economic prosperity. Beazley, the Minister for Defence and a senior member of cabinet, was the most outspoken proponent of the Prime Minister's position. Others, such as Susan Ryan and John Dawkins, as well as Clyde Holding, opposed the decision on the grounds that it conflicted with ALP policy and would undermine the federal initiative on land rights.

As Minister for Aboriginal Affairs, Holding held a minor cabinet portfolio and was not influential in making inner-cabinet decisions. Nevertheless, he opposed Hawke's decision by allying with Gerry Hand, the leader of the Victorian Socialist Left, and the left wing of the ALP (along with Aboriginal groups), to lobby within the ALP caucus against the Prime Minister's action.

Hawke's decision had the effect of undermining Holding's initiative on land rights legislation. While Holding did not openly challenge the Prime Minister, he opposed his decision by attempting to delay any action that would undermine the federal initiative. He tried to maintain the façade of implementing national land rights legislation. He sought to maintain the illusion that national land rights legislation was proceeding unchanged and according to schedule. However, once Holding gave in to pressure to publically endorse the Prime Minister's position as the federal position, Aboriginal members of the steering committee openly attacked him and the Hawke Government for succumbing to political expediency by selling out to the mining industry.

Removing the Mining Veto

At the steering committee of 4 October 1984, Holding gave a rambling explanation of developments during the previous three to four weeks (meeting of the steering committee, 1984). The Minister informed Aboriginal members that he and the Prime Minister were concerned about the distortion of land rights issues in Western Australia.

Holding erroneously mentioned television advertising by the AMIC (Australian Mining Industry Council) in this regard. The Minister said that both he and the Prime Minister told AMIC that the advertisements on television in Western Australia were not only inaccurate, but they were racist.[1] Holding said that the Prime Minister held two meetings with AMIC to discuss the issue. The first meeting was at The Lodge. It comprised Holding, James Strong, Executive Director of AMIC, along with a few directors of the large east coast mining companies, including the Chairman of the CMWA (Chamber of Mines of Western Australia) and Hugh Morgan, Executive Director of the Western Mining Corporation.

Holding said that a whole range of issues was canvassed and, essentially, AMIC presented its 'log of claims' as had existed since 1976, the date of the Northern Territory Land Rights Act. The Minister said that, at that meeting, he persuaded AMIC to withdraw its television advertisements. AMIC supposedly made this concession when Holding confronted them with the threat of NAC's television advertisements which were designed to counter AMIC's. Holding said that NAC's advertisements were equally racist. The Minister indicated that AMIC agreed to withdraw the advertisements out of concern for the industry's corporate image. He noted, however, that in his view the damage to land rights had already been done.

The Minister told the steering committee that AMIC later sent the Prime Minister a copy of its account of agreements reached at the meeting. Holding said that AMIC officials deliberately misconstrued what transpired at the meeting. He said that a whole range of issues had been discussed and AMIC had made an 'ambit claim' which was presented to the Prime Minister as representing the government's position. Holding said that he advised Hawke that AMIC's account of the meeting did not reflect the true position of the government, and the Prime Minister agreed with him. The Minister added, parenthetically, that this confirmed his previous experience with AMIC in relation to the federal heritage legislation. He said that the miners were very difficult to deal with, often distorting the facts to suit their own 'preconceived political position'.

Holding said that at the Prime Minister's second meeting with AMIC (which the Minister did not attend, on the somewhat disingenuous grounds that he had nothing more to say to them), Hawke underscored the inaccuracy of AMIC's notes of the previous meeting. According to Holding, Hawke told AMIC representatives that, while their concerns would be considered, he felt that the issue was 'more complicated than just simply the issue of veto rights'.

It is interesting to note in this regard that AMIC reportedly sent copies of the notes of the first meeting between AMIC and Hawke and Holding to the Labor caucus in Western Australia, where land rights legislation was then under discussion. The notes purported to show that an agreement had been reached between the federal government and AMIC. These were the notes that the Prime Minister had, according to Holding, repudiated. Holding said that the Prime Minister sent word to the Labor caucus in Western Australia disavowing the validity of the notes.

Holding explained that there were basically two 'thrusts' against national land rights legislation. One was directed by AMIC, the other by Brian Burke and the Western Australian government. The AMIC thrust was that they would support any form of land rights legislation, provided that Aborigines were not given control over their land. That is to say, that unless AMIC was assured that there were no veto rights (comparable with the Northern Territory Act), they would discontinue exploration and mining operations.

The Minister said that, in his view, AMIC had been in touch with 'its colleagues' in the Northern Territory to help them press their case with the federal government. For example, the day prior to the steering committee meeting, Holding received a telegram from Paul Everingham, Chief Minister of the Northern Territory, stating that the position taken by the Western Australian government on land rights had opened up a 'whole new ball game'. Everingham requested a meeting with Holding to discuss a 'whole new approach on land rights.' According to the Minister, AMIC was pressing the federal government to remove the veto from the Northern Territory Act, and to guarantee that it would not be included in the proposed national land rights legislation.

Holding's reaction to the so-called AMIC thrust was to point out that the Aboriginal leadership in Western Australia had reservations about the proposals of the Burke Government, and that the Aboriginal people of the Northern Territory had no confidence whatever in Everingham and his administration. The Minister said that if they put together all of their resources (i.e. Labor Party and the Aboriginal vote), they could defeat Everingham. He stated that this would be an 'enormous help towards solving all of these problems'.

In relation to AMIC, Holding said that their problem, as well as the farmers' problem (i.e. the National Farmers' Federation), was the perception that the Labor government would be returned in the next federal election. He said that both AMIC and the farmers were National Party voters. No matter what they were offered by a Labor government, they would remain National Party voters. In a meeting between the Prime Minister and the NFF (National Farmers' Federation), the farmers told Hawke that their criticism of national land rights legislation was part of the AMIC campaign in Western Australia. If their concerns were not accommodated by the federal government, they would consider mounting a national campaign against the legislation amongst their membership.

The Prime Minister responded to the threat by pointing out that there were certain risks connected with such a strategy. If they conducted a national campaign and, if, as expected, Labor won the forthcoming elections, then all government consultation with the farmers on land rights would cease. Furthermore, Labor would then feel they had a clear mandate to proceed with national land rights irrespective of the views of AMIC or the NFF.

The second thrust or source of pressure on the federal government's land rights legislation emanated from the Western Australian state government of Brian Burke. Holding said that the Seaman Report was issued in late September, and that the federal government received a copy of it two or three days later. The Minister pointed out that the Western Australian government did not adopt the recommendations of the Report, and this put the federal government under pressure. Holding described the nature of this pressure in terms of Burke's efforts to secure federal endorsement for his proposed state land rights legislation. Burke also sought assurances that, whatever legislation the federal government adopted, it would not apply in Western Australia.

In Holding's view, Burke confronted the federal government with a timetable for state land rights legislation (giving 1 December as the date he would introduce legislation), and he wanted federal backing for the legislation. The Minister was concerned that, by responding to the Premier's timetable, the federal government would lose its land rights initiative to him. Furthermore, Holding was concerned that, if Burke succeeded in his strategy, Western Australia's land rights legislation would become the model for other states and the Northern Territory, thereby replacing federal proposals.

Holding said that Burke's proposals were considered by the federal cabinet during lengthy meetings on 25 and 26 September. The Minister indicated that the outcome of the cabinet meetings was a stalemate and the issue unresolved. He noted, however, that cabinet decided that Holding should include AMIC, the farmers, and the states, along with the steering committee, in further consultation on land rights legislation. While Holding tended to discount this decision in his discussions with the steering committee, it signalled a significant shift in the federal initiative.

Originally, Holding's initiative on national land rights was to be developed in consultation with Aboriginal groups represented on the steering committee. Aborigines were supposed to determine policy in conjunction with the Minister. The panel of lawyers was to translate that policy into legislation. The NAC and the land councils were promised a veto power over the legislation, even a role in the federal government's negotiations with the states to ensure a uniform national standard for land rights throughout Australia.

After the federal cabinet meetings in September 1984, however, the process of formulating land rights legislation was substantially altered. Instead of Aborigines determining the principles of land rights legislation in consultation with the Minister, they became just one of several 'interest-groups' which included AMIC, NFF, and the states, all of whom were to have an input into the legislation. Therefore, instead of Aboriginal groups being represented in the federal government's negotiations with the states, Aborigines became just one interested group whose concerns and wishes had to be compromised in order to reach a 'balanced' position vis-à-vis other interest-groups.

Holding told the steering committee that cabinet was faced with two issues in relation to land rights legislation. The first issue was whether it accepted Burke's argument that Western Australia had an over-riding exemption in relation to national land rights legislation. He said that he thought the answer to this question would be 'no' because, if it gave one state such an exemption, the entire initiative for uniform land rights would be undermined.

The second political question facing cabinet was whether a statement would be issued (in Parliament or elsewhere) which outlined the government's final position on national land rights. Holding said that cabinet was under pressure in this regard as well (referring to pressure generated by the 1984 federal election campaign). He said that pressure was being applied to Aboriginal groups to make major concessions on land rights to Western Australia, AMIC, and the NFF. Holding expressed the view that Aboriginal groups should resist this pressure.

The Minister indicated that the best strategy for coping with the pressure was to avoid stating the steering committee's position on land rights legislation until after the forthcoming federal election. Holding said that he, in particular, was under pressure to 'come clean' and tell the special interests (i.e. AMIC and the NFF) what the federal government would do on land rights. However, Holding said that he preferred to stay in a 'back position' because he was under pressure to make concessions prior to an election. These concessions involved real limitations on what he and the steering committee were trying to achieve.

The Minister stated that if the steering committee resisted the pressure and waited until the election was under way, they would get uniform national land rights and the 'terror campaign' (presumably referring to CMWA's campaign in Western Australia) would stop. He proposed a strategy of maintaining that the federal government was committed to uniform land rights, and to continue with the processes and schedules the steering committee had set, i.e. to introduce legislation in the Parliament by March 1985.

The Fait Accompli

Although Holding assured the steering committee that it was not facing a *fait accompli*, the reality of the situation as he related it suggested otherwise. For example, the Minister informed the committee that the Prime Minister had decided that Aborigines should not have the power to veto exploration and mining on their land.

In response to a question from Pat Dodson about the status of the veto contained in the Northern Territory Act, Holding agreed that the Act as it presently stood was 'objectively' the best piece of land rights legislation achieved to date in Australia. However, he said that the Prime Minister would not support the retention of the veto in the Act, nor could it be included in any federal legislation. In other words, this was an established new ruling which could not be debated or negotiated.

Holding said that he had been instructed by the Prime Minister to consider a 'range of tribunal-type models' for the resolution of disputes between Aboriginal land owners and miners. He said that Hawke had expressed a personal preference for the South Australian arbitration system (i.e. the so-called Pitjantjatjara and Maralinga models).[2] However, he stressed that this was only the Prime Minister's personal preference, that other arbitration models could be considered for national land rights legislation.

The Minister tried to justify the Prime Minister's decision to drop the veto provision in the proposed national land rights legislation on the grounds that it was still possible for Aborigines to 'control' what occurred on their land without having the veto. In fact, he down-played the full significance of what had happened to the steering committee by incredulously suggesting that Aboriginal 'control' over their land under an arbitration system (i.e. tribunal) was more effective than it was under the existing veto mechanism in the Northern Territory Act.

Holding strained credibility, moreover, by arguing that the only way to remove unwanted pressure by the mining companies upon Aboriginal traditional owners who did not want mining on their land was to rely upon a tribunal. The Minister used the example of the Koongarra uranium mining project in the Northern Territory to make his point. He said that, after the TOs (traditional Aboriginal owners of land) refused to allow mining on their land, the company concerned, Denison Australia Pty Limited, continued to exert pressure on the Aboriginal land owners to agree to mining their land. Holding said that this situation created divisions within the community (ostensibly because unanimity concerning consent to mine is required).

John Ah Kit of the Northern Land Council of the Northern Territory discounted the example given by the Minister. Ah Kit said that the case of Koongarra was unique insofar as the company had already acquired mineral leases over the Koongarra deposit on Aboriginal land that had been excised from Kakadu National Park before the Northern Territory Land Rights Act had been adopted. The problem was that the company sought the use of additional adjoining Aboriginal land for its mining operations, but this land fell under the protection of the Land Rights Act. In other words, Denison had to have the consent of the local Aboriginal land owners in order to extend their original lease area. Ah Kit pointed out that, in this situation, the company, indeed, had access to the Aboriginal land owners. However, in more remote Aboriginal areas, such as the middle of Arnhem Land in the Northern Territory, companies did not have that kind of access to Aboriginal land owners.

The Minister responded by reiterating that the Prime Minister had decided that 'no group in the community ought to have a simple veto right' and that the federal government had a responsibility to the public to ensure that resource development projects were not blocked by any group. Holding equivocated, however, on this issue by saying that it was important for the steering committee to decide an appropriate arbitration model which would maximize Aboriginal 'control' over their land. He said that it was incumbent upon it to agree to an appropriate tribunal system in uniform land rights legislation to recommend to cabinet after the election. The Minister felt that if the steering committee did not move quickly to implement land rights legislation during the first term of the new Labor government the opportunity would rapidly slip away.

THE AUSTRALIAN LABOR PARTY'S
PRE-ELECTION ASSESSMENT

During the run-up to the federal elections held on 1 December 1984, the Special Minister of State, Mick Young, and his staff, developed a briefing paper regarding Aboriginal land rights (Young, 1984). The purpose of the paper was to assess possible election problems stemming from the land rights issue that the federal ALP would face. The paper provides an insight into the federal government's position on land rights just before the election.

The briefing paper began by re-stating the federal government's five principles for Aboriginal land rights which it embraced in 1983 soon after election to office. The paper noted the fact that the official opposition party formerly endorsed variations of the first four of these principles. It also indicated that more recent ALP policy emphasized 'secure' title rather than 'inalienable title', protection of sites of 'particular' sacred significance rather than the all-embracing protection of Aboriginal sites, and 'terms and conditions of entry and compensation for exploration, mining and other use of the land'.

It was pointed out that the federal Labor government had been discussing national land rights legislation with the NAC and Aboriginal land councils for over a year, and that draft legislation was scheduled for early 1985, although it could take longer. The paper also stated that there was existing legislation which met some or all of these principles in the Northern Territory, South Australia and New South Wales. Information compiled in the briefing paper on state and territory land rights legislation is reproduced in Table II.

The briefing paper explained that principle number three, relating to control of mining, was usually taken to mean that Aborigines had the power to consent or withhold their consent to mining on their land. While there was no absolute power of veto in existing land rights legislation, the over-ride provisions in the legislation were stringent. This meant that they were only intended for use in exceptional circumstances.

According to the paper, the Prime Minister stated that, due to pressure from the Western Australian government, which itself was under pressure from mining and pastoral groups, national land rights legislation would not include the right to veto mining on Aboriginal land. It also noted that Burke's proposed legislation was likely to fail in the upper house of state parliament.

However, this did not preclude the use of other measures to secure 'control' of mining on Aboriginal land. But it did mean that national land rights legislation would not over-ride Western Australia's decisions on land rights. Therefore, the federal government would not interfere with Western Australia's decisions concerning mining and exploration, resolution of access disputes, and land available for claim.

The briefing paper pointed out that legislation in the Northern Territory, South Australia and New South Wales required Aboriginal consent to mine on Aboriginal land, despite provisions for over-riding their refusal to give consent or 'veto'. However, the Prime Minister's decision had the effect of reducing the third principle. This meant that the proposed national legislation would be weaker than the legislation in three states/ territories.

Consequently, the national legislation would only have a major impact in Queensland and Tasmania, which have opposed land rights legislation consistent with the federal government's five principles. Furthermore, the government could expect pressure from the mining and pastoral industries

Table II
Federal Principles for State and Territory Land Rights Legislation

State or Territory	Land Claimable	Claim Process	1 Inalienable Title	2 Sacred Sites	3 Control Mining	4 Royalties	5 Compensation
Northern Territory (1976)	Unalienated Crown Land	Hearing by Aboriginal Land Commissioner	Yes	Yes Under Northern Territory legislation	Yes Veto can be over-ridden by the Governor-General	Yes	No Apart from wider distribution of royalties
South Australia (Pitjantjatjara, 1981, and Maralinga, 1984)	NA Separate Acts deal with specific areas	NA	Yes	Yes Under other South Australian legislation	Yes Appeals may go to an arbitrator	Yes	No But some royalties are redistributed
New South Wales (1983)	Unalienated Crown Land	Application to Crown Lands	Yes	Yes Under other New South Wales legislation	Yes Certain minerals excepted	Yes	Yes Via percentage of New South Wales Land Tax revenue
Western Australia (proposed)	Certain categories of Crown Land	Negotiated settlement or recourse to an Aboriginal Land Tribunal	Yes	Yes Under existing Western Australian legislation	No	Unclear	No
Victoria (under discussion)	Certain categories of Crown Land	Hearings by an Aboriginal Land Claims Tribunal	Yes	Yes Under existing state legislation (archaeological sites only)	Only over Sites of Significance. May be over-ridden by both Houses of Parliament	Yes	NA
Queensland and Tasmania	OPPPOSE LAND RIGHTS LEGISLATION						

Source: Office of the Special Minister of State, Mick Young, 1984.

in the Northern Territory, South Australia and New South Wales to weaken existing land rights legislation there to bring them into line with the proposed national legislation. The paper pointed out that the Prime Minister may not have anticipated the erosion of land rights on this scale. It also indicated that other state governments may rightly resent the privileged status accorded to Western Australia in relation to land rights legislation, when they have tried to comply with the government's five principles in the face of similar opposition from special interest groups. This may set the stage for increased pressure on the federal government to relax its other land rights principles.

Experience in the Northern Territory

The briefing paper indicated that, based upon the experience of the Northern Territory, the veto was unlikely to be used. However, its mere existence was a powerful factor benefiting Aboriginals in their negotiations with companies for favorable royalties and conditions of mining. According to the assessment, this increase in Aboriginal negotiating power had dramatically improved the mining companies' treatment of Aboriginal communities. And the benefits to Aborigines in the Northern Territory had spread to other states in Australia where the companies now understood the advantages of having good relations with Aboriginal traditional owners.

The briefing paper took exception to the claim made by the mining industry that exploration in the Northern Territory had declined seriously due to the Northern Territory Land Rights Act. It argued that in terms of value, exploration in the Northern Territory had increased by 400 per cent between 1974 and 1975 (despite the anticipated introduction of the land rights legislation), and that this increase matched that of the large mining states. The paper acknowledged that, while there had been interruptions to the process of granting ELs (exploration licences) due to actions by the companies, the Northern Territory Aboriginal land councils, and the Northern Territory government, this would 'smooth out' once the current backlog of exploration mining licence applications was cleared.

The paper pointed out that the Northern Territory government had made numerous attempts to subvert the federal land rights legislation enacted for the Northern Territory (i.e. the Northern Territory Land Rights Act of 1976). It specifically mentioned in this regard the Northern Territory government's alienation (i.e. selling) of land under Aboriginal claim, court challenges to the Northern Territory Aboriginal Land Commissioner's recommendations for granting title to Aboriginal land, court challenges to the decisions of the federal Minister for Aboriginal Affairs, violation of the Northern Territory Sacred Sites Protection Act (adopted by the Northern Territory government under federal duress) by desecrating Aboriginal sacred sites and threatening to amend the Act itself.

The observation was made that the most recent threat to amend the Northern Territory Sacred Sites Protection Act was connected with the political ambitions of the former Chief Minister of the Northern Territory, Paul Everingham. In other words, the Northern Territory government's attacks on Aboriginal land rights was politically motivated. The document also stated that the Western Australian government had, on occasion, ignored its sacred sites legislation. The Noonkanbah incident in 1980 was specifically mentioned in this regard.

The conclusion drawn from these observations was that the federal government could not assume that state and territory governments would exceed, much less maintain and observe, provisions beyond national land rights legislation. Therefore, while the federal government might regard its proposed national legislation as a minimum standard, in reality it was likely to be regarded as the maximum standard. In this regard, the document reiterated Holding's claim that the threat of imminent federal land rights legislation, with the example of Northern Territory legislation as its model, was a powerful incentive for states to proceed with their own land rights legislation.

Electoral Implications

The report noted the fact that public statements by the mining and pastoral industries on land rights legislation did not reflect their working relationships with Aborigines.[3] However, these statements served the purpose of 'fanning negative public feeling' toward land rights. The public was said to be easy prey to the unfounded fear that private land would be claimable under national land rights legislation.

The mining and farming peak organizations (i.e. AMIC and NFF) had also been successful in exploiting public fears that these industries would suffer under such legislation, to the extent that it would erode the standards of living of the general community. The paper mentioned the results of the ANOP (Australian National Opinion Poll) commissioned by the Department of Aboriginal Affairs in August 1984 as evidence for this fear. However, while the briefing paper acknowledged that thirty per cent of those polled were opposed to land rights, other figures in the poll were misrepresented by the media. For example, the paper pointed out that eighteen per cent of those polled 'strongly' favored land rights, and were not merely supportive of it as was reported in the press.

The briefing paper indicated that land rights was an electoral issue in Western Australia, Queensland, and the Northern Territory. However, whether it became a national election issue depended upon how much public debate it generated, and the extent to which the political opposition tried to take advantage of it. Already, it was noted, church groups and prominent Australians such as Dr. Coombs had begun to criticize the federal government's reduced commitment to land rights. And public statements had been made by opponents of land rights, such as Mr. Stone.

The paper noted that it was too late to assuage public fears regarding land rights before the federal election in December 1984. Furthermore, it was difficult to assess the impact of the Prime Minister's statement removing the veto from land rights legislation without knowing the effects of changes in electoral boundaries. Nevertheless, it was wrong to assume that it would necessarily cost the Labor Party many seats in the forthcoming election. For example, it was argued that it was erroneous to assume that the ALP would be vulnerable in remote area electorates where Aboriginal voting power is concentrated. The reason for this was that the veto issue was unlikely to change the overall perceptions of voters. In addition, Aboriginal voters have traditionally supported the ALP. And they had strong reasons to keep Labor in power, despite the Prime Minister's decision on the mining veto.

The briefing paper identified four federal electorates which had a high proportion of Aboriginal population and (with one exception, Leichardt) also contained large areas of land likely to become available for Aboriginal claim. Table III contains data presented in the paper on the Aboriginal population as a percentage of the whole in the four electorates. It estimated the voting swing required for the ALP to lose a parliamentary seat in these electorates.

TABLE III

ABORIGINAL ELECTORAL AREAS AND VOTING SWING

(Projected 1984 Federal Election)

Former Electoral Areas	Aboriginal Population	Swing Required to Lose Seat
	(%)	(%)
Northern Territory	23.7	2.0
Leichardt (North Queensland)	13.1	3.0
Kalgoorlie (Western Australia)	12.5	10.0
Grey (South Australia)	4.1	6.7

The document stated that the loss of Aboriginal votes could change the electoral balance against the Australian Labor Party in these electorates. And, in fact, it noted that land rights was probably the only issue which could alienate the Aboriginal vote from the ALP. Furthermore, it could be alienated from the ALP for a long time. The report also indicated that the removal of the veto provision from the proposed national legislation would be seen by the majority of Aborigines as a betrayal. Some would fear further compromises being made in the proposed legislation, and others would be alarmed that the legislation would not be enacted at all. The report noted that, if this happened, the government could not rely upon the continued support of Aborigines.

The non-Aboriginal voters in these areas, on the other hand, were likely to oppose land rights *per se* and, therefore, were unlikely to vote for the ALP because of modifications in land rights legislation such as removing the veto provision. It also noted that city voters were more likely to be sensitive to such modifications to land rights provisions. However, even in the urban areas there was a 'hard core' who resisted land rights *in toto*. In effect, this placed the ALP in a no-win situation.

The removal of the veto provision in land rights legislation would run the risk of alienating Aboriginal voters who were traditionally loyal to the Labor Party. On the other hand, since non-Aboriginal voters tended to oppose land rights legislation in general, they were unlikely to be won over to the ALP by simply amending the legislative proposals. The implication of this assessment was that land rights was an election liability. This was undoubtedly why Hawke and the national ALP leadership tried to play down the issue in order to minimize the electoral damage it could cause.

The Government's Dilemma

The paper identified the federal government's dilemma in relation to the land rights issue. It said that it was necessary to allay public fears and misinformation concerning the proposed national land rights legislation before the bill was introduced. At the same time, it was necessary to allay Aboriginal fears that national land rights would be eroded further (i.e. beyond removing the mining veto), or that it would not be implemented at all.

In order to reassure these divergent communities, the government had inaugurated a process of consultation with miners, farmers, and states, to assure them that their interests would be taken into account in the drafting of the legislation. The document specifically mentioned a meeting with the National Farmers Federation on 5 October as an example of the consultation process.

On the other hand, the briefing paper stressed the necessity of reassuring Aboriginals that 'no-veto' was not equated in the federal scheme with no right of control over Aboriginal land. In this regard, the paper specifically mentioned the Prime Minister's position that sacred sites were not negotiable with miners, and Senator Susan Ryan's statement that, while Aborigines will not have 'absolute rights of veto', they will have 'control of mining'.

Nevertheless, the federal government's new approach to the land rights issue decisively shifted the federal government's position against the Aborigines. For example, the mechanism suggested for addressing the dilemma facing the federal government was the adoption of a tribunal to resolve, along the lines proposed by the Western Australian government, differences over the use of Aboriginal land between 'sectional interests' and Aborigines. However, an important caveat was added. It was made in reference to the recommendations of Justice Toohey in his report 'Seven Years On'. Toohey supported the veto provisions in the Northern Territory Land Rights Act. However, he added that the forms of control over mining should not unduly delay exploration and mining. By emhasizing this caveat, the federal government tended to shift the burden of proof to Aboriginal communities to demonstrate that they were not delaying resource development on their land for pecuniary reasons.

The Aboriginal Reaction

The Aborigines' reaction to the change in the federal government's position on national Aboriginal land rights in the lead-up to the 1984 federal election was defensive. They recognized that they were faced with a government whose commitment to Aboriginal land rights was rapidly eroding. In the circumstances, they sought to develop a political strategy to arrest any further erosion in the government's position.

National Aboriginal Conference officials took a pessimistic view of the government's changed attitude towards land rights (Ryan, 1984). It concluded that its demands for land rights would not be met by the federal government, or any state government in 1985, nor by 1988 for that matter. The NAC felt that the 1984 federal election campaign demonstrated that Aborigines were losers in election campaigns. Therefore, simply postponing land rights legislation until 1987 would not solve the problem because the government would again be faced with an election. It concluded that it had to achieve national land rights legislation early in the term of the new Parliament (i.e. in 1985) so that the government would not bow to electoral pressure in the run-up to the next election.

NAC made the observation that Australian public attitudes toward Aborigines had changed dramatically since 1967 — the date that a referendum amended the Australian constitution to give the federal government jurisdiction over Aboriginal affairs.[4] The referendum passed by the largest margin of any constitutional referendum. NAC argued that this favorable public image of Aborigines had since changed to the point where they were now seen by many as 'privileged people' who unjustifiably enjoyed benefits (i.e. land, educational grants, affirmative job hiring, housing and business loans) which other Australians did not have.

The point was made that the Hawke Government had shown itself to be 'soft' on land rights. Therefore, Aborigines had to recognize that any national legislation they passed would be vastly different from what they wanted. This raised the question of what legislation would be minimally acceptable to Aborigines, and at what point national legislation would be worse than what now existed.

The NAC and the Federation of Land Councils faced that very question in January 1985 (shortly after the election), and decided that no national legislation was better than the one that the federal government was proposing. They strongly opposed the legislation since, among other things, it involved a weakening of existing land rights legislation.

The NAC in particular recognized, however, that there were certain advantages to having even a weakened version of the proposed land rights legislation. Specific reference was made in this regard to the fact that even weak legislation would give some Aboriginal groups land, and other groups more secure title to land (i.e. inalienable title), as opposed to the promise of deeds of grant in trust (referring to the Queensland Government). Furthermore, it was noted that such legislation might have the advantage of improving public opinion toward Aboriginal land rights.

According to this logic, when whites see that national legislation is not as 'bad' as they were led to believe, it would help defuse the anti-land-rights sentiment. However, they also noted the fact that the experience with the Northern Territory Land Rights Act threw this proposition into question. Whites in the Northern Territory had not become accustomed to the idea of land rights legislation and, in fact, have directed their efforts toward weakening the legislation rather than strengthening it.

The NAC felt that its position had been seriously compromised by the Prime Minister's actions. They feared that it would become the scapegoat no matter what they did. If, for example, national land rights legislation were not enacted, the NAC would be held responsible for that failure. On the other hand, if the NAC supported legislation which was viewed as a retreat from Aboriginal demands for land rights justice, it would lose Aboriginal community support. Also, NAC did not want to 'give in too early' to federal pressure, in the hope that it could win greater gains by standing firm a bit longer against pressure to weaken the legislation.

The End of the Federal Initiative

The break in Aboriginal support for the federal initiative came in January 1985 after a meeting between Premier Burke and a federal ministerial committee established to formulate the federal land rights legislation. Included on the committee were Prime Minister Hawke, Deputy Prime Minister Lionel Bowen, Clyde Holding, Minister for Resources and Energy, Senator Gareth Evans, Minister for Primary Industry, John Kerin, and three federal ministers from Western Australia—Senator Peter Walsh, Minister for Finance (who chaired the committee), Kim Beazley, and John Dawkins, Minister for Trade and Commerce.

The meeting was held on 23 January at the request of Burke. It was designed to gain federal support for Western Australia's land rights draft legislation which the Premier intended to introduce in the state parliament on 19 February 1985. (The bill was not introduced until mid-March, 1985.) According to news reports, Burke left the meeting claiming that the federal government would not force Western Australia to comply with four major elements of its national land rights policy. First, Aborigines would have no power of veto or *de facto* veto over mining on land to which they were given title. Secondly, they would receive no royalties from mining on their land. Any royalties associated with mining on Aboriginal land would be paid to the state. Thirdly, where mining was carried out on Aboriginal land, compensation payments to Aborigines for social disruption would be unrelated to the value of the minerals produced from land over which they held title. And, fourthly, Aboriginals would not be able to prevent mining exploration on their land (*Canberra Times*, 24 January 1985; transcript from 'A.M.', 24 January 1985; NAC, 1985)

However, Burke indicated that there were still two minor but unresolved differences between his position and that of the federal government on the land rights question. The first and most important difference was over Western Australia's wish to give the state Minister for Mines sweeping powers to excise from Aboriginal land any area which he believed had mining potential. The second area of disagreement was Western Australia's rejection of Aborigines' ability to claim compensation from mining companies for 'social disruption' stemming from mining on Aboriginal land, rather than compensation based upon the actual damage to the land caused by mining.

Reaction of the Left Wing

The reaction of the left wing of the Labor Party, plus elements of the Centre Left of the Party to these reports was sharp and hostile. The left, for example, was enraged that the Hawke administration had 'sold-out' once again to 'pragmatic' policies. It felt that the government had caved-in out of a concern that tough national land rights legislation would damage electorally a state Labor government.

This action particularly angered the left wing of the ALP since it followed similar recent reversals of ALP policy. Contrary to ALP policy, for example, the federal government allowed the Roxby Downs uranium project to go ahead in South Australia out of concern for the electoral situation of the Bannon Labor Government. And the Hawke Government took a strongly pro-United States stand on foreign bases and on disarmament issues. This was particularly upsetting to the left wing of the ALP. They perceived the federal reversal on land rights policy as yet one more example of Hawke's arrogance and disregard for democratic consultation within the party.

Gerry Hand, convenor of the left wing of the federal ALP caucus, attacked Premier Burke for an 'outrageous abrogation of Federal ALP policy' (*Sydney Morning Herald*, 25 January 1985). He accused Burke of conducting an 'underhanded' campaign, and not having the 'guts and integrity' to do so openly. He pointedly stated that there was no formal agreement between Burke and the federal government, implying that the content and status of federal land rights legislation had yet to be determined. He stressed that caucus would have to consider any agreement reached between the federal government and Burke (*The Australian*, 24 January 1985).

Hand said that what appeared to have happened was that Burke scored a victory for the mining industry over the Aboriginal community. He said that the miners were the 'big winners', that the Aboriginal communities were the 'big losers'. Hand argued that the cabinet decision had to do with winning the next state election in Western Australia. It had nothing to do with 'looking after people'. Other members of the left wing of the ALP attacked the Prime Minister directly for the federal government's concessions to the Premier. For example, Pat O'Shane, secretary of the New South Wales Ministry for Aboriginal Affairs, said that Hawke's actions represent 'the most disgusting political acts' ever witnessed (*ibid.*).

There was also widespread speculation among senior ALP politicians that Clyde Holding's ministerial status was in question. He had gone into the cabinet meeting of 23 January arguing that federal land rights legislation had priority over state legislation, and that the federal ALP policy on land rights could not be ignored. However, after the cabinet meeting (with Burke in attendance), Holding made no comment regarding the Premier's claims of federal support for his position. This not only raised serious doubts about Holding's future in the Hawke Government, but it put into question the whole notion of uniform national land rights.

This development presented the Minister with two options. One, he could resign his portfolio in protest against the political rebuff. However, if he followed this course, not only would it be viewed as an act of disloyalty to his 'mates' in the government, but it might effectively end his political career. Two, he could try to make the best of a bad situation and quietly fight a rearguard action to get the best land rights legislation possible and try to counter efforts to weaken existing land rights legislation.

Holding decided on the latter course and, it can be argued with some justification, he succeeded in this strategy. For example, in March 1986, when federal cabinet decided against proceeding with national land rights legislation, Holding successfully argued that the mining veto provisions in the Northern Territory Land Rights Act should be retained.

Withdrawal of Aboriginal Support

In a briefing paper from the land rights section of the NAC's research branch to all NAC members and all state secretariats, the organization's reaction to the federal cabinet meeting of 23 January was outlined (Ryan, 1985). The paper argued that the outcome of the meeting with Burke was that the federal government had caved-in on three of the five principles on land rights which they established in 1982 (i.e. failure to grant veto, compensation, royalties and conditions for mining). This amounted to a 'total sell-out' of Aboriginal land rights by the federal government. The NAC felt that, just as Burke caved-in to the mining industry in Western Australia, the federal government caved-in to Burke's position.

The report pointed out the fact that Minister Holding's office had made no comment regarding the cabinet meeting with Burke. This suggested to them that Holding had gone along with the Prime Minister in allowing Burke to have his way on land rights. Furthermore, it was explained that Holding had introduced new land rights principles to cabinet during the meeting of 23 January. According to the NAC report, these principles were different from Holding's original principles as outlined in the steering committee discussion paper of August 1984. However, not only had the Minister failed to explain the new principles to Aboriginal groups, but these principles were unknown to them.

The NAC took the position that if the Western Australian government was allowed to introduce its proposed legislation with the blessing of the federal government, it would become the model for national legislation. Burke's land rights bill would replace the federal model as the legislation which other states and the mining industry would demand. The NAC recommended, therefore, that all Aboriginal organizations reject not only the Western Australian legislation, but all state legislation because it was now clear that the federal government would not enforce its powers to over-ride states in the area of land rights.

The NAC decided to write directly to the Prime Minister protesting his government's failure to consult Aboriginal people on the current land rights proposals considered by cabinet (NAC, 1985*b*). It also demanded to know precisely how far the federal government would go toward meeting Aborigines' 'minimum expectations' for national land rights legislation.

In this regard, the NAC prepared a document listing twelve points comprising its minimum expectations for national land rights legislation (NAC, 1985*a*). Essentially, the list of minimum expectations for national legislation had been put to Minister Holding in response to his steering committee discussion paper of August 1984.

The only difference was a compromise on the veto power over mining on Aboriginal land. The National Aboriginal Conference shifted from its original position of insisting upon absolute veto power to endorsing the veto provisions contained in the Northern Territory Land Rights Act, which required an act of Parliament to over-ride the Aboriginal veto. In taking this position, the NAC said it was endorsing the stance of the Federation of Land Councils at the last steering committee meeting. It was described as a compromise between an absolute veto and a tribunal structure as proposed by the Prime Minister.

The NAC letter to the Prime Minister also included a request for a meeting between the steering committee and the recently established Aboriginal Affairs Sub-Committee of the ALP federal caucus which was chaired by Gerry Hand. In a telex dated 30 January 1985 from Rob Riley, National Chairman of the NAC, to the Prime Minister, the NAC made a further demand (NAC, 1985*c*). Riley requested that any future meetings of the federal cabinet sub-committee on land rights should include Aboriginal representatives on the steering committee. And on 8 February Riley sent a telex to Minister Holding making additional requests as a condition for the NAC's attendance at the next scheduled meeting of the steering committee.

The Break-down in Initiative

These requests included access to Holding's submission to cabinet on land rights as well as having federal cabinet ministers on the land rights cabinet sub-committee in attendance at the steering committee meeting scheduled for 13 February 1985. Holding refused these requests on the grounds that cabinet documents were confidential, and that the federal ministers who were requested to be in attendance could not be available on such short notice (Holding, 1985).

However, Holding did agree to show, on a strictly confidential basis, members of the steering committee the proposals which the Minister intended to make to cabinet. Holding agreed to show them cabinet's proposals two hours before the steering committee was scheduled to meet, and offered to make senior members of the Department of Aboriginal Affairs, including Graham Neate, available to answer any questions they had.

The NAC and the members of the Federation of Land Councils, Northern Land Council and Central Land Council met in Canberra on 12 and 13 February, to consider how they would respond to the Minister's proposed steering committee meeting scheduled for 13 February. At the meeting of 12 February the Aboriginal representatives decided to boycott the 13 February meeting with Holding and with the ALP caucus sub-committee on Aboriginal Affairs. These meetings were called by Minister Holding to discuss his proposed submission to the cabinet on national land rights legislation.

Aboriginal representatives decided to boycott the meetings because they were upset about Holding's rejection of the NAC chairman's requests. Specifically, they were angered that Riley's requests for unqualified access to cabinet proposals themselves, plus the request to have federal ministers in attendance at the steering committee meeting, were rejected (NAC, 1985c). They were outraged that the proposals had been circulated to ministerial departments for comment, yet, although the steering committee was supposed to be the Minister's chief adviser, he had not seen fit to even show them the document.

This marked the end of the federal initiative, at least as far as Aboriginal organizations were concerned. From this point on they felt that continued participation on the steering committee would only legitimate land rights proposals which they regarded as a 'sellout'. They took the position that Aboriginal land rights would be better advanced and protected if they undertook a public campaign against the federal government's actions. At the joint National Aboriginal Conference/Federation of Land Councils meeting held on 13 February 1985, they issued a five-point joint statement regarding the federal government's position on land rights (NAC/Federation of Land Councils, 1985). They called on the federal government to undertake the following course of action.

1. Use its constitutional power to intervene in Western Australia in relation to that government's proposed land rights legislation;
2. Make no changes to the Aboriginal Land Rights (Northern Territory) Act 1976 without consent of Northern Territory Land Councils;
3. Not proceed with national land rights at this stage;
4. Convene a national summit on land rights;

5. Take immediate action to ensure that Aboriginal and Islander people can develop acceptable national principles for a proper relationship between Aboriginal and Islander peoples and all governments.

The Aboriginal organizations did, indeed, mount a public campaign. It included, among other things, a National Aboriginal summit meeting in Canberra on 11 May 1985, and a delegation to the United Nations' Working Group on Indigenous People in Geneva in July 1985, to protest the actions of the Hawke Government. However, these actions appeared to have little impact upon the government's land rights policy.

In contrast, while the NAC was effectively terminated by the federal government in July 1985, the Northern Territory land councils (with the support of Minister Holding and the ALP Caucus Sub-Committee on Aboriginal Affairs), continued to lobby for the NAC's position within the federal ALP caucus. This campaign was ultimately successful in defeating the federal government's efforts to weaken the Northern Territory Land Rights Act (see Chapter Six).

CHAPTER FOUR

The Mining Industry Campaign in Western Australia

The mining industry's campaign against national Aboriginal land rights legislation in 1984 was the first major political campaign conducted by the industry.[1] While it proved to be a potent source of political leverage over both the Western Australian and federal governments, the unique circumstances surrounding the campaign, rather than the campaign itself, explains its effectiveness. The land rights issue was one on which there already existed widespread public opposition or skepticism even before the mining campaign was launched. Furthermore, the Western Australian government of Brian Burke was sympathetic to the miners' position toward land rights legislation.

Burke's support for the position taken by the mining industry in opposing the federal government's initiative was a critical factor in determining the outcome of the issue. There is reason to speculate, therefore, that without both of these conditions (i.e. the unpopularity of the issue, and a state Labor government opposed to federal legislation), the outcome of the national land rights issue would have been different.

In order to assess the political significance of the miners' campaign against land rights, it is necessary to examine the nature of the campaign. This chapter will discuss the industry's political strategy in Western Australia in 1984. The campaign had an additional significance: not only was it the first major political campaign conducted by the mineral industry in Australia, but it has been held up by them as a model for future political campaigns.

Awakening to Political Problems

According to Murray Hohnen, Assistant Director of AMIC (Australian Mining Industry Council), a fundamental shift occurred in the industry's style of political representation during the Whitlam Prime Ministry from 1972 to 1975 (interview, 4 March 1987).[2] During the 1950s and 1960s the industry was in a profitable situation. Customers would buy what the industry produced. Its profits were high. The fact that it was doing well made it feel that the political problems it had to cope with were not serious.

However, when the economy experienced a downturn in the 1970s, there was an awakening in the industry to the seriousness of the underlying political problems facing them. The miners began to see that for sometime into the future they would have financial problems. They began to feel that they could no longer afford to be complacent about the political issues affecting them. In April 1981 when Hugh Morgan, Executive Director of the Western Mining Corporation, took over the Presidency of AMIC, the industry began to think seriously about addressing the long-term political issues facing it.

Aboriginal land rights epitomized to the miners all that was politically threatening to the industry. The reason for this was that they threatened to restrict their access to land for the purpose of exploration and mining. Beginning in 1972 with the election of the ALP government of Gough Whitlam, the miners perceived that their access to land (Aboriginal plus park land) was increasingly restricted or 'locked away' from resource developers. In 1982, AMIC estimated that about 25 per cent of Australia's total land area was 'locked-up' or restricted. From their point of view, this situation reduced the industry's opportunities to discover new mines to replace current mines.

The mineral industry also saw itself as being at the center of a so-called 'trendy' debate (i.e. fashionable middle-class social issues). The miners were the objects of organized attacks by proponents of Aboriginal and conservation causes, as well as by opponents of uranium mining.[3] AMIC felt that it had to counter the 'unchallenged influence' that conservation and Aboriginal land rights proponents had with the government.

In late 1983 Aboriginal land rights were central to the miners' concerns. For example, they expected the Seaman inquiry to recommend that the Northern Territory Land Rights Act be extended to Western Australia. AMIC felt that it was one thing to 'lose the Northern Territory', but it was an entirely different thing to 'lose the rest of Australia' (interview with Hugh Morgan, 13 March 1987.) This was totally unacceptable to the miners. According to Morgan, the industry saw its campaign in Western Australia against land rights legislation as a fight for its very survival.

A NEW STYLE OF PUBLIC ADVOCACY

During the period of high profitability, the industry worked within existing governmental structures. It did not conduct public campaigns but, rather, lobbied the secretaries of relevant government departments. Before Whitlam came to office the public service was much stronger, so the industry sought to influence government policy through informal consultation with departmental secretaries over dinner and drinks, for example, at the Commonwealth Club (interview with Murray Hohnan, 4 March 1987).

The Whitlam Government changed that relationship. Under the new Labor government with R. F. X. Connor its Minister for Minerals and Energy, an adversarial relationship with the industry emerged. The government no longer felt that it was necessary to consult the industry on national economic issues. The miners felt that the Whitlam Government viewed the industry simply as a milch cow. If the government wanted cash it could simply get it from the industry.

The turning point in the miners' relationship with government came with a report by Tom Fitzgerald, a former journalist who worked for Rex Connor (Fitzgerald, 1974). The report criticized the mineral industry for being 'foreign owned' and for not contributing its fair share of tax revenue despite receiving generous tax concessions which no other industry received. Fitzgerald focussed his criticism upon Division 10 of the Income Tax Assessment Act which applied solely to the mining industry. Division 10 concessions enabled the industry to rapidly write-off their very large fixed capital investments made during the period of mining expansion in the 1950s and 1960s.

To support his contention, Fitzgerald calculated the difference between the industry's failure to pay tax and the companies' statements of high profits. What was not clear from his report, however, was the fact that the mining companies were on a different depreciation schedule from the government's tax schedule. Whereas the periods of capital depreciation were short-term, the corporate taxes were long-term. Furthermore, if the government was not a recipient of sizeable tax revenues during periods of capital depreciation, it also did not sustain losses during periods of low profitability in the industry, such as occurred during the 1970s and 1980s. Nevertheless, Fitzgerald concluded in his report that the 'opinions' expressed by the industry did not represent Australia's 'national interest' (Fitzgerald, 1974: 2-3).

According to Morgan, the industry was shocked by Fitzgerald's attack (interview with Hugh Morgan, 13 March 1987). It was not used to this kind of treatment by government. The miners thought that all they had to do was be good miners in a commercial sense and they would be regarded as successful, and be valued by the government. Fitzgerald's report destroyed that illusion, and it caused high tension within AMIC. AMIC tried to respond to the attack but found that it was not equipped to handle it.[4] G. Paul Phillips, Executive Director of AMIC at the time, tried to respond to the criticism, but his efforts were frustrated. Government pressure to discipline him was brought to bear upon Phillips through AMIC's company members. In effect. AMIC's defense of the industry was silenced by the government. It reduced AMIC's morale to an all-time low.

After this happened, AMIC took steps to defend the industry against future attacks. In this regard, it took three important steps. Firstly, it initiated the Coopers & Lybrand annual mining statements. The inaugural issue appeared in 1976. This enabled the industry to gather quantitative knowledge about itself. The statement gave it accurate and comprehensive information about the industry which helped it to respond to government criticism. Secondly, AMIC formed a public relations committee. The purpose of the committee was to conduct attitudinal studies of Australian society in order to get a qualitative view of the industry and its public image in the larger community.

Thirdly, AMIC launched its first national public relations campaign in 1982. Called 'backbone of the nation', the campaign was largely a public relations exercise designed to establish the public credibility of the industry and thereby improve its image. The campaign stressed the economic importance of the industry to the Australian economy. It pointed out the large welfare benefits derived from the industry, and the small amount of land used by miners. However, it had an importance beyond improving the industry's public image. It was a learning exercise for AMIC in preparation for mounting full-blown public advocacy campaigns such as the anti-land-rights campaign in Western Australia in 1984.

Hugh Morgan took over the chairmanship of AMIC's Public Relations

Committee in 1976. Morgan's view was that if the miners did not study the public mood they would not understand the industry's position in society. The minerals industry, in particular, had few customers and, on the whole, tended to be somewhat isolated from the main currents of public opinion in the country. Therefore, it was imperative for AMIC to study Australian public opinion. Morgan stressed the fact that the idea of the industry engaging in public advocacy was an alien concept to miners. In fact, it was only after much hesitation and resistence that the miners gradually came to understand the importance of such campaigns. The backbone of the country campaign played a central role in persuading the industry of the value of adopting a new style of public advocacy.

The backbone of the country campaign taught the miners a great deal. It showed them how to develop an advertising campaign using television. It brought home to the industry the importance of co-operating in a single campaign. The public relations departments of corporations tended to jealously guard their budgets. However, the backbone of the country campaign, under the umbrella organization of AMIC, showed them how much more could be achieved, in terms of getting the attention of national opinion leaders and politicians, by joining together. For the money spent on the campaign, it gave the industry a valuable case-study of how to influence public opinion.

The campaign was regarded by AMIC as an invaluable exercise in preparing for public advocacy campaigns. For example, it showed them that high profile campaigns involving television necessarily had to be short-term in nature. They were not only costly, but they could easily reach a point of saturation after about six months.

Industry representatives recognized that they could not change public attitudes by using television and the public media. For that they had to rely upon influencing the thinking of teachers and students in schools. Television campaigns were only suitable for short-term crises. It also convinced them that they had to go on the offensive and meet their adversaries head-on in public debate. By the time they came to the national Aboriginal land rights issue in 1984, they had matured in the realm of public advocacy. The industry had come to accept political campaigns as necessary. And AMIC had acquired the confidence to enter into public debate.

The Western Mining Corporation's Style of Leadership

When Hugh Morgan became President of Australian Mining Industry Council in 1981, he made important changes in the organization which inaugurated an entirely new style of political representation. It is important to note in this regard that the company which Morgan represented, WMC (Western Mining Corporation), was unique in the industry in terms of encouraging a highly political style of corporate leadership.

WMC was a relatively small, Australian-based and controlled mining company. It only had between 4,000 and 5,000 employees. This compared with approximately 20,000 employed by CRA Ltd, and 50,000 at BHP (Broken Hill Proprietary Co. Ltd)—two large international firms. WMC was characterized by decentralized policy making and the relative autonomy of its executives. For example, top Western Mining executives, Hugh Morgan, Sir Arvi Parbo, chairman of WMC, and Keith Parry, dealt directly with the press without consulting one another before issuing public statements on political issues.

Morgan and Parbo were based at corporate headquarters in Melbourne, while Parry operated from Perth. Parry was in charge of WMC's gold and nickel-mining operations in Western Australia and, in May 1981, became president of the Chamber of Mines of Western Australia. Therefore, shortly after Morgan took over the role of representing the mining industry in Canberra, Parry assumed a similar position in Western Australia.

WMC executives have performed a unique role in the industry. Duncan (1985a: 69) notes, for example, that when Morgan became President of AMIC, and when Parry became President of CMWA (Chamber of Mines of Western Australia), they acted as catalysts in encouraging other companies to become involved in social and political issues. Morgan, in particular, was animated by the philosophy that the times required corporate leaders to take public positions on a broad range of issues affecting them. He believed that it was necessary to influence public opinion on political issues. For this reason, WMC, and Morgan in particular, acquired a 'fundamentalist' reputation in the industry for political activism.

Hugh Morgan's Leadership of the Australian Mining Industry Council

Paul Phillips retired as Executive Director of AMIC when Morgan took over as its President in 1981. For sixteen months after Morgan assumed the presidency of AMIC he also functioned as its executive director. In February 1983 Morgan brought in James Strong as AMIC's executive director. Morgan and Strong teamed-up to develop a new style of getting out and mixing with politicians 'eyeball to eyeball'. Strong was ideally suited to the new, more aggressive style of AMIC leadership. He was a young, bright, articulate lawyer with a strong industrial relations background. he had mining experience at Gove in the Northern Territory and, therefore, had first-hand experience with Aboriginal problems and with the Northern Territory government. He also understood the political obstacles to uranium mining. Most of all, however, he was someone in whom Morgan had high regard, trust and mutual respect. Morgan's leadership of AMIC, his selection of James Strong as Executive Director of AMIC, and his collegial relationship with the President of the Chamber of Mines of Western Australia, Keith Parry, was the backdrop to the campaign against national land rights legislation in Western Australia.[5]

In one additional way Morgan's influence was central to the mining campaign in Western Australia; he provided the industry with an ideology for waging its campaign against land rights legislation. In May 1984, shortly after the Western Australian campaign began, Morgan delivered what can only be regarded as an exegesis for the religious basis of mining. His presentation was made at AMIC's annual minerals outlook seminar in Canberra. The seminar included top mining executives and key cabinet members such as the Prime Minister and Ministers Walsh, Holding and Cohen.

In that address, Morgan argued that it was necessary for the mineral industry to defend itself against efforts by the proponents of land rights and environmentalists to destroy its legitimacy. He said that it was incumbent upon the miners to 'rediscover the religious basis' of their own activity.

Morgan pointed out that the terms 'sacred' and 'spiritual' in connection with land rights were frequently used by government officials. Their use of these terms suggested to him that the industry had 'religious problems' in dealing with the government on this issue. In other words, the miners could only counter religious arguments for Aboriginal land rights with religious arguments of their own.

He asserted that those who attacked the miners for being materialist and non-spiritual were themselves 'heretical' in their religious philosophy. Morgan said 'they are followers of Manichean doctrines which have always been condemned by the Christian Church as heresy.' An exerpt from Morgan's address will illustrate the nature of this argumentation:

> The clash between the Christian orthodoxy of those who work including the miners, who, as St. Paul told us, are abiding in the same calling wherein we are called, and must perforce find the best ore bodies where ever they may be; and the Manichean style commitments of those who regard rivers, or trees, or rocks, or aboriginal sites as belonging to the spiritual world; who regard such sites as incommensurable, and seek to legislate such incommensurability into the statute books. (Morgan, 1984: 82)

The significance of Morgan's remarks was that it served an important function for the industry during its campaign against national land rights legislation. It legitimated the industry's stand on Aboriginal land rights and challenged the high moral ground which the proponents of land rights had taken in criticizing the industry. In other words, it gave the miners an ideology to support the industry's public advocacy campaign against the proponents of land rights legislation.

THE WESTERN AUSTRALIAN CAMPAIGN

The mining campaign in Western Australia against Aboriginal land rights in 1984 was a new development for the industry. The campaign was high-profile and market oriented, involving an expenditure of as much as a million dollars. It started at the grass-roots level then worked its way upward, building into a national issue. It was one of the first large-scale public advocacy programs carried out by an industry in Australia and it relied heavily upon television advertising. As such, it attracted a great deal of attention, including criticism and questioning the ethical propriety of an industry conducting such a campaign.

Nevertheless, there is general consensus among supporters and critics of Aboriginal land rights that the Western Australian campaign was the pivotal event in the entire push for national land rights legislation. For example, Garth Nettheim (1986: 71), Chairman of the Aboriginal Law Research Unit, argued that the mining lobby campaign in Western Australia 'created a major shift in public opinion, away from the widespread sympathy to Aboriginal aspirations'. Jennett (1985/1986: 12) explained 'the Hawke Government's backtracking on land rights' in terms of an 'aggressive media campaign conducted by the mining lobby in Western Australia'. Stokes (1986: 1) mistakenly attributed the mining campaign to

AMIC instead of the Western Australian Chamber of Mines. However, he argued that 'the most powerful campaign against the uniform legislation was instigated and conducted by the Australian Mining Industry Council'. The most well-informed observer of these events, Tim Duncan (1985: 3), made the following remarks about the mining campaign in Western Australia:

> The Burke Government had won power on a platform that included the granting of land rights and moved quickly to establish an inquiry as to how to go about providing them. But this time the mining industry took its case directly to the Western Australian public, advertising the 'equal rights' slogan. Opinion shifted so quickly that the Burke Government, fearing that the land rights issue might affect its chances of re-election, soon found itself opposing the Holding position on uniform national land rights.

The mining industry itself has argued for the effectiveness of the Western Australian campaign. It took the position that, because of the effectiveness of the campaign in Western Australia, it was not necessary for AMIC to run a national campaign against national land rights legislation. According to Hohnen (interview, 4 March 1987), the campaign in Western Australia was run at the 'belt level'. It did not hold back. The Western Australian television advertisements, in particular, tugged at raw nerves. By the time land rights legislation became a national issue, federal politicians knew that the industry could play 'hard ball'. Therefore, as a result of the Western Australian campaign, to achieve their objectives, they only had to threaten a similar campaign at the national level. The industry has also held up the Western Australian campaign as an implied threat against any legislation or government action they strongly opposed.

These claims for the effectiveness of the mining campaign in Western Australia in 1984 must be qualified, however. Examination of the campaign itself, including the results of opinion surveys conducted by the Chamber of Mines of Western Australia, raises questions about the claims for its success. For example, there is no evidence to support the assertion that the mining campaign in Western Australia fundamentally shifted public opinion on the Aboriginal land rights question.

To the contrary, the surveys show quite clearly that public opinion in Western Australia was strongly opposed to Aboriginal land rights before the campaign was conducted. Furthermore, while the campaign undoubtedly raised the profile of the issue to the electorate, the evidence suggests that CMWA (Chamber of Mines of Western Australia) could not control the issue. For example, after the miners, in consultation with the Western Australian government, agreed upon Aboriginal land rights legislation for Western Australia, that legislation was defeated by an opposition-controlled upper house.

In other words, after the industry publicly endorsed Western Australia's proposed land rights legislation as being acceptable to them, it was defeated. In addition, the surveys show that the public was not even aware that the CMWA had changed its position to support land rights legislation. This raises the question of whether CMWA was leading public opinion in Western Australia on the land rights issue, or whether its campaign simply tapped existing public opposition to a highly unpopular issue. Neither CMWA nor anyone else, including the opposition Liberal Party, could control the issue or use it for political advantage.

In this new and uncertain situation, the federal government threatened to come 'over the top' of the Western Australian government and introduce national land rights legislation. It was only the efforts of Brian Burke, leading a state Labor government, which prevented the adoption of land rights legislation. Therefore, it can be argued that the mining campaign in Western Australia backfired by helping to create an even more threatening situation.

It could even be argued that, if the Burke Government had not taken a strong 'states' rights' stance in opposing federal legislation, the mining industry might well have had what it regarded as disastrous land rights legislation imposed upon it. A related claim, that Burke's Government was pressured by the miners as well as pastoralists into opposing federal land rights legislation, will be considered in Chapter Five.

Rationale for the Campaign

The Chamber of Mines of Western Australia campaign against national land rights legislation was designed primarily by Duncan Bell, its public affairs executive officer. At a joint meeting between AMIC and CMWA on Aboriginal land legislation in February 1984, one month before the campaign was launched in Western Australia, he explained the rationale of the campaign (Bell, 1984).

Bell pointed out that, ever since the discovery of gold in the nineteenth century, the mining industry had been 'the major catalyst' in the economic development of Australia in general, and in Western Australia in particular. As a result of this the industry enjoyed 'pre-eminence and high visibility' in Australia. Industry leaders became accustomed to having power and influence in the economy and did not hesitate to take strong positions on political issues — at both the state and federal levels. Bell noted that, generally speaking, the industry had the support of governments which were committed to the economic growth of Australia, to full employment, and to an enhanced role for Australia in the world.

Since the 'resources boom' of the 1960s, the political climate of the industry's influence had changed. Political issues facing mining in Australia had become more difficult. The reason for the change was that the public no longer took for granted that mining was essential for the maintenance of their standard of living. Ironically, growing affluence in Australia was said to be responsible for this change in public attitudes. The public had lost sight of the fact that resource development during the past twenty years was largely responsible for the increased wealth in Australian society.

Bell explained that the public believed Australia was 'the lucky country' and that it had 'mineral deposits that were the envy of the world.' They did not understand, however, the potentially deleterious consequences of 'continually expropriating large areas of land from exploration and mining'. The public also did not understand the consequences of governments' increasing financial and administrative burden upon the mining industry.

Bell argued that the Australian public was ill-informed about these matters and, therefore, did not care. He offered a simple axiom: if the public is made aware that what affects the industry affects them, then they will care. He also quoted a statement made by Keith Parry the previous day: 'What is good for the miners is good for the welfare of the whole Australian community.'

The importance of the industry 'speak[ing] with one voice' was stressed. Bell pointed out that, until now, it was easier for companies to deal individually with the increased costs of government controls and requirements such as environmental protection, than it was for the companies to achieve industry-wide consensus. He noted that like any 'democratic organization' there was a wide range of opinions and objectives represented by companies in the industry. Consensus was now vital for the industry to be in the strongest position possible when dealing with governments, and presenting their case to the general public. By training and disposition, the industry had in the past tended to shun publicity. However, it could no longer afford this luxury. According to Bell, the very 'survival of mining as an industry' depended upon dealing with public opinion.

Bell explained that now, more than ever, public opinion shaped government policy. Therefore, any group in society which wished to influence the government must demonstrate that there is public support for its policy preferences. He said that, all too frequently, vocal minorities managed to manipulate the public media and convey the impression that there was majority support for their positions in the community at large.

He pointed out that during the past ten years the mineral industry has been the butt of severe public criticism. As a result, it had an 'image problem'. Bell noted that it had to change this negative image if it hoped to persuade the public that the industry was reasonable, and had the welfare of all Australians at heart.

Bell emphasized that the proposed new Aboriginal land legislation underscored the urgency of the industry becoming an 'active protagonist' in political debates affecting its future. He said that there was a real danger that those who did not respect the miners (implying the Labor government) would adopt legislation that would adversely affect the industry. In legislating they will be influenced by public opinion, or worse, by 'what they think the public wants'.

While the mining industry could, with justification, be proud of its technological and commercial achievements in Australia, it had been an 'unprofessional' or 'poor communicator' in the community. This called for a new competence or professionalism in communicating with the public. He said that the industry must become as professional in its communication skills as it was in exploring and mining. Bell stressed that the mineral industry must become the 'most competent communicator' in the community. Therefore, it must be prepared to commit the resources and have the spokesmen necessary to present their case to the public. He pointed out that failure to do this would cost it even more in the short term. And he placed Aboriginal land rights in the category of a burden that would cost it far more than any public relations campaign.

Bell emphasized that the industry should not allow itself to be placed on the defensive. He quoted C. Northcote Parkinson to support this proposition: 'In the modern world if an industry does not publicly defend itself it will be judged by the public as guilty by default.' Therefore, the accent should be upon a 'pro-active' and professional campaign on the Aboriginal land rights issue that presents the mining industry in a positive light. In order to do this, it was necessary to present the issue in such a way that the public could identify with it as vitally affecting its welfare. He said that the underlying objective of all good public affairs campaigns was to create a 'climate of awareness and understanding'. If the voters understood the important contribution of the mining industry to the economy, then the industry would have a 'positive opinion base' in the community upon which it could debate public issues. Therefore, if the general public had a positive image of the role of mining in the community, it would believe the miners when they said that a particular policy was in the best interests of Australia.

The Strategy of the Campaign

The significance of the Seaman inquiry (1984) to the mining industry was explained by Bell. He noted the fact that the inquiry (chaired by Paul Seaman, Q.C.) was the first public inquiry on Aboriginal land rights since the Woodward inquiry on Aboriginal land rights in the Northern Territory in 1974. Because this was a public inquiry, and because it was the first to be held in a decade, it had a special significance to the miners.

As a public inquiry, all submissions made to it would become part of the public debate. In this regard, Bell pointed out that the inquiry had already generated 'confrontation or near-confrontation between the state and federal governments'. Furthermore, controversy over the issue had expanded the debate beyond the confines of the inquiry itself. In this regard, it gave the industry an opportunity to demonstrate, not only to the state government, but also to the federal government, the extent of public concern on the issue of Aboriginal land rights. This was important to the industry in view of the proposed federal uniform Aboriginal land rights legislation which was looming on the horizon.

Bell argued that the media had 'fanned' the debate with editorials and cartoons. Despite the fact that the industry had 'briefed' the media, it had misconstrued the true position of the industry, making it necessary for the miners to state their views in the public forum.[6]

Bell indicated, however, that, despite the growing controversy over the Seaman inquiry, the Chamber of Mines of Western Australia intended to follow a policy program which was designed and approved by the Chamber in 1983. The key element of the program was to win public support for the principle of Crown ownership of minerals. According to Bell, there were four aspects to Crown ownership which were 'intrinsic and inseparable':

1. Over-riding government control to grant or deny access for exploration and mining;
2. Royalty payments only to government;
3. Compensation payments only for economic loss or for actual damage by the disturbance of the land;
4. No over-riding royalties or up-front payments.

He pointed out that CMWA intended to conduct a policy promotion program that was 'positive in manner'. Positive views were said to be more acceptable to the public than negative ones. The Chamber's 'positive view' on the land rights issue was that Aborigines should be granted land. However, they should have the same, not greater, rights than were available to all other Australians.

In order to design a policy promotion program which was acceptable to the public, and one that would win support for the industry's position on land rights, the public needed to have 'objective' information on the state of public opinion on Aboriginal land rights.

In order to acquire this information, the Chamber commissioned a professional survey research firm (Marketing Centre Research Pty Ltd of Western Australia) to conduct a survey of public attitudes on Aboriginal land rights. The survey was carried out on 1 September 1983 in response to the announcement of the Seaman inquiry. The results of the opinion survey were presented in a report titled 'Aboriginal Land Rights an Exploratory Study'. The purpose of the survey was to determine the attitude of the Western Australian public concerning the granting of land to Aborigines, and to giving them ownership of minerals on that land. Data was collected in the form of open-ended questions from metropolitan Perth and rural areas. The sample was 300, with 95 per cent accuracy and 3 per cent margin of error. This survey formed the basis of the Chamber's campaign. The poll was designed to determine public attitudes on the following five basic issues in the industry's policy program:

1. Did the public understand the principle of Crown ownership? (i.e. collectively they owned the minerals of the state).
2. Did the public support granting Aboriginal ownership or control over minerals in their land?
3. How important was the preservation of Aboriginal culture to the public?
4. Did the public know what was happening as a result of current Northern Territory land rights legislation?
5. Did they know the percentage of Aboriginal population in Western Australia?

As would be expected, the survey results showed that the general public was not as aware of the issues as the industry was. However, Bell expressed concern that the public was not aware that the principle of Crown ownership applied to all land—including freehold land. He said that, because the public was under the false impression that all private land owners also had ownership rights to minerals on their land, they were willing to concede to Aborigines the ownership rights to minerals on land which they owned.

He pointed out, however, that when the same respondents were informed that private land owners did not have title to the minerals under their land, 85 per cent of those surveyed (i.e. 255 in the sample of 300) were opposed to granting Aborigines title or control over minerals. On the basis of the survey, Bell outlined the emphasis the miners should give in their policy campaign. He said that they must make the public aware of the fact that the people of Western Australia collectively own the minerals of the state. He said that if the miners succeeded in this then the public would recognize that everyone had a financial stake or personal interest in supporting the industry's position on the issue.

Bell also noted that the survey results showed that Western Australians thought Aborigines constituted roughly 15 per cent of the total state population. However, in fact, they represented less than 3 per cent. He said that since people thought Aborigines constituted 15 per cent of the population they felt Aboriginals should be given between 12 and 15 per cent of the land area of Western Australia in the interests of justice.

Bell argued that if Western Australia had land rights legislation similar to the Northern Territory, then about 3 per cent of the population could claim almost half of the state's total land area (referring to the state's unallocated or 'vacant Crown land' (see Seaman, 1984: 19-20)). Bell observed that the industry must clearly explain in their policy promotion program that Aborigines represented only 3 per cent of the state's population. The implication was that they should not be entitled to more than 3 per cent of the state's land area.

On the question of whether Aboriginal culture should be protected, the survey showed that opinion was divided. One-third of the respondents believed that Aboriginal culture should be protected, even if it meant a loss of employment. One-third was undecided, and one-third of those polled felt that Aboriginal culture should be sacrificed if it meant a loss of employment. Bell interpreted this survey result as suggesting caution regarding the protection of Aboriginal culture. He said that the mining industry should stress its concern about disturbing sacred sites. The industry should emphasize the work already done by companies to identify Aboriginal sites, and it should support the work done by the Western Australian Museum in assessing the value of Aboriginal sites.

Bell summed-up the lessons from the September poll in the following way: the public believed that Aborigines should be treated equally with other sections of the community and not be given greater rights. He said that the Chamber of Mines of Western Australia fully supported this position and, therefore, the Chamber should stress this theme in its campaign. Bell pointed out that the general public was unaware of the amount of land granted to Aborigines in the Northern Territory, and possibly in South Australia as well. The public did not know that Aborigines had greater rights of titles in land under the Northern Territory legislation than non-Aboriginals had. Finally, those surveyed were not aware of the negative impact that the Northern Territory Land Rights Act had had upon the mining industry there and, therefore, upon the territory's economy.

The central theme of the CMWA's campaign against Aboriginal land rights legislation was to be based upon the concept of equality. This concept was said to be philosophically attractive to all Australians, and it had the added advantage of appealing to self-interest. That is to say, if people could not be more than equal they could at least be equal. Bell concluded by saying that the Western Australian promotional campaign would vigorously promote the concept of equality in a positive way. If it did that, he felt that the industry would win the public support they sought on the land rights issue. In a postscript, Bell said that the 'battle' in Western Australia was only part of the campaign. In order to be successful in the campaign against national land rights legislation it would have to have the support of the people of Sydney and Melbourne as well, where the bulk of the Australian electorate resided.

THE POLICY PROMOTION PROGRAM

The campaign in Western Australia was conducted over a period of seven months, from early March till mid-September 1984, with a two-month hiatus between May and July. The campaign was organized into two phases. The first phase ran for eight weeks, from 9 March to the middle of May 1984. The second phase was from mid-July to mid-September 1984.

First Phase of the Campaign

The first phase of the campaign had two principal aims. First, to make people aware of the Seaman inquiry, of the issues raised by it, and its impact upon the mining industry. According to Bell, many people had a far too idealistic or visionary view of land rights. The campaign had to break this down. Second, to exert public pressure upon the Burke Government in order to influence the final political outcome of the land rights issue. While the Chamber of Mines of Western Australia hoped that Seaman himself would listen to the miners' concerns (the Chamber had a public hearing before Seaman on 13 and 14 April 1984), that was not the purpose of the campaign. The purpose was to put political pressure on the Burke Government by winning public support for the industry's position against land rights legislation.

The CMWA did a variety of things during this phase of the campaign. It included the use of public affairs media in radio and television talk-back programs, letters to the editor, lobbying politicians, county shire councils, and regional development advisory committees, organizing seminars and speaking engagements, and mailing out tens of thousands of pamphlets. One pamphlet, in particular, that proved effective, included a map of unallocated Crown land in Western Australia that would be available for Aboriginal claims if legislation based upon the Northern Territory Land Rights Act were adopted (see Map 3). Twenty-five thousand copies of this brochure were distributed by the CMWA to mining company shareholders and others.

However, the most effective part of the campaign was the newspaper and television advertising. During phase one of the campaign, the advertisements on pages 70 and 71 were placed in major newspapers, beginning on 9 March. The one showing a check was placed only in newspapers. The so-called scales advertisement was placed in newspapers and run on television.

The scales advertisement on television ran for thirty seconds intervals. It began on 27 March and ran till 12 May. The newspaper advertisements were the lead-up to the campaign, starting before the television advertisements. The reason for this was that CMWA felt that, as soon as it put advertisements on television, it would immediately put pressure upon the government. The Chamber felt that this was particularly true of advertisements run by the mining industry because of its importance to the state's economy, and also because of the past controversy surrounding the industry in Western Australia. However, they were also aware that, until this campaign, there were few such television advertisements in Australia. Therefore, this was a new experience for them. They were feeling their way as they went along.

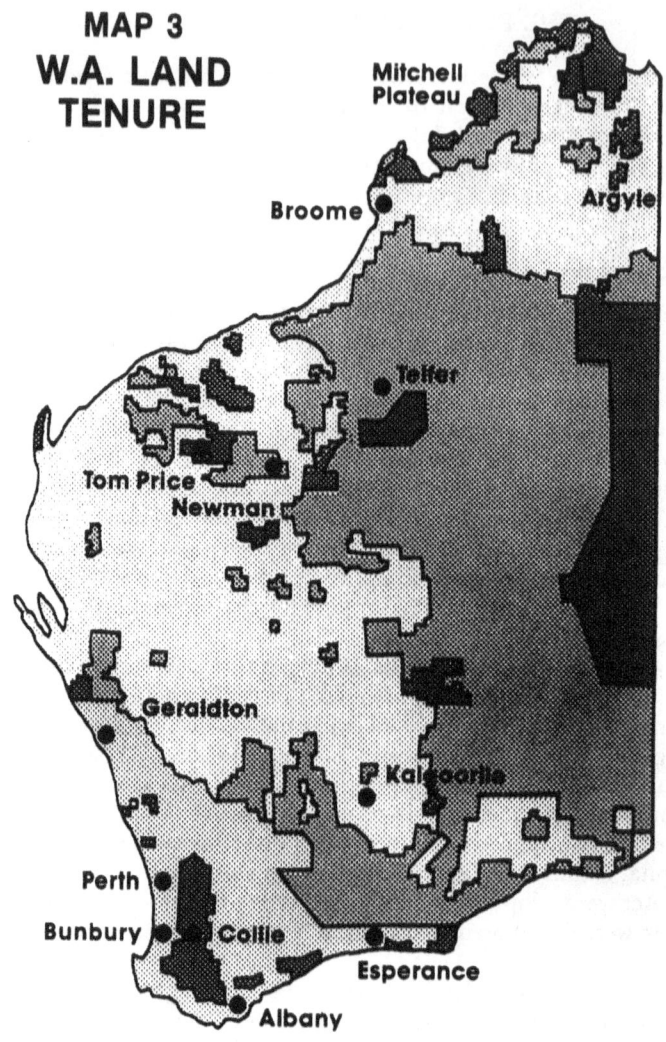

**MAP 3
W.A. LAND TENURE**

		km²	%
■	Aboriginal	219,000	8.7
▦	Vacant	1,010,000	40.0
□	Freehold	172,000	6.8
□	Pastoral	951,000	37.7
■	Parks/Reserves/Forests etc, (not all shown on map)	173,000	6.8
	TOTAL	2,525,000	100

The television advertisement ran several times each day for six weeks. It was shown during early morning, late afternoon (aimed at housewives), and during prime-time viewing. The advertisement was placed on both of Western Australia's commercial television networks (Channels STW-9 and TVW-7), plus regional networks such as GTW-11 Geraldton and VEW in Kalgoorlie. It also appeared on Mining T Network, the network which transmitted packaged television to mining towns.

THE SUCCESS OF THE FIRST PHASE OF THE CAMPAIGN

The Chamber of Mines of Western Australia made two related claims for the success of the first phase of its campaign. First, that it was having an impact upon the Burke Government; secondly, that public opinion in support of the industry's position on the land rights issue was growing, and that this had clear electoral implications for the state government. The second claim will be evaluated in Chapter Five.

Impact on the Burke Government

There is little doubt that CMWA campaign was having an impact upon the Burke Government. The most tangible evidence of the campaign's success was a meeting between the CMWA and Premier Burke, at his request, on 26 April 1984, to discuss Aboriginal land rights.

According to CMWA's account of the meeting, the Premier explained his concern about the campaign, especially, the paid newspaper and television advertising (Bell 1984a). Burke reportedly said that the Chamber's advertising campaign was placing him under extreme pressure. The Premier also said that, unless this pressure abated, he would have to consider abandoning the idea of state land rights legislation altogether and allow the federal government to introduce legislation in Western Australia. Burke warned CMWA that, if this happened, the consequences would be far more severe for it than those of the legislation he intended to introduce in Western Australia.

Chamber of Mines of Western Australia representatives responded to Burke's warning by saying that their program, including the paid advertisements, had at all times been objective, apolitical (meaning non-partisan), and constructive to public debate. The Premier acknowledged that the program had been objective and apolitical, but questioned its contribution to public debate. Burke said he was concerned that the strength of the public debate would 'overwhelm' the Seaman inquiry and its recommendations.

CMWA responded that it had grave concerns about the way the inquiry was being conducted (i.e. as a public forum for debate). It also stated that it was essential for the Chamber to counter public statements made by proponents of land rights legislation patterned after the Northern Territory model. Burke acknowledged the problems connected with the conduct of the inquiry, and also agreed that the Northern Territory Land Rights Act had been 'disastrous' for the resource industry in the territory. The Premier indicated that Seaman was also aware of the adverse consequences

Every time our mining industry makes a successful discovery, we all strike it rich.

Every year our mining industry contributes around $3 billion to Western Australia's economy.

In royalties alone, mining companies contribute nearly $100 million every year to this State's revenue. When you add company taxes, lease payments and the tax contribution of 125,000 Western Australians whose employment is linked to the State's mineral industry

In our democratic society this valuable principle also allows the Government, through Parliament to set rules for exploration, mining, compensation and royalty payments.

Although you may never personally work for a mining company or make a new mineral

THE WEST AUSTRALIAN MINING INDUSTRY 30-6-83
PAY *The people of Western Australia*
THE SUM OF *Three Billion Dollars* $ 3,000,000,000

it becomes clear how important a healthy mining industry is to us all.

In Western Australia, the rich mineral resource that attracts and continues to develop our mining industry belongs equally to every Western Australian through the principle of Crown ownership.

Crown ownership of minerals means that the State, on behalf of everybody, owns the minerals under the ground, irrespective of whether the land itself is owned freehold or leasehold.

discovery, through the principle of Crown ownership you benefit in a direct and personal way everytime our mining industry does.

The right to explore for minerals and develop their wealth for the good of everybody is a democratic principle that always has and always will benefit the people of this State.

Your part in the ownership of our State's mineral wealth works for a strong and secure future for every Western Australian.

The Chamber of Mines of Western Australia (Inc).

The mining industry is one of the most important contributors to the wealth of Western Australia. Last year, mining contributed almost $100m to the people of this State through the payment of mining royalties.

This unique contribution is based on the principle of Crown ownership.

What does Crown ownership mean?

Crown ownership simply means that the mineral resources of this State are owned equally by all of this State's citizens. The Government collects this royalty and decides on its use.

This principle of Crown ownership has allowed us all to enjoy a high standard of living without increasing the burden of tax.

Yet, despite these great benefits, Crown ownership could come under threat through legislation on Aboriginal Land Rights.

Land Rights should be Equal Rights.

The mining industry does not disagree with the principle of Aborigines owning land.

We simply believe that all rights in land should be equal. This means that regardless of who owns the land, Aborigines or non-Aborigines, the minerals below the ground are owned by the Crown on behalf of all people.

This democratic principle has always worked, and must now be allowed to continue to work, for every citizen.

If you support the equality of all Australians, we invite you to learn more about this vital issue by sending for our free brochure.

The Chamber of Mines of Western Australia (Inc).
231 Adelaide Terrace, Perth. Tel (09) 325 2955.

of the Northern Territory Land Rights Act for the mining industry in the territory.

CMWA explained to Burke that it was concerned about the Seaman inquiry recommendations (based upon the contents of the interim report, or discussion paper, issued by Seaman in January 1984). CMWA felt that, even if Seaman's recommendations were not adopted by the state government, they could still be used by Minister Holding to justify his federal legislation. Burke acknowledged that some 'pre-emptive action was desirable'. Within a week of the meeting with the Chamber of Mines, Burke appointed Graham McDonald as deputy commissioner to the Seaman inquiry. The purpose of McDonald's appointment was to speed-up the hearings in order to shut off public debate on land rights in Western Australia (interview with Graham McDonald, 16 February 1987).

The Chamber's assessment of the political situation was that the Burke Government had 'lost control' of the debate in Western Australia. It took the position that, since the government had initiated a public inquiry which was not scheduled to release its report until August 1984, the government was effectively gagged from making any comment on it. The Chamber felt that the January 1984 Seaman discussion paper was controversial and, therefore, had been counter-productive for the proponents of land rights. It had resulted in stimulating groups who were opposed to land rights.

Therefore, while the state government was gagged on this issue, various other interested parties such as Aboriginal groups, church and industry organizations, the Liberal Party and the federal government, were vocal participants in the growing debate in Western Australia.

CMWA felt that the principal reason for Burke's decision to meet with it was to stop the newspaper and television advertising campaign by assuring it that it had nothing to fear from his proposed Western Australian Aboriginal land rights legislation. To that end, the Premier had, in fact, outlined to the Chamber the relevant mining-related provisions in his contemplated state land rights legislation.

In addition to Burke's reassurances to the miners, there was an implied threat. It was that, if the Chamber's media campaign continued over the next few months, thus further hardening public opinion against land rights legislation, it could be counter-productive. It could undermine an opportunity for the Western Australian branch of the ALP to amend the party's national Aboriginal land rights platform (which is binding on states) at the federal Labor conference in July 1984. Burke raised the fear that a continuation of the Chamber's campaign could provoke opposition from the Victorian and New South Wales delegates to the Western Australian delegation's efforts to amend the party's land righs platform. This would inadvertantly strengthen support for Holding's position on land rights within the national ALP.

Weighed against these factors, however, the Chamber was reluctant to give up its leverage against the Burke Government without a political outcome favorable to the industry. CMWA decided, therefore, that, regardless of assurances given to them by the Premier, the proponents of land rights, such as Aboriginal groups, social science organizations, and churches, would continue to campaign for Aboriginal land rights. Therefore, if the Chamber were to terminate its campaign and 'vacate the field', the public momentum which the miners had generated against Aboriginal land rights would be lost. According to the Chamber, this would release the state government from the public pressure that had prompted it to moderate its stand on land rights in the first place.

Another reason why CMWA felt compelled to continue with its policy program was that it thought Minister Holding would continue to press for national uniform land rights legislation, regardless of what the state did. As evidence for Holding's intentions, CMWA mentioned the federal Aboriginal and Torres Strait Islander Heritage (Interim Protection) Bill of 1984. It felt that, in order to avoid criticism at the federal ALP conference in July 1984, the federal government had not honored its promises to Aborigines and that Hawke would be under pressure to adopt the Aboriginal Heritage legislation. According to the Chamber, this federal legislation would 'pre-empt' any action that the Western Australian government might have taken as a result of the Seaman inquiry.

The passage of the federal heritage legislation would have an added significance. The industry feared that the federal government could use the heritage legislation to control mineral development because federal approval would be required for any project which affected an Aboriginal site. CMWA felt that this made it incumbent upon it to keep up the pressure of public opinion against land rights legislation in Western Australia.

CMWA also noted that Senator Fred Chaney, a leader of the opposition federal Liberal Party, had advised them that the federal opposition would reject any uniform land rights legislation under its 'Federalism policy'. It felt that land rights was a matter for the states to decide. Chaney indicated that, with appropriate lobbying, support from the Australian Democrats to reject uniform land rights legislation could also be secured. Chaney's reasoning appears to have been that the Democrats would not support any land rights legislation which was not endorsed by the Aborigines themselves. CMWA felt that, if Chaney's assessment were correct, the miners would only have to ensure that state legislation which accommodated the industry's interests were adopted.

The Chamber concluded that the only real course of action open to the industry at this stage was to stimulate public opinion in all states on the land rights issue in order to counter action by state and federal governments to proceed with legislation. Therefore, the Chamber would continue with its policy promotion program in Western Australia. However, it emphasized the importance of appearing to be sensitive to the Premier's concerns regarding the advertising campaign. For example, it pointed out that the first phase of its advertising was scheduled to terminate in early May irrespective of the Premier's request of late April that the campaign be discontinued. There was a planned lull in the campaign of about two months. Therefore, Burke should be encouraged to believe that the cessation of the Chamber's paid advertising during the lull was due to his efforts to lobby the industry.

Public Support for the Chamber's Position

The Chamber of Mines of Western Australia claimed that its campaign was highly successful in terms of winning public support for its position on land rights. CMWA asserted that the general public was strongly supportive of the Chamber's public position, and that that support was steadily increasing as the public became better informed about the issues. CMWA indicated that its public opinion surveys demonstrated positive support for the industry's position, and that this support was equally strong among Labor and Liberal supporters. The Chamber claimed that the Burke Government was aware of this fact, and was concerned about the potential electoral impact of the land rights issue.

Indeed, the public opinion polls commissioned by the industry did show strong public support for the miners' position on Aboriginal land rights (see Table IV). However, the results of the polls conducted before and after the first phase of advertising in May 1984, suggest that that increase was only marginal. Furthermore, after the industry agreed to support an amended version of the proposed Western Australian state land rights

TABLE IV

EVALUATING THE IMPACT OF THE WESTERN AUSTRALIAN CHAMBER OF MINES ADVERTISING CAMPAIGN

(Comparison of the March and May Surveys)

Importance of Issues to be Addressed	March Support*	May Support†	Comments
	(%)	(%)	
1. Crown Ownership Awareness	52	68	Improved awareness
Crown Ownership Support	52	57	A need to continue exposure and education to increase support
2. Opposition of Right to Veto	62	64	Yet to address
3. Right of Access	76	79	Yet to address
4. Equality in Land Rights	79	87	Strong support increased. Maintain re-inforcement
5. Equality in Compensation	89	93	Strong support to consolidate
6. Importance of contribution of the Mining Industry	87	88	Strong support. Have established firm base on which to build

Source: Marketing Centre Research Pty Ltd, 1984: 8.

* The March survey was carried out the weekend before the start of the campaign on 9 March. There was a sample of 600 respondents with a 2 per cent variance.

† The May survey was undertaken on 28 and 29 April after the completion of the first phase of the advertising campaign. It had a sample of 400 and a 95 per cent level of confidence.

Both surveys used a 10 per cent validation procedure which is laid down by the Market Research Society of Western Australia.

legislation in 1985, public opinion (as reflected in the Chamber's polls) continued to oppose any form of land rights legislation.

Table IV summarizes the results of the opinion surveys conducted on behalf of the industry before the campaign began on 9 March, and at the end of the first phase of the campaign in May 1984. The survey results indicate that, with the exception of item one, awareness of the principle of Crown (i.e. state) ownership which increased from 52 per cent support to 68 per cent, support for the other issues increased by only a small percentage. For example, on the crucial question of public support for Crown ownership, there was only a 5 per cent increase, from 52 to 57.

Two things from the table stand out: the first is the high level of support for the position taken by the industry on all of the issues surveyed. Indeed, all issues received a positive response of more than 50 per cent from those surveyed, even before the advertising campaign was launched. For example, support for the idea of equality in land rights was 79 per cent and for equality in compensation was 89 per cent in the March poll.

The second thing is that, despite the high profile and expensive advertising campaign launched by the Chamber of Mines of Western Australia, there was little if any movement in public support for the mining position as reflected in its own polls. Indeed, after receiving 75 to 80 per cent or more support on items in the March survey, it is difficult to understand why it was even necessary to increase public support on these issues.

The one item where there was a significant level of increased support was awareness of the principal of Crown ownership. This increased by 16 per cent, from 52 to 68. Despite this, however, support for Crown ownership only increased by five percentage points. In other words, in March 1984, 52 per cent of those surveyed were aware of the principle of Crown ownership, and 52 per cent supported it. However, in May 1984, after the first phase of the campaign, 68 per cent of the respondents were aware of Crown ownership, while only 57 per cent supported it. This indicates that, while the Chamber's advertising campaign increased the public's awareness of the Crown ownership issue, its increased awareness did not translate into increased public support for the industry's position.

In other words, a high level of public support already existed for the position taken by industry, even before it ran its advertising campaign. This suggests that the Chamber may have had other reasons for undertaking the campaign. A likely reason was to create an illusion of being able to mobilize public opinion against government policies regarded as inimical by the industry.

The campaign was designed primarily to exert political pressure upon the Burke and Hawke Governments to abandon or modify land rights legislation to accommodate the industry's concerns. The industry sought to do this by running a high-profile public-affairs campaign and then selectively releasing the results of its public opinion surveys which purported to show the success of the campaign in mobilizing public opinion against land rights policy. In other words, the mining industry sought to take credit for the state of public opinion on the issue without ever producing the evidence to support its claim.

The Western Australian and federal governments equated the increased visibility of the land rights issue, and the growing debate over the Seaman inquiry, with increasing public opposition to land rights legislation. While there was some increase in public support for the position taken by the mining industry, the evidence does not support the claim that the Chamber's paid advertising campaign produced a significant shift in public attitudes.[7] Public opposition to Aboriginal land rights was already present; the Chamber's campaign simply made that obvious to everyone.

Nevertheless, since the Chamber of Mines of Western Australia never released its opinion surveys (except selectively), the industry was able to present an illusion of the political potency of its campaign. AMIC (Australian Mining Industry Council), in fact, exploited this perception in 1985 while attempting to persuade the federal government to abandon uniform national land rights legislation. AMIC threatened to run a fully fledged, nation-wide campaign against national land rights legislation based upon the policy promotion program conducted by the Chamber of Mines of Western Australia.

The Second Phase of the Campaign

The second phase of the CMWA's policy promotion program was also planned for a seven-week period. It ran from late July till mid-September 1984. Like the first phase of the campaign, it included paid advertising in newspapers and on television. During the second phase, the emphasis was upon the importance of industry access to all land for the purpose of exploration and mining, royalties paid to the Crown only, and compensation for damage to land due to mining based only upon physical damage, not spiritual or social disruption.

The Chamber placed two advertisements in newspapers and one on television. An artist's rendering of the television advertisement called the 'wall' advertisement is represented on the following page. It is probably the most famous political advertisement to appear on Australian television. It depicted a brown hand and arm building a brick wall dividing Western Australia in half. The advertisement conveyed the idea that land rights legislation in Western Australia would lock whites out of one-half of the state. It ran over a six-week period, following the pattern of the previous television advertisement. It appeared several times a day—morning, afternoon, and during prime-time evening viewing.

While the paid advertising campaign included newspaper advertisements which are also reproduced in the following pages, it was the 'wall' advertisement (or 'black hand' advertisement as critics called it) that captured the attention of the public and politicians. For example, Premier Burke personally requested that the Chamber withdraw it. And, at a meeting between CMWA, AMIC, Prime Minister Hawke and Minister Holding on 12 September, Hawke specifically referred to the 'wall' advertisement when requesting that the industry discontinue its campaign.

The advertisement on page 79 was run just after Burke announced on 27 September the elements of his proposed state land rights legislation. CMWA listed twelve points of Burke's recommendations which they found acceptable. It is noteworthy that point 11, reserves and vacant Crown land granted to Aborigines on the basis of ninety-nine year Crown lease, went beyond Burke's original statement of principles. This suggests that the miners were prepared to go further than the Burke Government in making concessions to demands for Aboriginal land rights.

The Mining Industry Campaign in Western Australia

As was the case with the first phase of the CMWA campaign, it allowed the paid advertising campaign to continue as planned. And it did this for the same reason that it did during the first phase. The Seaman inquiry was scheduled to be released in August 1984. The miners felt that they had to keep up the pressure on the Burke Government to get the kind of legislation that was acceptable to the industry. Therefore, since the Seaman Report was not released until 17 September, CMWA ran its advertising campaign almost until the report was made public.

SUCCESS OF THE SECOND PHASE

From the Chamber of Mines of Western Australia's perspective, the second phase of its campaign against national land rights legislation was even more successful than the first. It enabled the Chamber to achieve its objectives for the policy promotion program. CMWA felt that its campaign was responsible for creating political pressure on the Burke Government, which led to the moderation of its proposed state land rights legislation.

Can you afford to pay the price of unequal land rights?

If you don't know who actually owns and controls Western Australia's land the answer may surprise you.

Only 6.8% is owned freehold.

Around 8.7% is currently controlled by W.A.'s Aboriginal population.

The great percentage of this State's land is owned by the Government, which represents all the people of Western Australia.

And all the minerals below all of the land, regardless of who controls the land surface, is also owned by the people of this State.

Your right of ownership could be under threat.

Through Crown Ownership, the Government makes the rules on how the land can be used and who has access to the land.

We believe this system is fair and equal, yet soon it could come under threat.

The mining industry does not oppose the principle of Aborigines owning land. We simply ask that if land rights are granted that they should be granted under the same conditions as land held by non-Aborigines.

The unfair power of veto.

Some Aboriginal groups are asking for a power of veto that will require every Western Australian to apply for permission to be allowed to enter the areas of our State which are under Aboriginal claim.

This could mean that your current right of access to up to 50% of W.A. could be taken away from you. The same power of veto will also prevent all mineral exploration.

Land rights under these conditions are not fair or equal. They deny the great majority of citizens the right to benefit from royalty payments earned from minerals below the land.

What can you do?

If you believe in the principle of freedom of access and the democratic sharing of our mineral wealth we urge you to find out more about this vital issue by sending for our free brochure.

For the sake of your democratic rights we urge you to stake your claim for equal land rights and a better future for every Western Australian.

KEEP OUT
THIS LAND IS PART OF WESTERN AUSTRALIA UNDER ABORIGINAL CLAIM.

 The Chamber of Mines of Western Australia (Inc).
231 Adelaide Terrace, Perth. Tel (09) 325 2955.

Land rights should be equal rights.

The Chamber of Mines of Western Australia is encouraged by the strong public support for its positive position on issues related to Aboriginal Land Claims.

The mining industry has been consistent in its stance throughout the debate and continues to share with other sections of the community a recognition of the need to provide Aboriginal people in the community, many of whom are disadvantaged, with special forms of assistance and with security for significant sacred sites.

The mining industry has not opposed the granting of land as part of this assistance and its submission to the Seaman Inquiry and its contribution to the public debate, has been based on the following twelve (12) points:

1. Aborigines should be granted land with the same, but not greater, rights than a non-Aborigine can obtain for similar land.

2. There should be no veto over exploration or mining by any landowner because a veto would deny the principle of Crown ownership of minerals by placing de facto control/ownership in the hands of such landowners.

3. The mechanism for abitration of compensation agreements should be as proposed by the WA Hunt Inquiry, by the establishment of a judicial tribunal.

4. There should be no permit system for entry onto Aboriginal land. Aboriginal landowners should have equal but not greater protection under the law than other landowners with respect to access.

5. With respect to minerals on or under all land, these should remain the property of the Crown with State Government retaining the overriding authority to grant or deny access for exploration and development.

6. Only Government should have the right to negotiate and collect royalties for subsequent distribution of such monies as it so determines.

7. The right to demand overriding royalties should not be granted to any landholder.

8. Compensation for disturbance of land by exploration or mining should be based on actual disturbance or loss of surface usage and not related to the values of minerals.

9. Pastoral leases should remain pastoral leases with aboriginal pastoralists having the same rights and obligations as non-aboriginal pastoralists.

10. Freehold land obtained for Aborigines should be granted under a normal Torrens freehold title.

11. Reserves and vacant Crown land granted to Aborigines should be the subject of a 99 year Crown lease, giving the Aboriginal owners long term security.

12. Any single land area of over 200 square kilometres should be the subject of a "State Agreement" thereby allowing parliamentary review of the validity of the land grant and also allowing flexibility of the terms of the grant to meet the needs of individual Aboriginal communities.

If the aspirations of Aboriginal people and the needs of the wider community are to be balanced, then The Chamber of Mines believes all Western Australians should support the incorporation of the above principles in <u>any</u> land rights legislation.

The mining industry believes, and has always believed, that land rights should be equal rights - for <u>every</u> Western Australian.

The Chamber of Mines of Western Australia (Inc).
231 Adelaide Terrace, Perth. Tel (09) 325 2955.

The Chamber also felt that its campaign gave the industry leverage over the federal government. It helped to persuade Prime Minister Hawke to accommodate the miners' concerns by amending the principles for national Aboriginal land rights legislation.

Impact Upon the Burke and Hawke Governments

On 12 and 17 September 1984 (before the public release of the Seaman Report on 27 September), CMWA and AMIC held private meetings with the Prime Minister to discuss the mineral industry's concerns with land rights legislation. At a dinner meeting of 12 September, which included Minister Holding, the miners said that they did not want land rights legislation. However, if that could not be avoided, then they wanted to ensure that their interests were accommodated in the legislation. If that could be guaranteed, then the miners would be prepared to discontinue their advertising campaign in Western Australia, and would not conduct a similar campaign at the national level. It is important to note that, at the time of the dinner, the 'wall' (or 'black hand') advertisement was still being run on television in Western Australia.

From AMIC's point of view, it wanted the issue settled quickly. AMIC was worried that if Hawke started a negotiating process with them for amending the land rights principles which extended beyond the December 1984 federal election, the industry would lose whatever political leverage it had over the government. AMIC did not want to have to run a campaign against land rights legislation during the lead-up to an election. The reason was that, if Hawke won the election, as expected, it would be taken as a mandate for the federal government to proceed with uniform national land rights legislation.

During the dinner discussion Hawke asked both CMWA and AMIC to freeze advertising on the understanding that he would hold future talks with them to negotiate a new set of principles to govern exploration and mining on Aboriginal land. CMWA and AMIC acceded to the Prime Minister's request, and Holding gave assurances that Aborigines also would not run an advertising campaign on land rights. The National Aboriginal Conference had been planning to run a public media campaign in order to counteract the industry's campaign. It is important to note, however, that the Chamber's advertising campaign in Western Australia was already scheduled to end in mid-September. Therefore, in acceding to the Prime Minister's request, the Chamber did not actually depart from its previously planned policy promotion program.

The Prime Minister and the miners had broad-ranging discussions about the industry's concerns. The conversation focused upon four major issues:

1. The mining veto;
2. Sacred sites;
3. Crown ownership as opposed to Aboriginal ownership;
4. Who should control access to land for exploration and mining — the Crown or Aborigines?

They also discussed the issue of royalties. The miners expressed their strong preference for compensation based upon disturbance to land and not upon social or spiritual factors.

On 13 September AMIC supplied the Prime Minister with a draft proposal listing new land rights principles. It included all four of the major points of concern which the industry expressed to the Prime Minister.

On 17 September CMWA and AMIC again met with the Prime Minister to discuss the amendments to the proposed set of principles for land rights legislation. They had extensive discussions about a possible tribunal system to replace the veto. While there was no concrete meeting of minds at the meeting, Hawke agreed to float these ideas at the next cabinet meeting scheduled for 24 September. However, Prime Minister Hawke cautioned the miners that he was not confident he could deliver on the miners' proposed amendments to the principles for land rights legislation.

Of course the cabinet meeting of 24 September was the one at which Clyde Holding proposed a radical change in the government's attitude toward Aboriginal land rights. These new proposals would have significantly weakened Aboriginal control over mining on their land. In early October 1984, Holding and Hawke informed Aboriginal leaders that, in principle, their veto powers over mining on Aboriginal land would be removed and replaced by a tribunal system.

Premier Burke also attended the federal cabinet meeting of 24 September with a view toward getting federal support for his modified land rights principles for Western Australian state legislation. However, before Burke went to Canberra to hold discussions with Hawke and the federal subcommittee on Aboriginal land rights, he had reached agreement with the Chamber of Mines of Western Australia on acceptable principles for state land rights legislation. On the evening of 22 September Burke met with Keith Parry and other CMWA representatives and agreed upon a set of principles for state land rights.

On 24 September, after meeting with the federal cabinet, Burke sent the president of CMWA a letter confirming their agreed principles for land rights legislation in Western Australia (Burke, 1984). Five principles were listed in the letter:

1. Crown ownership of minerals.
2. No Aboriginal right of veto over exploration or mining.
3. The determination, collection and distribution of royalties to remain with the Crown.
4. Protection of sites of special significance.
5. *Bona fide* miners to have access to Aboriginal land by virtue of holding a miner's rights. Aboriginal land holders may object to and seek compensation for exploration and mining on the following criteria only:
   a. Sites,
   b. Improvements,
   c. Living areas, and
   d. Social disruption.

Burke emphasized the fact that claims for compensation would not relate to the potential value of minerals on the land. He also pointed out that, in cases where a negotiated agreement could be reached within the prescribed thirty-day period, the issues in dispute would be referred to a tribunal which had the power to recommend a decision to the state Minister for Mines. This would ensure that the state government had ultimate power to decide the outcome of mining disputes. The Premier also stressed that these principles accommodated 'all the concerns that the Chamber raised in relation to [its] original draft proposals' for land rights legislation.

Public Support for the Chamber's Position

The Chamber's final opinion survey was conducted in March of 1985, just after the first reading of the Western Australian Land Rights Bill in state parliament. It was designed to evaluate public attitudes toward Aboriginal land rights in Western Australia after the campaign. Table V gives selected survey results from the March 1985 survey and compares them with the survey results during the first phase of the campaign (i.e. March and May 1984).

TABLE V
EVALUATION OF PUBLIC ATTITUDES ON ABORIGINAL LAND RIGHTS
IN WESTERN AUSTRALIA

Issues Addressed	March 1984 Support	May 1984 Support	March 1985 Support*
	(%)	(%)	(%)
1. Opposition of Right to Veto	62	64	67
2. Right of Access	76	79	78
3. Equality in Land Rights	79	87	84
4. Equality in Compensation	89	93	94
5. Importance of Contribution of the Mining Industry	87	88	89

Source: Marketing Centre Research Pty Ltd, 1984, and Manners, 1985a.

* The poll conducted in March 1985 had a sample of 600 respondents. It was carried out after the first reading of the Aboriginal Land Rights Bill (1985) in the Western Australian Legislative Assembly.

The survey data do not show any significant change in public opinion. This merely confirms the pattern of results obtained during the first phase of the campaign. It suggests that the chief purpose of the second phase of the campaign, like the first, was not to shift public opinion on the land rights issue. Rather, it was designed to raise public visibility of the land rights issue to politicians, and to present the illusion of the industry's ability to mobilize public opinion on a political issue of major importance to it.

An indication of the Chamber of Mines of Western Australia's inability to significantly alter public opinion in Western Australia on the land rights issue came after the campaign. The Chamber ran an advertisement expressing the industry's support for the Western Australian Aboriginal Land Rights Bill which the Burke Government introduced into the state parliament in March 1985. However, the Chamber's March 1985 survey results showed that the Western Australian public continued to oppose Aboriginal land rights legislation. The Chamber concluded from this response that the public failed to grasp the fact that the mining industry had altered its position from opposing Burke's land rights legislation to supporting it (interview with David Fardon, 25 February 1987). However, an alternative interpretation is that the Western Australian public opposed Aboriginal land rights regardless of the position taken by the mining industry. If this interpretation is correct, it raises questions about the industry's claims for the success of its campaign.

Bell disagrees with this interpretation, however, and argues that the CMWA campaign was effective in producing a major shift in public opinion against granting 'land rights' (private communication, 18 April 1988). The evidence given for this is the Chamber's polling data. Table VI contains the data that Bell has used to support this interpretation.

TABLE VI

SUPPORT FOR GRANTING LAND RIGHTS

(Comparison of March and May 1984 Surveys)

	March 1984	May 1984
	(%)	(%)
In Favor	40.9	34.7
Against	41.6	56.3
Undecided	17.5	9.0

Source: Marketing Centre Research Pty Ltd, Western Australia, May 1984, p. 32.

The data indicate that in March 1984 (before the campaign) 41.6 per cent of those surveyed were against granting land rights to Aborigines while 40.9 per cent favored it, and 17.5 per cent were undecided. In May 1984 (the mid-point of the campaign), those against granting land rights increased to 56.3 per cent, while those in favor dropped to 34.7 per cent and 9 per cent were undecided. Therefore, the increase in those opposed to land rights rose from 41.6 to 56.3 per cent (14.7 percentage points). This reported increase in opposition to land rights is the industry's principal evidence for its claim that the campaign significantly altered public opinion on the issue of land rights.

CWMA argue, for example, that the people of Western Australia differentiated between 'land rights' and 'land grants'. While they were divided (45 per cent for and 45 per cent against) granting land to Aborigines, they were opposed to Aboriginal land rights which implies 'greater rights in land'—i.e. ownership of minerals (Manners, 1985a: 2).

However, there are problems with such an interpretation. For example, at no time did the miners' publicly oppose Aboriginal land rights. Instead, the campaign emphasized that Aborigines, like other Australians, should have equal, not superior, rights in land. However, the granting of land to Aborigines in itself is a right which non-Aborigines do not have. This was the campaign theme of the opposition Liberal Party. It flatly opposed Aboriginal land rights. And, in fact, the Liberals ran an election campaign in Western Australia based upon that issue.

Furthermore, even if the industry can take credit for at least some of the apparent increase in public opposition to Aboriginal land rights, this would not explain the fact that, in March 1985, after the industry publicly supported state land rights legislation, public opposition to land rights legislation remained high.

While there is no question that the Chamber's policy promotion program raised public awareness of the Aboriginal land rights issue, it does not necessarily follow from this that public sentiment on the issue was simply an expression of support for the mining industry's position on the issue. As the Australian National Opinion Polls study (1985) of national attitudes toward Aboriginal land rights revealed, public opposition to land rights in Western Australia was no greater than it was in Queensland and Tasmania, where the mining industry did not campaign against land rights.

CHAPTER FIVE

The Liberal Party Challenge to Premier Brian Burke

The Western Australian Liberal Party's electoral pressure on Brian Burke led his government to oppose the federal government's national land rights policy. Burke's opposition to uniform national land rights legislation was largely responsible for its defeat.[1] The mining industry's campaign against land rights legislation in Western Australia did not significantly alter public opinion on the issue (see Chapter Four). An underlying public sentiment against Aboriginal land rights already existed before the mining industry mounted its campaign. However, the industry campaign was effective in transforming an unpopular low-profile issue into an unpopular high-profile one which the opposition was able to exploit electorally. The success of the miners' campaign, therefore, was largely due to their ability to harness underlying social prejudice against Aborigines by focusing public attention upon a highly unpopular issue.

The Burke Government felt that, electorally, it was doing well in almost all policy areas except land rights. On this issue they felt vulnerable to the Liberal Party's campaign. In effect, the Liberals in Western Australia tried to make the state by-elections, the federal election in 1984, and the state election in 1986, into referenda on land rights. The issue was regarded by the state ALP as a vote-shifting one which, if not taken off the political agenda, could defeat them in elections. Therefore, Burke felt compelled to take drastic action in order to contain the politically damaging effects of the land rights issue.

He sought to defuse the issue by taking it out of the political arena. To this end, Premier Burke followed a two-fold strategy. First, he sought to take the issue out of the public media by winning the support of major interest-groups who were campaigning against land rights legislation, and who traditionally supported the Liberal Party (primarily the miners and pastoralists). This was partially achieved by establishing an Aboriginal land legislation drafting committee comprised of all major groups concerned with land rights legislation. The participation of industry groups on the committee not only succeeded in suspending their public criticism of Burke's Government, but it also secured their support for his Aboriginal land rights bill which they helped to draft. Secondly, after the opposition-dominated upper house of the Western Australian state parliament (i.e. the Legislative Council) defeated Burke's Aboriginal land rights bill in April 1985, the Premier waged a protracted and ultimately successful political battle against the federal government's attempt to impose land rights legislation upon Western Australia.

The political controversy between the Burke Government and the federal government on the issue of Aboriginal land rights can be understood primarily in terms of factional ALP politics. Burke was animated by the desire to contain an electorally damaging issue, one that he thought threatened the survival of his government. The Hawke Government, on the other hand, was primarily motivated by its desire to avoid factional conflict within the party between those who supported Burke and those who supported the Victorian SL and national left wing of the ALP. The latter sought to uphold the party's principles of (uniform) national land rights legislation regardless of the political costs. In the controversy, Hawke sought to avoid a major factional division within the Australian Labor Party. The conflict had the potential to become a 'states' rights' challenge by the Western Australian Labor government to the federal Labor government. The potential defeat of a state Labor government was too high a price for Hawke to pay for land rights legislation.

While the key industry groups concerned—i.e. the CMWA (Chamber of Mines of Western Australia), the PGA (Pastoralists and Graziers Association), and the PIA (Primary Industry Association)—supported Burke's challenge to federal land rights legislation, they played a minor role in the controversy. Their role was largely limited to private meetings with the Premier and his ministers, and the Prime Minister and federal cabinet members. They also made public statements in support of Burke, and threatened to run a policy promotion program comparable to the Western Australian campaign if the federal government proceeded with national legislation.

The interplay of factional ALP politics determined the outcome of the controversy. National Aboriginal land rights legislation was ultimately defeated by a compromise agreement between the Western Australian and the federal Labor parties just prior to the July 1986 national conference of the ALP. The over-arching threat of a major factional conflict breaking out at the conference was the incentive to work out a compromise solution to the land rights dispute.

The substance of the agreement was that Burke, who was supported by Prime Minister Hawke and Senator Evans, agreed not to attempt to remove or water-down the Aboriginal land rights plank in the federal ALP platform. And Hawke agreed to allow the mining veto to remain in the Northern Territory Aboriginal Land Rights Act (1976). The left wing, represented by Gerry Hand agreed, in exchange, to withdraw its insistence upon over-riding national land rights legislation, and not to oppose the government's efforts to 'streamline' the administrative provisions of the Northern Territory Land Rights Act.

The Labor Party's compromise satisfied the miners' wish to avoid national land rights legislation, and the Aborigines' desire to retain the mining veto in the Northern Territory Land Rights Act. However, both groups were dissatisfied with the outcome. The mineral industry felt betrayed by the Hawke Government's failure to implement its agreement to remove the veto from the Northern Territory Act. And the Aborigines felt betrayed by an ALP government that failed to implement national land rights based upon the Northern Territory model. Instead, the federal government ended by weakening the only legislation that it controlled—the Northern Territory Act.

The mining industry grudgingly accepted the outcome because it recognized that Prime Minister Hawke's declared intention to remove the veto from the Northern Territory Act was effectively blocked by opposition within the Labor Party. The Northern Territory Aboriginal land councils and elements of the ALP left wing, on the other hand, did not accept the outcome. They waged a lobbying campaign within the federal ALP caucus to prevent any weakening of Aboriginal powers under the mining provisions of the Northern Territory Land Rights Act (see Chapter Six).

Burke's Election Strategy

Brian Burke's election strategy for the Labor Party of Western Australia represented a new approach, or style of leadership. Before Burke entered state parliament in a by-election in 1973 and took over the leadership of the party in 1981, the Labor Party performed poorly in state and national elections. It was plagued by internal divisions (Kennedy, 1978). Party morale was low and, according to Pervan and Mitchell (1979), the Labor Party was in search of a new role and strategy which could unite the party-faithful and win electoral support. Burke's leadership of the party filled this niche. He was able to unite the party rank-and-file, and to persuade key industry groups and the electorate that he was the 'best new leader in Australia'.

Gallop (1983: 19-20) points out, however, that Burke's leadership of the Labor Party in Western Australia did not represent a significant departure from ALP ideology or policies. However, there was a major shift in Burke's leadership style. Brian Burke projected the image of a man who could lead the state out of its economic recession. By contrast, the incumbent Liberal-National Country Party coalition was widely perceived to be at an impasse. The Liberal's charismatic leader, Sir Charles Court, had retired from politics at the end of 1981. Ray O'Connor, a popular but less charismatic figure, took over the leadership of the party.

The Labor Party, under Burke's leadership, enjoyed successes in the by-elections of March and July 1982. In 1983 the Prime Minister, Malcolm Fraser (leading a federal Liberal coalition government), called an election. At the time the federal election was announced, the Western Australian state campaign for the February 1983 state election was already under way. This set the stage for a transition in political power in Western Australia. Burke launched a campaign strategy that was designed to rival the Liberal Party's claim that it could lead Western Australia to continued economic growth.

With state resource development in decline, and with the effects of a recession being felt in Western Australia, the Liberals were electorally vulnerable. They waged a low-key campaign in 1983, based upon their record of managing the state's economy. They hoped that the electorate would blame the federal Liberal government of Malcolm Fraser, and not the state Liberal government. However, the federal Labor Party under the highly popular and aggressive leadership of Bob Hawke, waged a vigorous campaign against the Fraser Government at the same time that Burke campaigned in Western Australia. This made it virtually impossible for the Liberals in Western Australia to keep the campaign low-key, and to insulate themselves from the unpopularity of the Fraser Government.

Burke capitalized on the Liberal's electoral weakness by projecting a leadership image of professionalism, moderation and, above all, managerial competence. He cultivated this image by proposing new government initiatives designed to stimulate regional economic growth. The principal means to achieve this was to provide incentives to the private sector. One major initiative was the 'Bunbury 2000 Development Strategy'. This proposal, along with one for the defense of Western Australia called 'Defence: Protecting the West', were revealed before the 1983 election date was even set. These programs were announced by Burke personally, and they were accompanied by detailed plans.

An indication of the importance of 'Bunbury 2000' in Burke's campaign, was the fact that, after the ALP's election in February 1983, Burke made Bunbury 2000 a special ministerial responsibility (Burke, 1984). In a subsequent policy document entitled: 'South-West Development Authority: Bunbury 2000', the Premier explained that 'Bunbury 2000' had 'top priority' in his government's program (South West Development Authority, 1983). He elaborated by saying that 'substantial progress' would be made during the first three years of his government. The importance which the Burke Government attached to 'Bunbury 2000' made it an electorally sensitive issue.

The 'Bunbury 2000 Development Strategy'

The government's policy document described Bunbury as an 'alternative urban capital' in Western Australia. An estimated 918,000 out of Western Australia's total population of 1,299,000 were said to reside in the Perth metropolitan area. 'Bunbury 2000' was designed to establish an urban alternative to Perth by diverting projects and people to the south-west. 'Bunbury 2000' was described as a model scheme which was to be implemented in other areas of the state. Bunbury itself was said to be the 'gateway' and 'service centre' for the entire south-west.

Burke created the South West Development Authority to design a master plan to encourage business and employment programs in Bunbury. Its functions included providing market information and feasibility studies for new business ventures in the area. It was designed to provide the agricultural, mining, and timber production industries with market information and advisory services to encourage them to locate in the region.

The economic diversity of the region was said to make Bunbury an ideal center for regional growth. For example, coal and bauxite deposits were being mined in the Collie Basin and Darling Escarpment, which is inland from Bunbury. These projects were attracting billions of dollars in investment. Bunbury was also the south-west's traditional export outlet. As such, roads and railway services converged there.

'Bunbury 2000' depended for its success upon the co-operation of neighboring shires (i.e. local government councils) which were described as constituting the 'Greater Bunbury'. These shires included Harvey, Dardanup, and Capel which together established a regional planning committee to handle Bunbury's expansion across city boundaries into their jurisdiction. It also included the suburbs of Australind, in the Shire of Harvey, Eaton, in the Shire of Dardanup, and Gelorup, in the Shire of Capel.

According to the report, Bunbury had intimate links with other neighboring shires, including Collie, Donnybrook-Balingup, and Busselton. An additional six shires were also effected by Bunbury's commercial and administrative zone. These included Waroona, Boyup Brook, Bridgetown-Greenbushes, Manjimup, Nannup, and Augusta-Margaret River. All of these shires were considered by the Burke Government to constitute the 'Bunbury Region'. The 'South-West Region' included the Bunbury region plus two local authorities, Mandurah and Murray.

Burke's campaign emphasis upon promoting regional economic growth by providing incentives for industrial investment paid off in the 1983 state elections. The Labor Party won thirteen new seats in parliament to become Western Australia's first Labor government in almost ten years.

For present purposes, what is significant about these new Labor seats is that some of them were in mining or farming districts, and several were in the 'Bunbury region' including Bunbury itself. Therefore, by virtue of Burke's campaign promise to foster Western Australia's economic growth, the new ALP government had a commitment to retain these seats in state elections. However, these parliamentary seats were marginal, or 'swinging seats'. They were regarded as being extremely sensitive to shifts in public opinion on major political issues. The land rights issue became just such an issue. It became a 'vote-shifting' issue that could potentially swing against Labor and perhaps lose them elections.

The Election Results of 1983

According to Gallop (1983: 11), the ALP won the 1971 election in Western Australia with a swing in the popular vote of 3.6 per cent and a gain of three seats in the Legislative Assembly.[2] The outcome of the 1971 election gave Labor a slender one-seat majority over the coalition parties. By contrast, the Burke Government was elected to office in 1983 with a 7.2 per cent swinging-vote increase over their 1980 election results. This gave the ALP what appeared to be a comfortable seven-seat majority in the Legislative Assembly. The distribution of seats in the assembly before and after the 1983 election by party affiliation is given in Table VII.

TABLE VII
DISTRIBUTION OF SEATS IN THE
LEGISLATIVE ASSEMBLY BY PARTY
BEFORE AND AFTER THE 1983 ELECTION

Party	Before	After
ALP	23	32
Liberal	26	20
NCP*	4	3
NP†	2	2

Source: Gallop, 1983: 11.
* National Country Party
† National Party

However, the size of the ALP's majority in the Legislative Assembly was deceptive. Of the nine seats Labor gained in the 1983 election, five were marginal. Table VIII gives a break-out of the nine assembly seats gained by the ALP according to electoral zone. The newly won Labor seats included Bunbury, Mitchell, and Mundaring. Whitford and Joondalup were also new Labor seats. They are located in the northern corridor of metropolitan Perth (the so-called 'mortgage belt', named after the high mortgages of suburban home-owners).

TABLE VIII
DISTRIBUTION OF LABOR SEATS GAINED IN 1983 BY ELECTORAL ZONE

Metropolitan	Agricultural Mining and Pastoral	North-West Murchison-Eyre
Whitford	Bunbury	Pilbara
Scarborough	Mitchell	
Joondalup	Mandurah	
	Mundaring	
	Esperance-Dundas	

Source: Gallop, 1983: 12.

The Burke Government was particularly concerned to retain Labor control of these seats. Their loss would not only represent a failure of the government's highly publicized 'Bunbury 2000' development strategy, it could potentially bring down Burke's Government. Therefore the Labor Party was sensitive to its standing in these electorates.

The Aboriginal land rights controversy was regarded as the only major issue on which the electorate in these districts and elsewhere in the state could swing against Labor. As a result of this concern, the state ALP commissioned ANOP (Australian National Opinion Polls), a public polling company under the managing directorship of Rod Cameron, to conduct a series of opinion surveys of marginal electorates. It is important to note in passing that Cameron is a key campaign advisor to the ALP, and the Labor Party relies upon the ANOP for most of its polls.[3] The purpose of the surveys was to determine whether the land rights issue was a major vote-shifting issue in these electorates.

Land Rights: a Vote-Shifting Issue

ANOP surveyed marginal electorates in Western Australia and the state as a whole in mid-1984, late 1984, mid-1985, and in late 1985 during the lead-up to the state election which was held in February 1986. A state-wide ANOP opinion survey of Western Australia in mid and late 1985 highlighted the electorally damaging nature of the land rights issue to the ALP.

Table IX summarizes the results of the state-wide survey. The table lists the major campaign issues, and estimates the extent of the lead or lag that the Labor Party had in relation to the Liberal Party on the issues surveyed.

The data in Table IX clearly show that, with the exception of the development and land rights issues, respondents favored the Labor Party's position over the Liberal Party's stance. Of the two issues on which the Liberal Party was preferred, land rights was the greater electoral liability.

TABLE IX
COMPARATIVE ADVANTAGE OF THE LABOR AND LIBERAL PARTIES IN W.A. BETWEEN JUNE AND OCTOBER 1985

Issue	Party	June	October	Switchers
Unemployment	LABOR	46	53	Labor is performing strongly on this issue.
	LIBERAL	20	19	
	LABOR LEAD	+26	+34	
Land Rights	LABOR	27	22	Still a very vulnerable spot for Labor.
	LIBERAL	42	47	
	LIBERAL LEAD	+15	+25	
Strikes — Industrial Relations	LABOR	46	54	Situation has improved greatly.
	LIBERAL	28	23	
	LABOR LEAD	+18	+31	
Development	LABOR	23	32	Static, no movement.
	LIBERAL	44	40	
	LIBERAL LEAD	+21	+8	
State Taxes/ Charges	LABOR	29	36	A good result. Holding the line.
	LIBERAL	27	34	
	LABOR LEAD	+2	+2	
Petrol Prices	LABOR	16	31	Very good result. Cut back Liberal lead.
	LIBERAL	36	27	
	LABOR LEAD	−20	+4	
Education	LABOR	33	31	Holding ground but room for improvement.
	LIBERAL	29	23	
	LABOR LEAD	+4	+8	
Interest Rates	LABOR	31	34	Static, potentially serious position.
	LIBERAL	25	27	
	LABOR LEAD	+6	+7	
Cost of Living	LABOR	30	33	Marginal improvement.
	LIBERAL	25	23	
	LABOR LEAD	+5	+10	

Source: ANOP Survey of Western Australia, mid-, and late, 1985. As a matter of policy, ANOP does not publicly release information on the samples of its surveys. However, according to Lois Anderson, Electorate Officer to Senator Michael Beahan, the samples of ANOP polls in Western Australia were comparable to the polls conducted in Western Australia by the Marketing Centre Research on behalf of the Chamber of Mines of Western Australia (see Chapter Four) (private communication from Lois Anderson, 2 June 1988).

In the October 1985 survey, the Liberal Party had a 25 per cent lead over the Labor Party on the land rights issue. This compared with the Liberal Party's 8 per cent lead over Labor on the issue of development.

Therefore, not only was land rights potentially the most damaging election issue for the Labor Party but, according to opinion surveys carried out in June and October 1985, the Liberal Party's margin of preference on land rights over the Labor Party increased from 15 to 25 per cent. This signaled a serious potential election problem to the Burke Government.

The increase in public opposition to the Labor Party's handling of the land rights issue during this period was undoubtedly related to the fact that Burke's land rights legislation was defeated in the Liberal-controlled Legislative Council in April 1985, with the federal government subsequently threatening to impose national land rights legislation upon Western Australia. Such a development would inevitably have raised the profile of the land rights issue further by transforming it into a states' rights issue. State-federal rivalry over constitutional powers has historically been a sensitive issue in Western Australia, which once sought to secede from the federation.

ANOP also conducted surveys of marginal seats (i.e. ones recently won by the Labor Party) in the northern suburbs of the metropolitan zone, such as Joondalup; in outer urban districts, such as Mundaring; and in the South-West—Mitchell and Bunbury. It is significant that the latter two electoral districts were located in the Bunbury region. Therefore, they were not only marginal seats, but were located in an area of the state in which the Burke Government had invested a great deal of its political stock in its 'Bunbury 2000' regional development program. The loss of these seats would have been a particularly damaging political blow to the Burke Government.

Opinion surveys of these electorates persuaded Burke and the state Labor Party that land rights posed a serious election problem for the government. For that reason, and also because widespread skepticism had been expressed about the seriousness of the electoral threat that the land rights issue posed to Burke, it is instructive to examine these surveys in some detail.

Surveys of Marginal Electorates

One survey of Bunbury and Mitchell was conducted in late 1984. Voters were asked whether they were basically in favor or not in favor of land rights for Aborigines—and how strongly they held that view. They were then asked their reasons. The results of that survey are presented in Table X. The data indicate that the total average support for Aboriginal land rights in Bunbury and Mitchell combined was only 6 per cent. In contrast, total opposition to land rights (i.e. 'soft' and 'strongly opposed') in these two electorates was a staggering 90 per cent. The reasons given for respondents' opposition to land rights related to the Chamber of Mines of Western Australia's slogan, 'equal rights for all Australians': the belief that Aborigines should work and earn the right to own land; the fear that Aborigines would not use land productively; and the feeling that Aborigines had already received 'too many hand-outs' (i.e. social welfare).

In mid-1985, ANOP conducted a similar survey of the Mundaring, Joondalup, and Mitchell electorates. The results of that survey are presented in Table XI. The survey data in the table are similar to those in Table X for Bunbury and Mitchell. The data indicate overall opposition to Aboriginal land rights in all three electorates. Combined opposition to land rights (i.e. 'soft' and 'strong') in Mundaring, Joondalup, and Mitchell

TABLE X
LAND RIGHTS IN BUNBURY AND MITCHELL
BASIC ATTITUDES AND WHY

	Bunbury	Mitchell (as a percentage)	Total	Potential Swinging Voters
In Favor	5	7	6	7
Opposed but Soft-Lean to Opposition	49	37	43	42
Strongly Opposed	41	53	47	49
Undecided	5	3	4	2

Source: ANOP, late 1984.

was 84 per cent, with potential swinging voters registering total opposition to land rights of 87 per cent.

Comparable with the survey results in Table X, the respondents for the data presented in Table XI gave similar reasons for their opposition to land rights: which also related to the CMWA's slogan, 'equal rights for all Australians': the fear that Aborigines would not use land productively; and that Aborigines already received 'too many hand-outs'.

TABLE XI
LAND RIGHTS IN MUNDARING, JOONDALUP, AND MITCHELL
BASIC ATTITUDES AND WHY

	Mundaring	Joondalup	Mitchell	Total	Potential Swinging Voters
		(as a percentage)			
In Favor	16	14	7	12	9
Opposed but Soft-Lean to Opposition	41	48	40	42	49
Strongly Opposed	38	36	50	42	38
Undecided	5	2	3	3	4

Source: ANOP, mid-1985.

After the Legislative Council defeated Burke's Aboriginal land Rights Bill in April 1985, the Labor Party commissioned another survey of Mundaring, Joondalup, and Mitchell, to assess the impact of that development upon public opinion. Voters were asked whether they thought it was a good or a bad thing that the state government's land rights bill was defeated in Western Australia's upper house where Labor does not have a majority. The data in Table XII summarize the results of the survey.

Sixty-six per cent of the respondents who felt that the defeat of Burke's land rights bill was a good thing gave as reasons the ones that had been given in previous surveys. They mentioned the equal rights slogan, felt that Aborigines should work for the land, and stated that they were fundamentally opposed to the concept of land rights. The voters in these three elec-

TABLE XII
REACTION TO THE DEFEAT OF THE LAND RIGHTS BILL
IN THE LEGISLATIVE COUNCIL

	Mundaring	Joondalup (as a percentage)	Mitchell	Total	Potential Swinging Voters
Defeat of Land Rights Bill is a:					
Good Thing	61	63	72	66	68
Bad Thing	22	26	16	22	19
Unconcerned or Undecided	17	11	12	12	13

Source: ANOP, mid-1985.

torates were also asked what the state government's course of action should be now that the land rights bill was defeated. Voters were presented with four possible courses of action for the state government in the land rights area and were then asked to indicate their preferences. Responses to that opinion survey are presented in Table XIII.

TABLE XIII
PREFERRED ACTION FOR THE STATE GOVERNMENT ON LAND RIGHTS

	Mundaring	Joondalup (as a percentage)	Mitchell	Total	Potential Swinging Voters
W.A. Government should forget Land Rights	32	31	49	38	33
Both State and Federal Governments should delay for a year or so and decide what to do then	29	29	21	26	30
W.A. Government should try again soon to have its Bill passed	25	26	19	23	20
The Federal Government should introduce a National Land Rights Bill which would apply to W.A.	13	17	7	12	16
Other	5	6	*		
Unsure	8	5	4	6	5

Source: ANOP, mid-1985.
* Less than ½ a per cent.
Note: Percentages may exceed 100 because some respondents gave more than one preference.

The surveys showed that land rights was potentially the single most damaging election issue facing the ALP in Western Australia. While the issue appeared to recede somewhat as an electoral problem in late 1984 (after Burke rejected the Seaman inquiry recommendations, and after the CMWA discontinued its publicity campaign), it continued to be a problem in 1985.

For example, there was strong public approval of the defeat of Burke's Aboriginal land rights bill in April 1985, and strong opposition to any further attempts to introduce land rights legislation in Western Australia.

In particular, the public appeared to oppose any attempt by the federal government to impose land rights legislation on Western Australia. This was evident in the increased opposition to land rights legislation reflected in the surveys immediately after federal cabinet announced its support for Minister Holding's preferred national land rights model legislation in August 1985. For example, the percentage of respondents in Mundaring, Joondalup and Mitchell who were 'strongly opposed' to land rights increased from 42 per cent in mid-1985 to 48 in November 1985. Likewise, combined opposition to land rights in these electorates (i.e. 'soft' and 'strongly opposed') increased during the same period from 85 per cent to 88 per cent of the total.

ANOP's analysis of the electoral difficulties which land rights posed to the ALP in Western Australia was consistent with the shifting but negative results of their opinion surveys. For example, in mid-1984, during the Chamber of Mines of Western Australia's campaign, ANOP pointed out that land rights was a much misunderstood issue which was 'causing real electoral problems among middle-class voters' who recently voted for the Labor Party. The report noted that these 'swinging voters' had little sympathy for Aboriginal land rights. It pointed out that if the Liberal Party in Western Australia was 'smarter' than it was federally over the immigration issue, it would allow the land rights issue to simply brew and become 'distorted' in the suburbs through rumor and local community action.

In late 1984, however, after the Burke Government had managed to win the support of the miners and pastoralists for his state land rights legislation, ANOP made a somewhat different assessment. It said that the issue had been 'temporarily defused' and, therefore, was now a small vote loser. The report asserted that while it was still 'an issue', the state government had neutralized the issue by late 1984. ANOP concluded that, for the time being at least, the vote relevance of land rights was not great. The report recommended that the federal government carry out an information campaign of 'mammoth proportion and impact' in 1985 to lay the issue to rest.

It is interesting to note in passing that the federal Labor Party did not regard land rights as a national election issue. Bob McMullan, national secretary of the Labor Party, conceded that there were a number of federal seats in the Perth metropolitan area which were vulnerable (between two and five, including Stirling and Canning in the northern suburbs). However, land rights never became an electoral problem for the federal government. It was not a major political issue, for example, to the voters in New South Wales and Victoria, where most of the country's electors were (interview with Bob McMullan, 12 March 1987).

The federal ALP was primarily concerned in avoiding land rights becoming a states' rights issue between Western Australia and the federal government. The ALP also felt that the pro-land rights publicity campaign proposed by ANOP would not be successful in any case. The reason was that the miners anti-land-rights campaign was based upon pre-existing hostility and prejudice toward Aborigines. Therefore, in order to counter the effectiveness of the CMWA campaign, the federal government would be faced with trying to change fundamental social attitudes. It did not believe that this could be achieved through a publicity campaign. It would take far more than a few months' advertising to change basic social attitudes.

After the defeat of Burke's land rights bill in April 1985, however, ANOP's opinion surveys began to indicate strong anti-Labor sentiment based upon the land rights issue. For example, in a survey of Avon, a rural Labor seat held by a Minister in Burke's Government, in late 1985, land rights was found to dominate the political agenda. The Avon survey revealed that 87 per cent of respondents were opposed to land rights (57 per cent strongly so), and 94 per cent of the swinging voters opposed land rights. ANOP's report on the Avon survey pointed out that land rights constituted most of the swing against the state government. It stated that, among the swinging voters, 42 per cent had 'doubts' about voting for another Burke Government, as opposed to only 20 per cent having doubts about voting for a Liberal government. The report stressed that land rights dominated doubts about the Labor Party.

Any significant rural reaction against the Labor Party would be amplified by the zonal electoral system for the Legislative Assembly, which divided the state into Perth metropolitan, country, and northern areas. In the 1983 election, 457,000 metropolitan voters elected thirty Members of the Legislative Assembly, while an estimated 182,000 decided twenty-two country seats, with one sitting member going unchallenged. Only 26,000 voters elected four northern members.

As a result of the 1983 election, the ALP held twenty metropolitan seats, ten country seats, and won two seats in the northern area. A voting swing against the Labor Party of only 4.4 per cent, or the loss of Mundaring, Mandurah, Bunbury and Avon, might have been fatal. Their loss would have cost the ALP its majority and, in normal circumstances, brought down the government.

LIBERAL PARTY OPPOSITION TO THE BURKE GOVERNMENT

The official opposition party in Western Australia during the land rights controversy from 1984 to 1986 was the Liberal Party. As of 19 February 1983 it had twenty out of fifty-seven seats in the Legislative Assembly (compared with the ALPs thirty-two seats) and nine out of seventeen seats in the Legislative Council (compared with seven seats for the ALP). During this period, the Liberal Party was led by Bill Hassell, a solicitor and former Minister under the Court and O'Connor governments. Hassell was supported for the leadership of the state Liberal Party by the former Liberal Premier, Charles Court — a legend in Western Australian politics.

Within five years of entering Parliament in 1977, Hassell emerged as the key minister in the Court Government. He held three cabinet portfolios. In 1980 his ministries included Chief Secretary, Minister for Police and Traffic (later Police and Prisons), and Minister for Community Welfare. As the Minister for Community Welfare, Hassell had responsibility for Aboriginal affairs. When Ray O'Connor became Premier in early 1982, Hassell also became the Minister Assisting the Minister for Emergency Services. And, at the end of 1982, just prior to the 1983 state election campaign, Hassell became the state's first Minister for Employment.

Hassell admits to being strongly influenced by his experiences handling the ministries in the Court Government. For example, just before Hassell was defeated by Ray O'Connor to succeed Premier Court after his resignation in 1981, Hassell described his leadership self-image:

> My personal image was moulded by those portfolios. I identified myself with tough campaigns aimed at lowering the road toll, controlling illegal gambling, racing, film censorship and social issues. (*Sydney Morning Herald*, 24 January 1986)

Hassell was criticized from within his own party for presenting an uncompromising 'purist' or fundamentalist style of leadership. He was also criticized for making dogmatic pronouncements. For example, he was reported to have said that the Liberal Party offered a 'return to decent, ordinary values where family comes first, and a place where militant unionists, homosexuals and criminals would be shown their place' (*ibid.*). He had called for the removal of peace studies from the public school curriculum, and was an uncompromising champion of privatization. Hassell's style of party leadership was a combination of unwavering commitment to ideals, and tough-minded, aggressive election campaigning. Both of these qualities were brought to bear in the Liberal Party's anti-land-rights election campaign against Brian Burke's Government.

Hassell attacked the Burke Government for being inconsistent and opportunistic in its policies. He specifically singled-out for attack so-called 'secret deals' between the Burke and Hawke governments. These deals were alleged to occur 'almost daily' in response to political pressures, and were designed to ensure that Labor remained in power in Western Australia.

Under Hassell's leadership, the Liberals focused upon Aboriginal land rights as a major campaign issue. It was an important issue to Hassell because it represented to him the clearest policy difference between the Liberal and Labor parties. The unpopularity of the issue for Burke's Government was undoubtedly another major reason for the Liberals' campaign against land rights.

Hassell repeatedly challenged Burke to call an early election (the next election was constitutionally required on or before March 1986) on the basis of the land rights issue. After the Premier's land rights bill was defeated in the Legislative Council in April 1985, and after federal cabinet endorsed Minister Holding's 'preferred' model for national land rights in August 1985, the Liberal Party elevated Aboriginal land rights to the major campaign issue in the lead-up to the 1986 state election.[4]

Liberal Opposition to Land Rights

The position of the Liberal Party in Western Australia on the issue of land rights differed from the federal Liberal Party's position and, indeed, from the position taken by its counterpart in other states. For reasons of 'principle', the Western Australian Liberal Party categorically opposed any form of Aboriginal land rights. Western Australian Liberals spoke out against land rights in 1976, the date the Fraser Liberal-Coalition Government enacted the Northern Territory Aboriginal Land Rights Act (1976). Despite the fact that two Western Australian Liberal politicians, MHR, Ian Viner, and Senator Fred Chaney, were instrumental in implementing the Northern Territory Act, they did not have the support of the Western Australian Liberal Party for that legislation.

State Liberal Premiers, including Sir Charles Court and Ray O'Connor, plus Bill Hassell (leading the party in opposition), took doctrinaire positions against Aboriginal land rights. For example, at the party's 1983 state conference, delegates voted 594 to 6 against the concept of land rights (Hassell, 1986).

The Liberal Party in Western Australia reaffirmed its categorical opposition to Aboriginal land rights, despite the fact that federal Liberal Party policy supported an amended version of the Labor Party's Northern Territory Land Rights Bill and recommended that the federal government adopt land rights legislation after consultation with the states (Liberal Party, 1983: 12-14). The Western Australian branch of the Liberal party was even more doctrinaire than the NP (National Party) of Western Australia on the question of Aboriginal land rights. For example, unlike the Liberals, the NP supported Aboriginal ownership of land on their reserves (National Party, 1982: 21).

A clear indication of the Western Australian Liberal Party's position on land rights was given by Bill Hassell during the airing of a panel discussion in Western Australia in 1985 (see *West Australian*, 18 November 1985). The program featured four state Liberal Party leaders: Hassell, Greiner of New South Wales, Kennett of Victoria, and Olsen of South Australia. In the interview Hassell 'disowned' Malcolm Fraser's land rights policy. He said that under Fraser's leadership the Liberals had lost federal and state elections, and lost public credibility. Hassell stressed that 'there is no such thing as land rights', and the sooner the federal government understood that the better for everyone.

As the leader of the Liberal Party in Western Australia, Hassell's position on Aboriginal land rights was consistent. The logic of his position was straightforward, albeit simplistic. Hassell and Norman Moore, the Liberal Party's Shadow Minister for Aboriginal Affairs in Western Australia, argued that, by definition, land rights was a racist proposal. They described it as a plan to divide the country along racial lines which would inevitably produce a racist backlash which would do irreparable damage to the state.

They pointed out, however, that they were not opposed to the state granting leases on Aboriginal reserves. Indeed, during Hassell's tenure as Minister of Community Welfare, he obtained land (both reserves and pastoral leases) for a number of Aboriginal communities, such as the pastoral lease land for the Cundeelee Aboriginal community. However, he maintained that if the state granted Aborigines rights in land that other Australians did not have, it would have a devastating impact upon the Western Australian economy and community. Furthermore, he and others maintained that if land rights were carried to their logical conclusion, they would create a separate state for Aborigines which was condemned as paralleling apartheid in South Africa. This theme was hammered home repeatedly at seminars organized by the Liberal party throughout the state, during question time in parliament, in information pamphlets, and in newspaper, radio and television advertisements and appearances.

During the parliamentary debate in 1985 over Burke's Aboriginal land bill, the Premier outlined what he regarded as the substance of the Liberal Party's criticism of land rights in Western Australia. Burke said that the Leader of the Opposition used three arguments to justify Liberal opposition to land rights:

1. there was widespread public opposition to it;
2. state legislation would simply lay the basis for the federal government to impose more stringent legislation upon Western Australia; and
3. in principle land rights were discriminatory since they created different laws for blacks and whites.

(*W.A. Parliamentary Debates*, 26 March 1985.)

Hassell argued that his party did not take up the issue simply because it was politically opportune to do so. The Liberals in Western Australia had always opposed land rights. What happened was that the public did not awaken to the implications of such legislation until it threatened them directly. For example, Sir Charles Court openly criticized the Northern Territory Act in 1977. However, it was only with the release of the interim Seaman Report in January 1984 that the issue hit home in Western Australia. At that point the public began to understand the implications of applying the Northern Territory Act to Western Australia (interview with Bill Hassell, 19 February 1987).

In February 1984 Hassell took over the leadership of the Liberal opposition in Western Australia. Under Hassell, the Liberals set out to defeat land rights both in Western Australia and federally. He rejected Burke's argument that land rights legislation was inevitable, and that it was better to have state legislation which was tailored to local conditions than Holding's national land rights legislation which was not. Hassell argued to the contrary. He asserted that, if the Liberals accepted state land rights it would virtually guarantee federal legislation to 'top up' Western Australia's bill in order to bring it up to uniform national standards. Hassell argued that this was all the more certain given the fact that both Burke and Hawke led Labor governments, and both the Western Australian and federal ALP platforms called for Aboriginal land rights legislation based upon the principles of the Woodward Report (i.e. the Northern Territory model).

THE LIBERAL PARTY'S CAMPAIGN

The opposition followed two main strategies in its anti-land-rights campaign. First, it sought in its campaign to gain the backing of the major industry groups effected by the proposed legislation. The major industrial bodies concerned were the miners, pastoralists and farmers, represented by the Chamber of Mines of Western Australia, the Pastoralists and Graziers

Association of Western Australia, and Primary Industry Association of Western Australia respectively. The membership of these associations historically supported the Liberal-coalition parties. Therefore, all things being equal, the Liberals should have been able to win their support on a major political issue of concern to their members. The second strategy was to undermine the credibility of the Burke Government by trying to turn the land rights issue into a states' rights issue, and characterizing Burke as siding with the federal government against the interests of Western Australians.

The Liberals tried to do this by arguing that Burke's loyalty was primarily to the Labor Party, whose state and federal platforms called for land rights legislation based upon the Northern Territory Act. The opposition stressed that opinion surveys had demonstrated beyond doubt that the citizens of Western Australia opposed any form of land rights. Therefore, if Burke proceeded to adopt land rights in whatever form, he was betraying the wishes of the people of Western Australia in the interests of appeasing the left wing of the ALP, whose base of power was in the eastern states. This proved to be an effective campaign criticism of the Burke Government, one that ultimately forced Burke to openly repudiate any form of land rights legislation.

Securing Industry Support

The first major thrust of the Liberal anti-land-rights election campaign was to secure the support of industry groups that had traditionally supported the Liberal Party. This was important to the Liberal Party for several reasons. It represented electoral support, plus it would provide badly needed funding for the Liberal Party's election campaign. In addition, industry support for the Liberal Party was essential for the credibility of the Liberal's anti-land-rights campaign.

A central element of the Liberal's argument against land rights was that it would seriously damage Western Australia's economy. However, if the major industry groups which would be effected disputed this contention, it would tend to undermine the entire thrust of the campaign. For that reason, it was essential for the Liberals to have industry support for their position.

Hassell and other Liberal spokesmen appealed for the support of industry groups by arguing that, when it came to land rights in particular, they could not trust a Labor government to protect their interests. Indeed, from the beginning of the Liberal anti-land-rights campaign in January 1984, until the meeting between Burke and the federal cabinet on 24 September 1984, the positions of the Liberal Party and major industry groups in Western Australia were basically complementary.

For example, in a letter from Norman Moore, the Liberal's shadow Minister for Aboriginal Affairs, to the chairman of the Pastoral Division of the PGA, Moore pointed out that, in the initial stages of the anti-land-rights campaign, industry groups supported the Liberal position. He said that the public 'opposes land rights becuse they oppose the principle of granting land to Aborigines on the basis of their race. The PGA, the Chamber of Mines and the opposition have all argued this line' (Moore, 1985).

However, after Burke's meeting with federal cabinet in late September, these organizations abandoned their support for the Liberal Party. This was due to their agreement with Burke to participate on a state drafting committee set up on 28 September by the Premier to prepare (through parliamentary counsel) the Aboriginal land rights legislation for Western Australia. On the basis of Burke's statement of ten principles for Aboriginal land rights in Western Australia, which was released on 27 September along with the Seaman Report, major industry groups agreed to participate in the drafting of the legislation.

The drafting committee met for six months, from late September 1984 to early March 1985, and produced an Aboriginal land bill which was ultimately defeated by the Liberals in the Legislative Council. The committee was chaired by Graham McDonald of the Department of Premier and Cabinet (who was the deputy to Seaman in his inquiry), and comprised representatives of all interested groups: PIA (Primary Industry Association); PGA (Pastoralists and Graziers Association); DAA (Commonwealth Department of Aboriginal Affairs), represented by Graham Neate; CMWA (Chamber of Mines of Western Australia); AMIC (Australian Mining Industry Council); APEA (Australian Petroleum Exploration Association); the state Aboriginal Advisory Council and Aboriginal Land Trust; and AMEC (Association of Mining and Exploration Companies).

NAC (National Aboriginal Conference) initially agreed to participate but withdrew at an early stage, charging that the exercise was a sham designed to legislate land rights for miners and farmers, and not for Aboriginals. However, NAC did retain an observer status until 24 November when it was expelled from the committee for an alleged leak of confidential committee information to the press.[5] The Liberal Party declined to participate in the drafting committee for the same reason they refused to make a submission to the Seaman inquiry: it opposed in principle any form of land rights.

Despite some disagreement between the major industry groups represented on the committee, once they agreed to participate they felt obliged to support the Aboriginal Land Bill which they had helped to draft. This was acutely embarrassing to Hassell and the Liberal Party. Since they had elevated land rights to a leading campaign issue, the issue tended to alienate the party from the core of its political constituency.

Because the Liberal Party could not claim to have the support of the industrial groups concerned, it was forced to make the improbable claim that the Liberal Party represented the 'ordinary Western Australian' on the land rights issue. Also, the party was starved of campaign funding since these industry groups had been major contributors to Liberal Party election campaigns. For example, the Liberal Party in Western Australia did not have sufficient funding to commission its own opinion surveys. it was forced to rely upon opinion surveys reported in *The Bulletin*, and those conducted by the Chamber of Mines. Hassell estimated that Labor outspent the Liberal Party in the lead-up to the 1986 election by a margin of about five to one.

Out of frustration, the Liberals eventually resorted to public criticism of the industry groups which had defected to Labor and now supported Burke's land rights legislation. One illustration of the open conflict between the Liberal Party and industry groups which traditionally supported the Liberals was a dispute involving Hassell and the PGA in March 1985 — just before the land rights legislation was defeated in the state parliament. Hassell publically referred to the PGA president, Max Cameron, as an apologist for the Burke Government. He said that Cameron was pushing the 'old Burke line that failure to swallow state Labor's land rights poison will result in a lethal dose from federal Labor' (*Western Farmer*, 28 March 1985).

This elicited an immediate and violent reaction from the PGA. It demanded a retraction and apology from Hassell. The pastoralists justified their support for Burke's land rights legislation on the grounds that it was inevitable, and it was their duty to protect their membership by ensuring that unacceptable and damaging legislation was not passed.

In an open letter by the PGA to members of the Western Australian parliament, it argued for passage of Burke's Aboriginal land bill on the grounds that it represented a moderate approach in contrast to extreme positions in the debate. One extreme position was said to be characterized by those espousing the issue in 'narrow philosophical terms' who rejected the concept of Aboriginal land grants. This was an obvious reference to Hassell and the Liberal Party. The other extreme was represented by those who believed that Aborigines should be given land as a 'right' — a reference to Clyde Holding.

Pastoralists and Graziers Association put its dilemma to the opposition party in the following way:

> If the Liberals could 'unequivocally guarantee' that they could protect land-holders' rights from federal intervention, then they should reject the bill. However, if they could not give that guarantee, then their rejection of the bill would 'recklessly' expose land-holders to the dangers of unsuitable and potentially damaging federal legislation. If the latter occurred, it would be entirely due to the opposition's pursuit of a gratitutious 'whim'. (PGA, 1985)

After the Liberal Party defeated Burke's Aboriginal Land Bill in April 1985, the industry groups which had supported the legislation continued to support Burke's efforts to prevent the federal government from imposing land rights legislation on Western Australia. In this regard, they continued to criticize the Liberal party for defeating the Labor government's legislation in the first place.

For example, in June of 1985, the CMWA, PGA and PIA all expressed their disapproval of the opposition's intransigence toward the land rights issue. Neville Munns of the PGA said, 'We are holding the Liberal Party responsible for any draconian federal legislation'; Stephen Malley of the PIA said, 'We have missed the boat and I'm sorry that the federal government has become involved; and Jack Manners of CMWA said, 'The mining industry would have been comfortable with the State government's proposed legislation' (*West Australian*, 18 June 1985).

During the lead-up to the February 1986 state elections, the Liberal Party and the other conservative coalition parties also openly quarrelled about the importance of land rights as a campaign issue. For example, in January 1986, the Liberal Party argued that 'land rights are a major election issue'. While the National Party declared that 'land rights are no longer an election issue' (*West Australian*, 14 January 1986). Therefore, not only were the major industry groups which traditionally supported the Liberal Party alienated, but the conservative coalition parties were at odds over the land rights issue.[6]

Land Rights: A States' Rights Issue

The opposition pursued its second campaign strategy against the Burke Government by attempting to convert the land rights issue into a states' rights issue. It sought to identify Burke's position with that of the federal ALP against the interests of Western Australia. The opposition was largely successful in this undertaking by repeatedly accusing Burke of carrying out an ALP land rights policy (both state and federal) which was opposed by the majority of Western Australians. In effect, Hassell and others in the Liberal Party put great pressure upon Burke to demonstrate that his political responsibilities as the Premier of Western Australia superseded his Labor Party commitment to implement the ALP's land rights platform.

Burke was vulnerable to this criticism. Since all the polls showed that Aboriginal land rights legislation was highly unpopular in Western Australia, the onus was upon him to prove that his government was not toadying to pressures from the federal ALP to adopt land rights in Western Australia. One measure of the effectiveness of this criticism by the opposition was the lengths to which Burke went to get assurances from the Prime Minister and federal cabinet that the federal government would not impose over-riding national land rights legislation upon Western Australia.

At one stage, in August 1985, after federal cabinet endorsed Minister Holding's 'preferred model' for national land rights, the Premier felt obliged to go so far as to declare that he would resign if the federal government imposed land rights legislation on Western Australia. He also vowed to challenge the constitutionality of such legislation, and said he would demand compensation for all Crown land in Western Australia which was designated by the federal government for that purpose. In fact, Burke's ultimate success in answering the opposition's campaign criticism largely explains the defeat of uniform national land rights legislation in Australia.

Most of Burke's actions and public statements on land rights can be explained, in part at least, by the Premier's efforts to respond to attacks by the Liberal Party. Hassell summarized the opposition's criticism of Burke's handling of the land rights issue in his speech against the Aboriginal Land Bill in the Parliament on 26 March 1985 (Hassell, 1985: 17-21).

Hassell criticized Burke for playing a 'political trick' on the people of Western Australia by raising the threat of federal intervention in Western Australia, and by claiming he had a 'deal' with the Prime Minister which did not exist, and which Hawke could not fulfil in any case. Hassell argued that Burke's Government was acting contrary to the wishes of the people of Western Australia by proceeding with land rights legislation. The only thing that would prevent the federal government from enacting its legislation was for them to be 'stopped politically'. Since the federal government was controlled by Burke's 'mates', he was incapable of stopping federal legislation.

According to Hassell, the Premier was guilty of playing a political trick on the people of Western Australia by claiming that the adoption of state

Aboriginal land legislation would immunize or protect the state from federal legislation. He argued that the federal government never gave Burke such a guarantee. Hassell challenged Burke to produce a letter, signed by the Prime Minister and all members of the ALP caucus, to support his contention. He said that these were the people who would make the federal land rights policy, therefore, there could be no guarantee against over-riding federal legislation without their approval.

Hassell claimed that the Premier could not produce such a letter. Despite Burke's strenuous attempts to secure such assurances (involving numerous ministerial trips between Perth and Canberra), and Burke's repeated warning of the political fall-out in Western Australia of having federal land rights legislation forced upon them, all of Burke's efforts failed. According to Hassell, the reason for this was that the Prime Minister did not have the 'political will' to confront the 'left-wing caucus' and the 'left wing of the party' to make good on such a promise. And even if he did, the Prime Minister did not have the political capacity to fulfil such a promise. Hassell stated that the left wing of the Labor Party would go ahead with its national legislation regardless of what Burke and his government did.

The leader of the opposition also claimed that Burke's threat of federal intervention in Western Australia had a weak constitutional basis, and was unfeasible. He argued that there was really only one constitutional basis upon which the federal government might intervene in Western Australia in order to grant land to Aborigines. That was under section 51 of the Constitution. Under this provision, the federal government had the power to 'make laws for the peace, order and good government of the Commonwealth with respect to the people of any race except the Aboriginal race'. The 1967 referendum amended section 51 by removing the phrase 'except the Aboriginal race' from the Constitution so that the federal government could make laws for people of any race.

Hassell said that was the only constitutional basis upon which the federal government had the authority to justify its land rights legislation. However, he added that this constitutional grant of authority was too limited to justify the kinds of sweeping changes envisioned in the proposed national land rights legislation. For example, the federal government would not have the power, based solely upon this provision of the Constitution, to grant 40 per cent of the land area of Western Australia to Aborigines.

If the federal government wanted to grant land it would first have to resume or acquire it. And to do that it would have to establish that the land was required for the 'public purposes' of the nation. According to Hassell, even if the High Court by some 'twist of interpretation' did agree that granting the land to Aborigines was 'within the public purposes of the Commonwealth [of Australia]' the federal government would still be required to pay compensation to the government of Western Australia for the land acquired. In this regard, Hassell said that, while the Hawke Government was a 'spendthrift, profligate government with no regard for the taxpayers' money', he did not think that the Labor government could finance the resumption of about 45 per cent of the land of Western Australia; it was simply worth too much for the federal government to afford that. Therefore, Hassell concluded that the foundation upon which the federal government proposed to grant land to Aboriginals was very much in doubt.

Hassell stressed the fact that 'even politicians in Canberra' must eventually respond to the pressure of public opinion. They must recognize that their seats (and livelihoods) are at risk if their actions are in opposition to 'persistent, informed public opinion' which was against granting land rights. However, he emphasized that 'the lunatic left and lunatic fringe', which were combined in the ALP caucus in Canberra, were not cognisant of this fact of political life. Therefore, unless they were stopped politically, they would proceed with uniform national land rights.

According to Hassell, Burke's Labor Government was not politically capable of defeating his federal ALP 'mates' in Canberra on the land rights issue. Hassell argued repeatedly that only a Liberal government which was unalterably opposed to land rights legislation (implying his leadership) was capable of defeating land rights legislation both in Western Australia and federally.

BURKE'S POSITION ON LAND RIGHTS

In order to understand Burke's response to the Liberal campaign against his land rights policy, it is necessary to appreciate the fact that he was relatively new to politics when he became Premier of Western Australia. He was elected to the premiership in 1983 without any previous government experience, and he had no direct involvement in Aboriginal affairs.

At the time of election, Burke had little knowledge or interest in Aboriginal affairs. He was not involved in proposing the amendment to the ALP's platform to include land rights, and his only real activity in the land rights debate before his election was to give ceremonial allegiance to the ALP's land rights platform.[7]

However, even this symbolic involvement in Aboriginal affairs was in deference to idealistic sentiment within the ALP, shared primarily by the rank-and-file of the party (interview with Julian Grill, Western Australian Minister for Regional Development, 17 February 1987). An often-quoted example of Burke's support for the ALP's land rights platform was his speech of 16 November 1982 to the Ngaanatjarra Aborigines at the Claremont Showgrounds in Perth. Burke promised the Aborigines gathered there the title to their traditional western desert land. And he naïvely said that 'the land you want is not wanted by white people' (*Western Mail Weekend*, 25-26 January, 1986: 20).

While Aboriginal land rights was in the state Labor Party platform during the 1983 election campaign, it was not an important issue. In fact, it was not until the mining industry launched its anti-land-rights campaign in May 1984, and after the Liberal Party made land rights a major campaign issue, that Burke was forced to give the issue serious attention.

The basis of Burke's 1983 campaign was his promise to stimulate the economic growth of Western Australia. In order to do that, he emphasized the importance of state incentives for private sector investment and expansion. Of course, in order to achieve that goal, Burke had to have the cooperation of major industries in the state.

Mining was critical to the state's economic growth. For example, in 1984, mining, oil and gas production was worth more than $4 billion to

Western Australia, with about 18,000 people employed in those industries. It was estimated that the mineral industry spent about $500 million annually in exploration. It was understandable, therefore, that Burke did not want to alienate this important industry from his government.

After the Premier became aware of some of the issues raised by the land rights debate, he became concerned that the impasse in new exploration and mining in the Northern Territory did not emerge in Western Australia. Hence Burke rejected out-of-hand the Northern Territory Land Rights Act as a model for Western Australia. He regarded it as being responsible for the stagnation of mining activities in the Northern Territory. In this regard, Burke removed the reference to the territory's land rights model (i.e. Woodward Report) from the state ALP platform in 1984. He also threatened to make a similar change to the federal ALP land rights platform at the next national Labor Party conference, in July 1986.

Nevertheless, Burke was prepared to enact an Aboriginal land bill in Western Australia provided that it did not jeopardize his government electorally. However, this is precisely what happened. Even the most passionate Labor supporters of land rights in Western Australia, such as Tom Stephens, the Member of the Legislative Council for North Province, and the Aboriginal Affairs Minister, Keith Wilson, ultimately agreed with Burke's assessment. After the defeat of the government's Land Rights Bill in April 1985, they concluded that it was not feasible for the Labor Party to enact land rights legislation and remain in office. Stephens blamed this situation upon the Liberal Party. He said that their 'hate politics' had made metropolitan voters fear land rights, and it was unreasonable to expect the government to 'go down on the issue' (*Western Mail*, 25-26 January, 1986).

Burke's Delayed Involvement in the Issue

The Premier's late involvement in the land rights issue was evident in his government's inadequate preparation for it. The principal reason for the Premier's decision to establish the Seaman inquiry was to sound-out the views of major concerned groups in Western Australia in order to arrive at a 'balanced' piece of legislation. In this regard Burke was primarily motivated by the desire to formulate land rights legislation which had political support from all major interest-groups in Western Australia.

Burke and his ministers did not have any clear views on Aboriginal land rights legislation. In fact, their lack of real understanding of the issues raised by the land rights debate was evident, even after the announcement of the Premier's statement of principles which was attached to the Seaman Report released in September 1984. For example, Hassell and other Liberal spokesmen repeatedly embarrassed the Burke Government in parliament and elsewhere by requesting detailed information on the kind, size, and location of land which would be available for claim under the government's announced principles for land rights legislation.

These questions caught Burke and his ministers completely unprepared and led to a series of vague and seemingly contradictory statements by government spokesmen, such as they did not know how much land would be available for Aboriginal claim and, later, that about 30 per cent would be available and, still later, that 40 per cent plus would be available. The opposition had a veritable field day quoting the government's vague and conflicting statements.

The opposition also challenged Burke's blasé references to the areas of Western Australia which would be subject to Aboriginal claim as being 'mainly desert' that whites did not want. For example, Hassell compared the 40 per cent of Western Australia which would be subject to claim (an estimated $1,000,000 \text{ km}^2$—more than the size of South Australia, and almost equal to the combined area of New South Wales and Victoria) to Saudia Arabia and Arizona in terms of potential mineral wealth. He said that mineral-rich areas of Western Australia such as Kalgoorlie, Kambalda, the Pilbara and the Kimberleys were, at one time, desert areas before they were developed.

The Liberals also used the government's lack of attention to the practical implications of their policy by arguing that the Burke Government was intentionally refusing to answer detailed questions about its land rights policy because it was part of a cover-up. Hassell argued that Burke was silent on the issue to avoid exposing a politically unacceptable land rights policy which could cost him the up-coming state by-elections in 1984 and the elections in 1986, plus, it could lose Western Australia for the federal ALP in the December 1984 elections.

Burke's Response to the Campaign

Burke followed a two-fold strategy in coping with the Liberal Party's anti-land-rights campaign against his government. The first strategy was to isolate the opposition politically by winning the support of major industry groups for state land rights legislation. Once they agreed to participate on the drafting committee for Aboriginal land legislation, they were not only co-opted into supporting Burke's position on land rights, but they were immediately placed in opposition to the Liberal Party.

This would enable Burke and his government to claim that they were pursuing reasonable and moderate legislation which all major groups in Western Australia supported. It would also enable them to claim that the only major 'group' refusing to participate in drafting suitable state legislation, the Liberal Party, was following an extreme and politically uncooperative policy toward land rights which would inevitably invite punitive federal land rights legislation. The second strategy followed by Burke was to press the federal government for assurances that it would not impose over-riding uniform national land rights legislation upon Western Australia.

Burke was ultimately successful in both strategies. An indication of this was the fact that Aboriginal land rights ceased to be a threatening campaign issue in the February 1986 state elections. The Burke Government had managed to defuse the issue, and won the election easily. However, a major casualty of Burke's strategy to cope with the Liberal challenge was the defeat of national land rights legislation.

Forging Consensus

Burke's chief strategy for isolating the opposition politically was to win the support of major industry groups in Western Australia for his land rights legislation. Burke initiated this strategy by rejecting the recommendations of the Seaman inquiry on the grounds that they were politically unacceptable in Western Australia. The statement of principles, which the Premier issued simultaneously with the Seaman Report, set the political limits for land rights legislation in Western Australia. It was designed to win the support of industry groups, most of whom had strongly opposed the recommendations of Seaman's discussion paper issued in January 1984. All of the ten groups involved (with the important exception of the National Aboriginal Conference) agreed to participate on the Premier's drafting committee on the basis of Burke's new guidelines for land rights legislation.

The Premier's strategy was to moderate the demands of each group by bringing them into alignment with his statement of principles.[8] Burke felt that if they arrived at a consensus position on appropriate land rights legislation for Western Australia (including the state Aboriginal Lands Trust, the Aboriginal Advisory Committee and the National Aboriginal Conference), this would kill land rights as a political issue. Burke felt that if he could get draft legislation through the committee, it would put pressure upon the Liberal Party to accept the legislation in the Legislative Council and, in effect, remove land rights as a campaign issue. The committee would also dissuade the federal government from proceeding with national land rights legislation which would be politically unacceptable in Western Australia. In other words, Burke felt that, if he could get an Aboriginal land rights bill that had been drafted by the major groups concerned, including the federal government, he could then go to the electorate and say that the bill was acceptable to all major interests.

According to Bob Pearce, the Western Australian Minister for Education, Burke advised the Aboriginal groups to accept this process of drafting land rights legislation on the grounds that 'they should take what they could get now and then go for more later' (interview, 18 February 1987). The government pointed out to the Aboriginal groups that Western Australia was way ahead of public opinion on the issue and, indeed, was even leading the federal government in terms of legislation. The Aboriginal Lands Trust and the Aboriginal Advisory Committee accepted this argument on the grounds of political realism. However, the NAC rejected the advice, hoping that Burke's legislation would fail, and that the federal government would then move ahead to fill the vacuum with its national land rights legislation.

Each of the groups which participated on the drafting committee made concessions to bring itself into alignment with Burke's political guidelines. Indeed, it is untrue to say, as many critics of the Burke Government have, that the mining industry drafted the Western Australian Aboriginal Land Bill. In fact, the miners made two major concessions to Burke in the process of formulating the draft legislation. They reversed their positions on permits to enter Aboriginal land, and they agreed to compensate Aboriginal communities for social disruption arising from exploration and mining on their land. These concessions were made in response to Aboriginal protests to the Burke Government, with the backing of the federal government.

Nevertheless, it is also true to say that the major mining provisions in the legislation on which industry insisted (viz., Crown ownership of minerals, no veto, royalties paid only to the Crown, and compensation unrelated to mineral values), were all supported by Burke's statement of principles. In other words, the Premier arbitrarily removed the major mining provisions in Holding's five principles for land rights before the drafting committee was even convened.

Burke was successful in his strategy to win the support of major industry groups for his legislation, and thereby changed the nature of the land rights debate in Western Australia. He shifted the ground away from industry criticism of land rights in general, to a consideration of the most appropriate form of land rights legislation for the state. For example, after the drafting committee began deliberations on an Aboriginal land bill for Western Australia, Burke claimed that 'all of the people acting on behalf of their constituencies have come together to produce what I will be sending to the Prime Minister for the federal government's approval' (*W.A. Parliamentary Debates*, 28 November 1984: 655).

In effect, through this consensus-building strategy, Burke staked-out the middle ground in the political spectrum on the land rights issue in Western Australia. This enabled him to characterize the opposition as representing an extreme and negative position on the issue for reasons of political opportunism. For example, speaking in parliament in November 1984, Burke said that the Chamber of Mines of Western Australia, Australian Mining Industry Council, Pastoralists and Graziers Association, Australian Petroleum Exploration Association, and the Primary Industry Association, as well as the federal Liberal Party's ex-Minister for Aboriginal Affairs, Senator Fred Chaney, and the Leader of the federal Opposition, Andrew Peacock, all supported the Premier's 'constructive approach' to the land rights problem. Burke contrasted this with the Western Australian Liberal Party's 'fear-mongering tactics' in which they claimed that not even peoples' homes were safe from Aboriginal claim (*ibid.*).

Resistence to Federal Intervention

The second strategy followed by the Burke Government in coping with the Liberal Party's campaign against land rights was to obtain assurances from the federal government that it would not adopt over-riding land rights legislation. The Liberal Party stimulated intense public pressure against Burke's land rights policy by arguing that he could not stop federal land rights legislation from being imposed on Western Australia.

The opposition's pressure on the government's land rights policy was so intense that Burke was placed on the defensive and forced to react to Liberal Party criticism. For example, the opposition made repeated charges that Burke supported the federal ALP's land rights policy. And even if he did not, the federal government would proceed with uniform national land rights legislation.

Burke sought to counter this attack by persuading Prime Minister Hawke to issue a public statement to the effect that the federal government would not over-ride any land rights legislation that Western Australia adopted. In fact, it was due largely to Burke's influence that Hawke issued the unilateral campaign statement in October 1984 in Perth, to the effect that the federal government would not over-ride Western Australia's land rights legislation. Hawke issued a similar statement in January 1986 in Perth during the lead-up to the 1986 state elections (*The Age* 2 February

1986). Hawke's campaign statements were part of a strategy devised by Burke and Hawke to minimize the electoral damage of the land rights issue.

For example, in return for Hawke's 1984 statement (which had neither cabinet nor caucus sanction), Burke undertook to enact state land rights legislation. The Prime Minister's assurance that the federal government would not over-ride Western Australian legislation was crucial to Burke's effort to achieve state land rights legislation. Without that, no one would have supported the Burke Government in the undertaking. For example, why should the major industry groups participate on the drafting committee if the federal government would simply over-ride the legislation produced by the committee? (Interview with Bob Pearce, W.A. Minister for Education, 18 February 1987.)

During the parliamentary debate on the Western Australian Aboriginal Land Bill in March 1985, the opposition attacked the Burke Government. Hassell quoted a statement made by the acting federal Minister for Aboriginal Affairs, Susan Ryan, in the Senate that day. The Leader of the Opposition asked the Premier whether he was aware that Senator Ryan stated that the federal government had not abandoned its land rights policy. She was reported to have said that it intended to have further discussions with state governments to ensure that Minister Holding's five principles for land rights were upheld, either through state legislation or complementary federal legislation (*W.A. Parliamentary Debates*, 26 March 1985: 896).

Burke responded to this criticism by stating that it was all the more reason for Western Australia to pass its own land rights legislation in order to avoid the necessity for over-riding federal legislation. However, he disputed Hassell's implied argument that the federal government would pass over-riding national legislation regardless of what happened in Western Australia. Burke went on to make the following statement:

> It was the Commonwealth [i.e. *federal government*] who initially proposed there would be a veto. That has gone out the window. Do members know why? It has gone out the window because we pursued the contrary point of view with the Commonwealth. The Commonwealth also proposed that compensation should be paid on the basis of the value of minerals discovered and exploited on particular areas of grant land. That is no longer the case. Why? Because we pursued the contrary point of view with the Commonwealth. (*Ibid.*)

Factionalism in the Federal Government

The Prime Minister's unilateral campaign statement not to over-ride Western Australia's land rights legislation, brought out into the open a factional conflict in the federal government. The division was between Prime Minister Hawke, Ministers Evans, Beazley, Walsh, Keating, and other senior members of cabinet affiliated with the right wing, some members of the Centre Left faction, and Minister Holding backed by a few cabinet ministers such as Senator Ryan (who was also in the Centre Left faction), with the support of the left wing, plus some members of the Centre Left of the ALP caucus. The conflict represented two competing positions on the land rights issue.

The Prime Minister and his supporters were prepared to compromise the Labor Party's land rights policy as represented by Holding's five principles, in the interest of the political survival of the Burke Labor Government. Holding and his supporters, on the other hand, argued that the Burke Government was exaggerating the electoral threat the land rights issue posed to it. They were dubious about single-issue campaigns, and did not think the land rights issue would bring down Burke's Government.

Therefore, there was the spectacle of Prime Minister Hawke making campaign speeches, and giving private assurances in contravention of ALP land rights policy, as interpreted by his Minister for Aboriginal Affairs, but without the endorsement of his own cabinet, let alone the ALP caucus. On the other hand, Minister Holding and his supporters continued to make public statements which contradicted the Prime Minister by reaffirming the federal government's commitment to his five principles for national land rights. This confused and contradictory situation continued for over a year until it was finally decided in negotiations between the Western Australian and federal ALP in April 1986. The basis of the compromise agreement was confirmed by the party in June 1986, just prior to its conference in Hobart in July 1986.

This protracted factional division in the federal Labor Party explains, for example, the difficulties federal cabinet had in making decisions on the land rights question. On numerous occasions it was scheduled to decide the issue, only to postpone action or to make tentative and contradictory compromise agreements. This played directly into the hands of the Liberal opposition in Western Australia.

Hassell focused upon the contradictory signals emanating from the federal Labor government on the land rights issue to accuse Burke of 'conning' Western Australia into believing that it had agreed to Burke's request not to intervene in Western Australia. Alternatively, the opposition accused Burke of not having the political will and clout to prevent the federal government from 'interfering' in a states' rights issue (i.e. granting title to state land).

Examples of factionalism in federal cabinet which increased the opposition's political pressure on Burke were Holding's refusal to endorse Burke's proposal to the cabinet in January 1985, and cabinet's August 1985 decision to endorse Holding's five principles for national land rights. Hassell and the opposition interpreted these decisions as a repudiation of Burke's land rights policy. Hassell and others offered this as evidence that the federal Labor government would indeed impose uniform land rights legislation upon Western Australia.

While federal cabinet decisions did not allow for that interpretation, the ambiguous nature of them tended to strengthen the opposition's argument against the Burke Government. The August 1985 cabinet decision, in particular, forced the Premier to retreat into an extreme and defensive states' rights position in order to defuse the issue in the up-coming state elections of February 1986.

Factionalism and Support for the Opposition

Examination of federal cabinet's ambivalent decisions regarding national land rights policy in January and August 1985 will illustrate how the opposition in Western Australia used them to good advantage in the campaign against the Burke Government. The stalemate within federal cabinet on the issue of land rights first came to the surface in a January 1985 meeting of the federal ministerial committee on land rights.

The federal cabinet sub-committee was established to work out a compromise among factions in cabinet after they failed to agree on Burke's proposed draft legislation on 14 December 1984. The first meeting of the cabinet sub-committee was held on 17 January 1985, but it soon became apparent that there was an impasse, primarily on the question of concessions to mining interests in Burke's proposed legislation for Western Australia. The sub-committee meeting was followed by a full cabinet meeting on 24 January, and it included Premier Burke.

It was after the 23 January meeting of federal cabinet that Burke declared that the federal government had endorsed his proposal for land rights legislation in Western Australia. The Premier said that, with the exception of 'two minor issues' (i.e. exempting mineral prospective land from claim, and compensation for social disruption), the federal government supported his proposal. Burke's claim was immediately challenged by Holding who said it was not correct to say that there were only two differences between the governments.

This exchange was followed by Burke's statement that 'Mr. Holding and the truth are complete strangers' (*The Australian*, 30 January 1985). Burke elaborated by saying that Holding 'was clearly not listening during the discussions I had with the Prime Minister' (*ibid.*). He pointed out that the minutes of that meeting were published in the *Commonwealth Record* (1984: 2069-70).

The Leader of the Western Australian Opposition immediately seized upon the controversy to accuse Burke of 'hysterical hypocrisy'. Hassell said that, while the Premier had condemned Holding for 'pumping up expectations that are unreal', he was guilty of the same thing himself (*The Australian*, 1 February 1985). This public dispute required the intervention of the Prime Minister himself who declared that 'there was no area of dispute between [his] and Mr. Burke's government'.

A similar, only more serious, dispute arose after the 13 August 1985 meeting of federal cabinet. Cabinet announced its decision to endorse the principles of the preferred national land rights model as proposed by Minister Holding. However, as was the case with the January decision, it was another compromise, with ambiguity and contradiction accompanying it. For example, while Holding received cabinet endorsement for national legislation, it was with the proviso that the eventual legislation be implemented by state action that was 'broadly consistent' with the federal principles. However, since there was no state land rights legislation in Western Australia, and since Brian Burke had vowed not to reintroduce such legislation, it was impossible to implement cabinet's decision.

Nevertheless, the opposition in Western Australia was given a powerful issue on which it could mount an election campaign in 1986. Hassell immediately picked up this development and charged that there was no difference, either in principle or substance, between Burke's and Holding's land rights proposals. He argued that this demonstrated that 'Mr. Burke is not capable of fighting Canberra over land rights' (*West Australian*, 15 August 1985). Therefore, only a determined Liberal state government would be able to 'stop all this nonsense'.

Burke's reaction to the cabinet decision was immediate and emotional. The Premier claimed that the federal government had 'pulled out' at the eleventh hour of a four-point compromise on Aboriginal land rights. He said that this was a 'slap in the face', and his government would strongly oppose any federal land rights legislation imposed on Western Australians.[9] In other words, the federal cabinet decision forced Burke into taking a states' rights position in opposing the federal government on land rights.

Premier Burke vowed to challenge any federal 'interference' in the High Court. He argued that laws regarding the tenure and transfer of land were the province of the states. Furthermore, if his challenge in the High Court failed, Burke declared he would demand compensation payments from the federal government for any Crown land appropriated. He argued that such payments would involve enormous sums that would be well beyond the financial capacity of the federal treasury (Burke, 1985).

On 30 December the Leader of the Opposition released the results of an opinion survey he said was carried out by 'independent market researchers' in late November and December on the issue Aboriginal land rights. According to Hassell, land rights turned-up as one of the top three 'un-prompted' campaign issues, along with interest rates and unemployment.

He said that the survey showed that 70 per cent of the voters surveyed feared that a Labor government would introduce land rights legislation in Western Australia if it were returned to power after the February 1986 election. Hassell also said that there was no doubt that Burke would introduce land rights if he won the election. The reason that Burke and Hawke were down-playing land rights was that this was part of a secret deal to put the issue on the backburner until after the election. This strategy was similar to the one Hassell accused them of following just before the 1984 elections.

The next day Burke declared that he would resign from office if the Labor Party (implying the Western Australian ALP), ever instructed him to reintroduce land rights legislation. Furthermore, Burke promised to try to remove the land rights policy from the federal Labor Party platform at its national conference in July 1986. Brian Burke went to great lengths to spell out his government's opposition to any attempt by the federal government to impose over-riding land rights legislation upon Western Australia. For example, he made the following statement:

> Both the Minister with responsibility (for *Aboriginals*) and myself are on record as saying we will not have land rights after the election and we will fight any federal government attempts to override state responsibilities (*The Australian*, 1 January 1986).

Burke maintained his uncompromising states' rights position on the land rights issue. The election was held on 8 February. Burke easily won re-election. The Labor Party maintained its thirty-two-seat majority in the Legislative Assembly, the Liberal Party lost one seat (from twenty to nineteen), and the ALP won nine out of seventeen seats in the Legislative Council, while the Liberals lost two seats and went from nine to seven.[10]

In the light of Burke's election victory on a platform opposed to any form of land rights legislation, the pressure on the federal government to concede was irresistible. Burke also warned the federal government that if it tried to pursue national land rights it would encounter the same kind of political opposition that it experienced in Western Australia.

A compromise deal was finally worked out between the Western Australian and federal ALP shortly after the 8 February election. Negotiations were between Hawke, Burke, Holding, Bob McMullian (national secretary of the ALP) and Michael Beahan (secretary of the Western Australian branch of the ALP) (interview with Michael Beahan, 24 February 1987). It is interesting to note that, with the exception of Holding, all of the participants were Western Australians.

The meetings were held on 6 March, 14 April, and 27 June. The first two meetings worked out the basis for the compromise. The last meeting gave the party's endorsement to it. There were four elements of the agreement:

1. No over-riding federal land rights legislation.
2. Progress for Aboriginal land rights on a state by state basis. There was to be a package of goods for Western Australia. It was land rights by administration.
3. Retention of the mining veto in the Northern Territory Land Rights Act (1976), but allow changes in the administration of the act to streamline the legal machinery.
4. No change in the national Labor Party's Aboriginal land rights policy.

While Burke succeeded in forcing the federal government to abandon its uniform national land rights legislation, he proposed a policy package which, from his point of view, at least, was designed to achieve the same ends. On 20 May 1986 an agreement was reached between Western Australia and the federal government which involved a package of a $100 million expenditure over five years. This financing was to go partly towards the purchase of land and partly towards the provision of infrastructure and support services on Aboriginal land. The Western Australian government also agreed to give 'secure title', i.e. ninety-nine-year leaseholds to Aborigines occupying their traditional land (reserves and missions constituting roughly 8.7 per cent of the total area of the state).

CHAPTER SIX

Australian Mining Industry Council's Offensive and the Aboriginal Counter-Offensive

The Australian Mining Industry Council sought to apply pressure upon the federal government to either drop its proposed uniform national land rights legislation or make it as consistent as possible with the principles of the Western Australian Aboriginal Land Bill (1985). It also sought to have the mining veto provisions removed from the Northern Territory Aboriginal Land Rights Act (1976). AMIC's strategy to influence the government consisted of lobbying the Prime Minister and his ministers — primarily Senator Gareth Evans — and threatening to run a national campaign against federal land rights legislation, patterned after the Chamber of Mines' campaign in Western Australia.

The compromise agreement reached between the Burke and Hawke governments on an acceptable land rights package after the Western Australian state elections in February 1986 resulted in the abandonment of national land rights legislation and the retention of the veto in the Northern Territory Land Rights Act (1976).

AMIC regarded this both as a victory and a defeat for the mining industry. It was pleased that the federal government dropped the preferred model for national land rights, however, it was frustrated in its efforts to remove the mining veto provisions from the Northern Territory Act.

As part of the ALP factional compromise, the Hawke Government reneged on its promise to AMIC to remove the veto from the Northern Territory Act. The government reversed its position and justified the action by arguing that the removal of the mining veto from the Northern Territory Aboriginal Land Rights Act could only be achieved in the broader context of the introduction of national land rights legislation. Therefore, without national legislation, it would be too sensitive politically for the federal government to water-down the Northern Territory Act alone.

The reason for this was that such an action would have violated the compromise agreement within the ALP. Strong left-wing support within the ALP for the Northern Territory land councils' opposition to removing the veto (which also had support from other party factions), would have provoked cross-factional opposition to Hawke's government if the veto provisions of that Northern Territory Act were removed. While the federal government did amend the Northern Territory Aboriginal Land Rights Act in June 1987, the changes did not meet the demands of the mining industry.

The government's sudden decision to introduce the amendment to the

Northern Territory Act into the Senate in May 1987, after reaching agreement with the Northern Territory land councils, and without consulting the mining industry, was undoubtedly motivated by political factors. Hawke wished to have the land rights legislation out of the way before federal elections were held in July 1987, and before Australia's bicentennial celebrations began in 1988.

While the Hawke Government allowed the mining veto provision of the Northern Territory Act to remain (albeit in modified form), it sought to appease the miners by 'streamlining' the Act in order to eliminate the so-called 'log jam' in mining EL (exploration licence) applications. Nonetheless, AMIC threatened to wage a national campaign against the replacement of the veto in the land rights legislation.

However, the industry did not launch such a campaign against the retention of the veto in the Northern Territory Act. There were two reasons for this. The first was that there was no support for removing the veto at this time within the ALP, and the opposition parties had little prospect of defeating the ALP in national elections. The second was that the Hawke Government promised the industry that, after two years from the date of the amendment (i.e. 1989), it would review the legislation to assess the amendment's success in eliminating the log jam in exploration applications in the Northern Territory. In other words, AMIC decided against running a campaign against the veto in the Northern Territory Land Rights Act because it did not believe it would be successful, and also because the government agreed to re-evaluate the legislation within two years.

AUSTRALIAN MINING INDUSTRY COUNCIL'S POLITICAL STRATEGY

The political concerns of AMIC in relation to federal land rights legislation were presented to Prime Minister Hawke and Holding at their meetings of 12 and 17 September 1984, and at a subsequent meeting held on 4 October 1984. The Prime Minister responded to the miners' concerns by giving them assurances that his government was sympathetic to their complaints, and would try to accommodate them. However, Hawke noted that the Aborigines also had legitimate concerns about mining their land and, therefore, a 'balance' would have to be arrived at among the major groups concerned.

AMIC tried to get a firm commitment in writing from the Prime Minister to implement the policy he had outlined to the miners at these meetings. They were primarily concerned to ensure that Hawke's verbal undertakings would become government policy. However, Hawke was unable to do that because he did not have control of the land rights issue in his own government.

Reactions to the Preferred Model

Minister Holding announced the government's preferred model for national land rights legislation on 20 February 1985. The mining industry was not only not consulted about the contents of the document prior to its release, but it was given to the press before AMIC received its copy. AMIC officials expressed their disappointment and strong opposition to the preferred model saying that it was 'totally unacceptable to the mining industry' (AMIC, 1985). The miners felt that the preferred model completely disregarded the understanding they thought they had arrived at with Prime Minister Hawke at meetings in September and October 1984.

In an address to the annual mining industry seminar in Canberra on 2 May 1985, the Executive Director of AMIC, James Strong, explained the industry's dissatisfaction with the preferred model. He said that it was primarily based upon the Northern Territory and South Australian land rights legislations, which were unworkable. Strong pointed out that the original intention of the Northern Territory legislation had been completely subverted. It was designed to reconcile two competing interests in land use.

The government granted land to Aborigines for the purpose of protecting their spiritual and cultural life. However, the government also sought to encourage mineral development to ensure its contribution to Australia's economy and the welfare of Australians as a whole. In this regard Strong pointed out that, during 1984, for example, the mining industry earned 44 per cent of Australia's export income of over $11 billion and paid 63 per cent of its profits (before tax payable and resource taxes were deducted) to governments. This amounted to $1 billion in tax.

The government's effort to reconcile these competing interests in land use, however, completely failed. The legislation created a legal/commercial system which placed 'total negotiating power' in the hands of Aborigines and their advisors. In effect the government surrendered its control over the development of mineral resources to Aborigines. Instead of facilitating 'workable arrangements' for mining development, the Northern Territory Aboriginal Land Rights Act (1976) gave Aborigines such a tactical advantage in negotiations with the mining companies that it paralyzed exploration and mining in the territory. According to Strong, the industry was being 'choked' by barriers to access to land for the purpose of exploration.

Indeed, one of the principal objectives of Minister Evans' amendments to the mining provisions of the Northern Territory Act in 1986, was to remove the log jam in export licence applications. As of 1986, there were 103 EL applications lodged with the Northern Territory land councils (nineteen with the CLC and eighty-four with the NLC). Many of the applications were lodged by mining companies as far back as 1982. As of June 1986, only one mining exploration licence agreement had been successfully negotiated under the Northern Territory Act. Strong said that more and more companies were 'voting with their feet' by abandoning the Northern Territory. Stagnation of the industry would not benefit Aborigines, or Australia's economy, which depends heavily upon mineral development for its prosperity.

Strong indicated that the federal government was now faced with a dilemma. The Northern Territory Land Rights Act was not achieving its idealistic objective of protecting the spiritual and cultural life of Aborigines, and it was doing irreparable damage to the mining industry. Faced with this dilemma, the government felt obliged to improve the system and, at the same time, extend it to Australia as a whole.

Executive Director Strong argued that the mining industry was extremely unhappy with the government's approach to this problem. The preferred model did not correct the 'imbalance' in legal/commercial negotiating power between the miners and Aboriginal interests. Furthermore, the federal government was now proposing to extend this unsatisfactory legislation to the country as a whole. Strong said that, at the very least, the federal government should ensure that the Northern Territory legislation was workable in a commercial sense before imposing this flawed regime upon other states.

Effects of Land Rights Legislation

James Strong argued that there was convincing evidence of the paralysis of exploration and mining under the Northern Territory legislation. He noted that there was a government freeze on the issuance of exploration licenses (designed to enable the land councils time to identify the traditional Aboriginal owners of land within their jurisdictions), until mid-1981. In almost four years since the freeze was lifted the Northern Territory government offered forty-two mining companies 165 exploration licences. However, not a single agreement had been negotiated with traditional Aboriginal owners as of early 1985.

Strong also countered claims by pro-land rights groups that Aborigines favored mining on their land by emphasizing that the only agreements negotiated for mining projects on Aboriginal land in the Northern Territory were concluded before the Northern Territory Land Rights Act came into force. He noted in this regard that the Gove Project, Groote Eylandt, Ranger, and the Granites operations were based upon mining titles that were granted by the federal government before the Northern Territory Act came into existence. Therefore, since Aboriginal groups did not have the veto power over these projects, they could not use the projects as evidence of their pro-mining attitude.

Strong also sought to rebut the claim made by pro-land rights groups, that the mining companies were reluctant to reach agreement on exploration and mining rights on Aboriginal land. He said that AMIC conducted a recent survey of the forty-two companies that were offered licences by the Northern Territory government to explore Aboriginal land in the Territory. According to the AMIC survey, half of the companies were willing to negotiate with the land councils for Aboriginal consent to explore and mine on their land. He said the willingness by the companies to negotiate with the land councils can hardly explain the failure to conclude a single agreement in almost four years.

Executive Director Strong also noted that exploration activities in the Northern Territory had fallen dramatically during the past three years. He provided data contained in Table XIV to support the claim.

Strong argued that apologists of land rights explained this decline in exploration expenditure in the Northern Territory upon low market prices, especially for uranium. However, according to Strong, the decline in exploration expenditure during this period averaged less than 30 per cent for the country as a whole, while the decline in exploration expenditure in the Northern Territory was greater than 60 per cent.

He concluded that the effect of the Northern Territory Land Rights Act was detrimental to the Territory's mining industry. It would continue to have serious and harmful effects upon one of the Northern Territory's

TABLE XIV
DECLINE IN EXPLORATION
EXPENDITURE IN THE
NORTHERN TERRITORY

($m)

1981/82	$32.0
1982/83	$25.6
1983/84	$11.8[1]

largest revenue earners and, therefore, upon the economic growth of the Territory as a whole. Strong made a similar claim about the deleterious consequences of South Australian land rights legislation upon the mining industry there. He said that the only 'real test' of the Pitjantjatjara legislation (enacted in 1981) resulted in an oil exploration company 'walking away from grossly excessive demands for compensation' and the uncertainty surrounding the outcome of arbitration by the South Australian land rights tribunal which had not heard a single case.[2]

Strong summarized his case against land rights legislation by saying that the mining companies were discouraged by prolonged delays, frustration, and uncertainty about future Aboriginal title to land, and by the increased cost to miners stemming from land which may be subject to Aboriginal claim. Furthermore, he added that, regardless of what developments occurred with respect to federal land rights legislation, the government should amend the Northern Territory land rights legislation to resolve the current paralysis of the industry there. If that were done, and if time were allowed to see the results, the federal government would then have transformed a flawed piece of legislation into a 'workable formula'.

The Federal Government's Actions

However, instead of striving to develop a 'workable' legal/commercial system in the Northern Territory, the federal government was proposing to make minor amendments to the Northern Territory Land Rights Act and then extend it to the whole of Australia. According to AMIC, the preferred model was nothing more than a modification of the Northern Territory legislation to bring it into alignment with the South Australian legislation—both of which were failed legal/commercial systems for negotiating mining agreements.

Strong pointed out that in proposing the preferred model, the federal government had missed an excellent opportunity to consider an entirely new approach—the Western Australian model. He argued that if the federal government had considered Burke's proposed draft legislation as a model for land rights, instead of the legislation in the Northern Territory and South Australia, the 'disastrous effects of the legislation' could be avoided. He noted that while the Western Australian Aboriginal Land Bill was defeated by the parliament in Western Australia it was still worthy of consideration by the federal government.

AMIC argued that the Western Australian draft land rights legislation was an alternative to the Northern Territory approach. As far as the mining industry was concerned, the Western Australian approach was fundamentally different from the Northern Territory approach. Under the Western Australian approach, the importance of mining to the entire community was recognized. The Western Australian draft legislation was based on the presumption that exploration and mining would proceed with protection for Aboriginal sites of significance, living areas, and compensation for actual damage caused by exploration and mining.

Strong contrasted the federal preferred model with that of the Western Australian model. He said that the federal approach took as its point of departure the existing Northern Territory Land Rights Act and considered 'how far it could claw back that unsuccessful regime'. In contrast to the Western Australian approach, instead of removing barriers, the preferred model created barriers to exploration and mining by giving Aborigines the right to refuse them entry onto their land. Having given the Aborigines this power, the proposals then provided a tortuous path to overcome these barriers. They made it necessary for a tribunal and the government to over-turn the original Aboriginal refusal to allow exploration and mining on their land.

AMIC took the position that the tribunal approach to resolving conflict between Aborigines and mining companies would not work. In fact, if anything, it would add to the conflict. It placed the companies in an adversarial relationship to Aboriginal groups, involving delays, legal costs, animosity, and uncertainty regarding the outcome. It had the added handicap of involving the government in discretionary decisions on a case by case basis on a politically sensitive issue and, all the while, the companies would be prevented from exploring on Aboriginal land. Strong stressed that this amounted to a '*de facto* veto' which the government had promised to avoid.

Opposition to National Legislation

The mining industry took the public position that it was categorically opposed to the concept of national land rights legislation. They argued that such legislation was not necessary, that it would: cause constitutional difficulties (creating chaos with existing state and territory legislation); contradict and derogate from state laws; introduce greater complexities; and increase litigation and costs. The fact that the proposed national legislation was the preferred model added to the miners concerns. In other words, AMIC was opposed to the concept of national land rights, and particularly opposed to the extention of the 'unworkable' Northern Territory Act to Australia as a whole. Strong warned that the industry would regard such legislation as a serious threat to the industry, and would act accordingly.

SPECIFIC OBJECTIONS TO THE PREFERRED MODEL

In order to understand the reasons for AMIC's opposition to the preferred model, which they regarded as a variation of the Northern Territory Land Rights Act, it is necessary to examine the four major points of concern which the miners raised in meetings with the Prime Minister during

September and October 1984. The issues were: (1) Crown ownership of minerals; (2) the power of veto; (3) compensation; and (4) protection of existing mining titles.

Crown Ownership of Minerals

AMIC argued that mineral rights (i.e. on-shore) have always been vested in state governments. The miners reaffirmed this principle, and said that the federal proposals compromised the principle. Strong pointed out that Aboriginal land legislation should not permit Aborigines to exercise powers as if they owned minerals on their land. That is to say, Aborigines should not have the power to control miners' access to land in order to obtain a share of mineral wealth as compensation for granting access. Instead, governments should continue to exercise control over access to land. They should be responsible for the exploration and mining of state land for the benefit of the general community. Strong added the proviso that state and territory governments should also provide protection for Aboriginal sites of significance, and provide adequate living areas for them.

The Power of Veto

AMIC stressed the fact that Aborigines did not have the power of veto in land rights legislation. However, in the Northern Territory Land Rights Act, Aborigines had the power to prevent any access to their land without consent. In other words, they had the power to withhold their consent to access to land for exploration and mining purposes. This power to withhold consent has been described as a right of 'veto'. Section 40 of the Northern Territory Aboriginal Land Rights Act (1976), sets out this right of veto.

SECTION 40:

1. A mining interest in respect of Aboriginal land shall not be granted unless:
   a. both the Minister (Federal) and the Land Council for the area in which the land is situated have consented, in writing, to the making of the grant; or
   b. the Governor-General has, by Proclamation, declared that the national interest requires that the grant be made.

Strong argued that the Northern Territory's concept of Aboriginal consent being required before any exploration could be carried out was included in the preferred model. This was evident in paragraphs 9.7, and 9.8 of the proposed national legislation.

PARA. 9.7: Title to prospect or explore for minerals or petroleum on Aboriginal land not to be granted except with the prior consent of the Aboriginal land holder and agreement as to the terms and conditions on which such exploration is to take place.

PARA. 9.8: In the event that either consent of the Aboriginal land holder is withheld.

These two paragraphs also included provisions for a tribunal mechanism if Aboriginal consent were refused. This tribunal process was a departure from the Northern Territory Act, however. The preferred model would empower the tribunal to review either a refusal to give consent, or to review unreasonable conditions attached to the consent. Strong emphasized that, in the industry's view, a tribunal mechanism which allows for a decision by a judge and/or the Minister to over-ride an Aboriginal veto is cumbersome, time-consuming, expensive and unpredictable. It also introduced the potential for political pressures on the government against reversing an Aboriginal veto.

AMIC was strongly opposed to the preferred model on the grounds that it gave Aboriginal groups what the miners referred to as a '*de facto* veto'. Strong cited paragraph 9.3 of the proposed national legislation in which the federal government guaranteed that 'mechanisms to resolve disputes over access to Aboriginal land not to constitute a *de facto* veto'. However, he pointed out that nowhere in the proposals was the concept of *de facto* veto defined. AMIC defined the *de facto* veto as follows:

> Any procedure required before gaining access to land which is likely to cause such delay, extended court proceedings, legalities, negotiations, increased costs and uncertainties as to deter exploration and mining on that land.

Despite the fact that the Hawke Government gave AMIC assurances that it would not allow an Aboriginal veto over exploration and mining (including a *de facto* veto), the preferred model contained just such a veto. In the miners' view, the required consent for entry onto Aboriginal land, despite provisions for over-riding the veto, constituted a *de facto* veto. The proposed legislation gave Aboriginals the power to refuse access which could only be over-ridden by a tribunal process, and then only with government approval.

AMIC stressed the fact that, in the miners' experience, any requirement for consent inevitably became part of Aboriginal claims for compensation. It was a powerful 'bargaining weapon' to be used by Aboriginal groups against the mining companies in order to extract financial compensation. Strong doubted that any 'appeal procedure' involving tribunals and government approval to over-turn Aboriginal refusal based upon cultural or spiritual justification would prevent the use of consent as a bargaining tool.

Strong indicated that the Western Australian model was designed to address this problem. It was based upon the assumption that the government wanted exploration and mining to proceed. It provided safeguards for Aboriginal culture and life, yet ensured that miners would be given '*prima facie* right' of access to Aboriginal land. The obverse of this (i.e. that Aborigines had a *prima facie* right to refuse access) constituted a *de facto* veto.

Compensation

AMIC emphasized the fact that the question of compensation for access to Aboriginal land went to the heart of the commercial viability of mining.

Strong stressed that the normal compensation for exploration and mining was based upon restoring any damage caused to the land, or damage arising from the owners being deprived of the use of land. However, he pointed out that under the federal proposals (para. 9.15), compensation was allowed for spiritual and social criteria. This left the mining companies open to virtually limitless claims for compensation.

Strong pointed out that, despite the government's assurances that compensation would not be based upon the value of minerals, there was no protection for the miners against open-ended claims for the disruption of Aboriginal culture. The Western Australian proposals were mentioned in this regard as an acceptable approach to the question of compensation. The Western Australian model was designed to place limits on the basis for claims. Under that proposal, claims could be made only for actual damage to land, and actual damage to neighboring Aboriginal living areas.

AMIC under-scored the fact that under the preferred model (para. 9.5), the basis for mining compensation to Aboriginal communities was unclear. The relevant section in the model read as follows:

> PARA. 9.5: Aborigines to have access to payments in the nature of mining royalty equivalents, i.e. a payment made by Government which represents a proportion of the ordinary royalties received by Government in respect of mining on Aboriginal land. The relevant Government to determine the proportion to be so paid and the distribution of such payments to the Aboriginal people, including those affected by mining operations.

In fact, it appeared to the miners that Aboriginality was itself the rationale for mining compensation in the federal model.

Protection of Existing Mining Titles

The mining industry also strongly opposed the preferred model's failure to provide protection for the companies' applications for mining titles to land under Aboriginal claim. The federal model did offer protection for exploration or mining leases which were in existence before Aboriginal claims were made to the land concerned. These leases would continue to be valid and, therefore, the companies would not be obliged to re-negotiate the terms and conditions for the leases with the new Aboriginal owners.

However, any title less than a mining title (including existing applications for the right to explore and mine), and any renewal of a mining title, would be subject to re-negotiation with the new Aboriginal owners of the land claimed. The re-negotiations would involve additional terms and conditions, new compensation costs and, perhaps, tribunal hearings. None of these was required at the time of the initial exploration, or when the feasibility study was undertaken.

In other words, after a mining company had spent millions of dollars establishing the commercial viability of a project, it would suddenly be faced with new additional costs and conditions for mining due to Aboriginal claims to the land. AMIC argued that this was unfair to the industry. It represented a 'retrospective change of rules and conditions, and a penalty beyond the control of the title holder'. AMIC pointed out that this placed unforeseen additional costs and obligations upon a company which had taken financial risks in good faith. Strong noted that this would not be tolerated in any other area of business.

The executive director concluded his comments by saying that Aboriginals and miners should be 'partners' in resource development. They should not be adversaries in a 'commercial/legal power game'. However, for as long as the federal government continued to use the unsuccessful Northern Territory Land Rights Act (1976) as its model for land rights legislation, a threat to the industry remained.

Australian Mining Industry Council's Recommended Action

At a meeting of AMIC's Aboriginal affairs committee on 7 March 1985, the recommended course of action regarding land rights was considered.[3] The committee, which makes recommendations on Aboriginal policy to AMIC's supreme executive committee, endorsed AMIC's actions regarding the federal government's proposed national legislation.

The Aboriginal affairs committee affirmed AMIC's objective of defeating the concept of national land rights legislation. Alternatively, they agreed that if such legislation were actually introduced by the government, it should be as consistent as possible with the principles contained in the Western Australian draft legislation. The committee confirmed four specific points of AMIC's strategy:

1. Reject the concept of national legislation;
2. Reject the federal government model of national legislation as being 'totally unacceptable' on fundamental issues including access, compensation and protection of interests;
3. Revive the decision for a national media campaign by AMIC to oppose the proposed national model and explain the mining industry position; and
4. Ask AMIC member companies to contribute funds for that advertising campaign, as soon as possible.

AMIC's executive committee confirmed the recommendations of the Aboriginal affairs committee on 13 March 1985. It also noted that the Western Australian Aboriginal land bill looked as if it would be defeated in the upper house of the Western Australian parliament. Nevertheless, AMIC would continue to adhere to the Western Australian model, regardless of its fate in parliament, and the miners would publically endorse it the following week.

However, prior to commencing their plan of action, AMIC decided to request a meeting with Ministers Evans and Holding during April 1985. The purpose of the meeting was to express the industry's misgivings about the preferred model, and to request permission to submit to Holding a formal response to the proposed legislation after the 31 March date for submissions, specified in his letter accompanying the proposals.

The meeting between executive committee members of AMIC and Senator Evans and Clyde Holding was held on 17 April 1985 (AMIC, 1985a). Evans opened the meeting by reviewing the federal position in the light of the rejection of the Western Australian legislation. He indicated that the government was trying to accommodate the mining industry and, for that reason, had agreed to the exploratory meeting with AMIC to assess the differences between the government and the industry.

Evans said it was unlikely that the Western Australian government would make another attempt at introducing land rights legislation. This left the issue in the federal government's court. Therefore, it was in everyone's interest to settle down and debate the issues, perhaps by focusing upon the differences between the federal and Western Australian models. Senator Evans went on to imply that the government was committed to diluting the Northern Territory Land Rights Act. However, he pointed out that the federal government would encounter difficulties in doing this without applying a uniform standard for land rights throughout the country as part of a package approach.

Holding reminded AMIC that the public relations campaign which the Chamber of Mines of Western Australia conducted had produced the political climate in which Burke's legislation was defeated. Therefore, the mining industry had to take responsibility for the increased tension over the land rights issue.

Strong responded to Minister Holding's comment by saying that AMIC had participated in the formulation of the Western Australian draft legislation. He stated that the industry saw the proposed legislation as a basis for a 'workable system'. Despite the defeat of the legislation in Western Australia, it had forced the parties to resolve their differences in detailed legislation. The executive director outlined AMIC's four major points of criticism of the preferred model. He suggested that the industry saw merit in 'fixing up' the Northern Territory legislation and then, after having demonstrated that the model worked, applying it to other states.

Holding responded by saying that the mining industry continued to use worst case scenarios when discussing land rights. The Minister stated that anthropological evidence would already be on file at the time that a tribunal was expected to resolve a refusal to consent, so it should not unduly delay a hearing. Minister Holding asserted that what the miners were demanding was the right to over-ride everyone else in the community. He suggested that, with good faith and common sense, agreements could be reached between the miners and Aboriginal land owners, who were basically pro-mining in outlook.

AMIC's Hugh Morgan questioned several of the Minister's statements. He said that the mining industry could produce incontravertible evidence that, where governments were involved in a land rights issues, the worst case scenario was the most likely outcome. Morgan said that it was extremely unlikely that appropriate anthropological evidence would already be on file with a tribunal. And he said that the miners did not detect a pro-mining bias in the Aboriginal communities with whom they had attempted to deal.

Senator Evans stressed that rights of compensation in the federal legislation would be based upon the actual damage caused, however, 'spirituality' would be one basis for claiming compensation for damage. Evans also indicated that AMIC's 'laboratory test approach' for the Northern Territory would be politically unacceptable unless uniform national legislation was also introduced. He pointed out that the legislation could perhaps be proclaimed first in the Northern Territory and, at some later time, proclaimed in the Australian states.

Senator Evans also underscored the fact that the federal government had already made substantial concessions to the mining industry, and that this would cause it considerable concern when its performance was measured against Labor Party platform promises. Therefore, he asked AMIC to accept the political realities of the situation, and to respond constructively to the government's proposals.

Strong pointed out that there would also be 'social costs' connected with the government's failure to accommodate the mining industry's desire to maintain 'uncomplicated access' to all land in Australia. He said that if the government 'got it wrong', then exploration in Australia would come to a halt. An inevitable result of such a development would be a drop in receipts from mineral exports, and a fall in the standards of living of all Australians. He stressed that if this occurred, there would be an enormous backlash from the Australian electorate, that this would be to the severe detriment of the Aboriginal people, whom the government was attempting to help.

Strong concluded by saying that, in the following week, AMIC would submit its detailed response to the preferred model. Senator Evans suggested that discussions should continue at the departmental level (i.e. Departments of Aboriginal Affairs, and Resources and Energy), with a view toward holding another ministerial meeting in about three weeks.

Consultations with the Prime Minister

On 7 May, AMIC formally submitted its response to Holding's preferred model, and expressed its hope that its comments would constitute the basis for further consultation. That consultation occurred on 4 June 1985 between Prime Minister Hawke, Senator Evans, their advisers, and executive committee members of AMIC, including Sir Bruce Watson, President of AMIC, and James Strong. Significantly, Minister Holding was absent from the meeting.

The executive committee members of AMIC outlined the industry's principal dissatisfaction with the preferred model (viz., the power of veto, compensation, and protection of existing mining interests). It argued that the proposed legislation did not reflect the position that AMIC thought they had reached at the last meeting, of 4 October 1984, with the Prime Minister. AMIC expressed the view that the tribunal mechanism proposed in the federal model constituted a *de facto* veto in favor of Aboriginal land owners. With the exception of the Northern Territory and parts of South Australia, the industry had a presumptive right of access to land for exploration and mining purposes. However, it could lose that right if the proposed legislation were enacted.

AMIC stressed that the basic flaw in the model was the retention of a consent provision. That is to say, once Aborigines refused to allow mining companies access to their land, that refusal could only be over-ridden by a tribunal/government decision. Instead, they asked whether it was not possible to reverse the process by giving the miners access to Aboriginal land, and then giving Aborigines the right to object to the mining proposal in a tribunal hearing. This would place the government in the role of upholding (or denying) an Aboriginal objection, instead of upholding the objection of the miners to an Aboriginal veto. AMIC representatives underscored the proposition that, in taking this position, it was merely advancing the argument that resource development was in the national interest.

AMIC officials presented two sets of documents at the meeting to support their contention that the *de facto* veto provision in the preferred model would have the same devastating impact upon the industry nationally that the Northern Territory Act had had upon the industry in the territory. One document was appended to a letter from Sir Bruce Watson, President of AMIC, addressed to the Prime Minister. It consisted of two tables showing the relative decline in exploration activity in the Northern Territory compared to the nation as a whole—especially from 1981 to 1984 (after the freeze was lifted in the issuance of exploration licenses). Tables XV and XVI were the ones submitted to Hawke. The data in Table XV was interpreted by the miners as representing a decline in exploration in the Northern Territory in terms of drilling for prospective ore bodies. The decline was said to be minus 34 per cent from 1981 and 1982, and minus 52 per cent from 1982 to 1983. In 1984, there was a modest increase of 7 per cent in drilling over the precipitous decline registered in 1983. This contrasted with an increase in exploration drilling of 2 per cent in 1982, a decline of 32 per cent in 1983, and a recovery of 16 per cent increased drilling for Australia as a whole.

TABLE XV

MINING EXPLORATION IN AUSTRALIA

METERS DRILLED

('000)

	71-2	72-3	73-4	74-5	75-6	76-7	77-8	78-9	79-80	80-1	81-2	82-3	83-4
NSW	360	291	333	289	290	323	423	391	453	658	730	468	364
Vic.	17	21	39	40	27	21	13	39	48	79	126	48	50
Qld.	567	602	360	441	537	325	631	674	753	1057	1127	579	504
SA	123	343	207	199	142	104	144	161	281	409	374	227	151
WA	1996	1393	1255	1266	877	922	904	821	1091	1423	1409	1266	1950
Tas	60	60	96	80	45	41	55	66	76	113	110	93	90
NT	116	171	112	86	92	98	159	175	215	226	149	71	76
Aust.	3235	2880	2403	2401	2010	1834	2329	2328	2917	3965	4025	2752	3186

PERCENTAGE CHANGE

(Northern Territory and Australia Compared)

NT	+47	-35	-1	+7	+7	+62	+10	+23	+5	-34	-52	+7
Aust.	-11	-17	-1	-16	-9	+27	0	+25	+36	+2	-32	+16

Table XVI contains data on total private expenditure for mining exploration in Australia from 1971 to 1984. According to the table, there was a sharp decline in expenditure, from $32 million in 1982 to only $11 million in 1984, for exploration in the Northern Territory. During the same period, there was a decline from $575 million in 1982 to $416 million for Australia as a whole. In terms of percentage change in dollars expended for private exploration, the decline in the Northern Territory was minus 22 per cent in 1983 and minus 56 per cent in 1984. This contrasted with declines of 24 per cent in 1983 and minus 5 per cent in 1984, for Australia as a whole.

TABLE XVI
PRIVATE EXPLORATION EXPENDITURE
($m)

	71-2	72-3	73-4	74-5	75-6	76-7	77-8	78-9	79-80	80-1	81-2	82-3	83-4
NSW	15	12	11	11	13	23	25	27	44	69	89	65	55
Vic.	1	1	2	2	2	2	1	2	7	13	25	18	11
Qld.	22	15	15	21	18	21	35	37	62	96	124	88	80
SA	4	5	4	5	5	6	9	10	18	26	64	50	54
WA	62	51	54	57	50	64	64	75	118	178	216	170	184
Tas	3	3	4	5	4	4	7	9	12	19	22	18	18
NT	8	9	9	6	6	11	13	17	21	29	32	25	11
Aust.	117	99	101	110	99	133	158	181	286	430	575	437	416

PERCENTAGE CHANGE
(Northern Territory and Australia Compared)

NT	+13	0	-33	0	+83	+2	+31	+24	+38	+10	-22	-56
Aust.	-15	+2	+9	-10	+34	+19	+15	+58	+52	+33	-24	-5

The message conveyed to the Prime Minister by AMIC's presentation of these tables was that mining exploration was in decline throughout Australia. However, it was down by the greatest margin in the Northern Territory. The inference which AMIC drew from this data was that the Northern Territory Aboriginal Land Rights Act was responsible for the sharp decline in the territory's mining exploration. And the clear implication was that exploration activity in Australia as a whole would decline by the same margin as it did in the Northern Territory if the government's preferred model were enacted.

By way of evidence for the adverse impact of the Northern Territory's Land Rights Act upon exploration in the territory, AMIC showed the Prime Minister copies of a *pro forma* letter sent by the NLC (Northern Land Council) of the Northern Territory to ten companies rejecting their applications for exploration licences. The NLC had supported the decision of traditional Aboriginal owners in Central and Eastern Arnhem Land (in the Northern Territory) to reject twenty exploration licence applications at a meeting held on 8 May 1985. AMIC made the point that these rejections were proof that Aborigines were not favorably disposed toward mining on their land.

Senator Evans indicated that, under the preferred model, the mining industry would be better off in the Northern Territory than it was at present, however, they would be worse off in Queensland and Western Australia. The Prime Minister expressed the government's view that *prima facie*, mining development should go ahead, and that the onus was upon

Aborigines to show that such development should not proceed. He also pointed out that the government did not want a *de facto* veto through time delays in a lengthy tribunal process. However, he indicated that he thought the model met the undertakings which he had given to the industry during the last meeting (viz., that miners should not be prevented from viable access to Aboriginal land).

The Prime Minister cautioned AMIC, however, that Aboriginal groups had also expressed their strong opposition to the preferred model. He indicated that Aborigines felt even more strongly about retaining their veto powers in land rights legislation than the miners did about removing them. Nevertheless, it was essential that development proceed in order to increase the nation's wealth. He indicated that this position would be reflected in the land rights legislation which would ultimately emerge. Senator Evans was asked by the Prime Minister to prepare revised wording for the proposed legislation which would take into account their discussions with particular reference to the *de facto* veto issue.

Australian Mining Industry Council's Strategy Following Consultations

The Aboriginal affairs committee met on 7 June to consider its strategy in the light of the meeting of AMIC representatives with the Prime Minister on 4 June (AMIC, 1985c). During the meeting it was noted that Prime Minister Hawke and Senator Evans had merely noted AMIC's opposition to the concept of national land rights legislation. However, AMIC felt that they did appear to have a better understanding of the industry's dissatisfaction with the model — especially regarding access, compensation and protection of existing interests.

Specifically, the committee noted that Hawke and Evans accepted the difference between the requirement for Aboriginal consent to miners' access (with recourse to a tribunal), compared to Aborigines' right to object to applications for exploration and mining titles. Nevertheless, the committee felt that some amendment to the preferred model would be required in this regard.

On the issue of compensation, AMIC felt that the government appreciated the industry's concern with the open-ended nature of claims made on the basis of 'spiritual' damage or disruption. However, it felt that the industry would have to understand that Aborigines had a 'special affinity' with the land, and that this would have to be taken into account in any consideration of claims for compensation. AMIC also indicated that more attention would have to be paid in further discussions with the government to the protection of title holders who had spent funds on exploration, and had proved the commercial viability of mineral deposits and development projects. The committee made the pointed observation that all these matters would have to be confirmed by the government in writing, and that it would be necessary to assess the real extent of government concession on the issues.

Tactical Issues

The Aboriginal affairs committee identified three major tactical questions facing AMIC. First was whether it should concentrate upon attacking the concept of national legislation by launching a publicity campaign including advertising. Alternatively, should they continue efforts to make the proposed legislation acceptable to the industry? Secondly, AMIC had to consider whether continued discussions with the government (on modifying the model) would compromise the industry's ability to oppose the concept of the legislation. Thirdly, AMIC had to consider which policy should be followed with regard to advertising (which could prejudice discussions with the government). This was especially important in the light of a possible pro-land-rights government advertising campaign which was recommended by the ANOP opinion poll on attitudes toward Aboriginal land rights in late 1984. The committee apparently thought that the federal government would act on the ANOP recommendation and would launch a large-scale nation-wide land rights publicity campaign.

In addressing these tactical questions, the committee discussed what they regarded as factors which would prevent federal legislation from being enacted. They noted that Aboriginal groups had already succeeded in delaying national legislation. In response to Aboriginal protests against the preferred model in Canberra in May 1985, the Prime Minister promised Aborigines that the government would delay the introduction of the legislation until the following year to allow for further consultation with them.

The observation was also made that the Australian Democrats would have seven senators after July 1985, and that they had been attacking the government for not adhering to Holding's five principles. This raised the possibility that they could defeat, or try to amend, any proposed national legislation on land rights which deviated from the government's original position.

Therefore, the committee concluded that the more acceptable any proposed legislation was from a mining industry point of view, the greater would be Aboriginal and Democrat opposition to it. It observed that the more concessions which were made by the government to the mining industry, the greater would be the opposition to the legislation from Aboriginals, the Democrats, and from the left wing of the ALP. Committee members concluded that this was a powerful reason for AMIC to continue to negotiate on the terms of the model, as opposed to attempting to defeat any national legislation outright.

The implication of the committee's assessment was that, by trying to defeat federal legislation, the industry could precipitate a countervailing reaction which might neutralize whatever influence the miners had in determining the nature of legislation which would emerge. The committee also considered the political advantages and disadvantages of proceeding with a national advertising campaign. It noted the fact that any attack against the government after it had responded positively to industry demands could cause the government to change its policy and damage industry-government relations. While this was a risk which AMIC ran on any public issue at any time, if the prime Minister thought that the mining industry was conducting a racist campaign after securing concessions from the government, he would undoubtedly react strongly against the industry's position. The committee pointed out that, while the industry had clearly stated its opposition to the concept of national land rights legislation, it would be much harder for it to act against 'reasonable legislation' (i.e. legislation that accommodated their interests).

On the question of the timing of AMIC's advertising, should they decide to launch a campaign, the committee made the following observations. The committee noted that timing was crucial for any advertising campaign, and this included the government's plan as well as the industry's. The state elections in South Australia and Western Australia (anticipated in March or April 1986) would be crucial in the timing of advertising. One view was that, unless the industry 'gets in first' to state its case, it would never regain ground lost to a government campaign. The Chamber of Mines of Western Australia strongly supported this position (Manners, 1985).

In opposition to this view was the argument that a pre-emptive campaign by the industry could provoke a government response which could swamp the industry's message. The proposed legislation was many months away from coming before Parliament. From experience, many changes would be made in the legislation by that time, and the industry would be better advised to wait until the bill was actually introduced into parliament before advertising. Tactically, it would be better for the industry to state its case at that time and, therefore, it should conserve part of its campaign funds for that eventuality.

Factors For and Against Advertising

The Aboriginal affairs committee thought that there were four factors supporting an advertising program and four factors against it. The factors favoring an advertising campaign were as follows:

1. Due to the state elections in South Australia and Western Australia which were expected by March or April 1986, the federal government would be vulnerable to the mining campaign. At this time, the states' rights issue would be heightened, and latent opposition to land rights would be at its greatest. Furthermore, the fact that the federal government's own opinion surveys showed that there was widespread opposition to land rights made the miners' campaign based upon the slogan 'equal rights' all the more threatening to the government.

2. There is a 'first strike' benefit accruing to the industry resulting from establishing its case on the issue rather than reacting to the government's campaign.

3. The mining industry's fundamental objection to the concept of national land rights legislation fully justifies such a campaign.

4. Advertising may gain for the industry greater concessions in the model.

The arguments advanced against an advertising campaign were the following:

1. The total defeat of the preferred model might mean that there would be no improvement in the Northern Territory legislation. However, even if this occurred, the industry would continue to press for changes in the Northern Territory Act. In this regard, the committee noted the possibility of statehood for the Northern Territory (perhaps by 1988), and the expectation that this would bring hoped for improvements in the Act.

2. An aggressive advertising campaign which was based upon 'equal rights' would be portrayed as racist by many politicians—including the Prime Minister—and it would therefore be attacked on that basis. In addition, the industry would be characterized as not being capable of compromise if it rejected a reasonable balance, involving a tribunal system, between Aboriginal and mining interests.
3. Advertising might bring to an end all negotiations with the government on further improvements in the model, or it could possibly prejudice progress already made.
4. The national legislation might be defeated ultimately by Aboriginal opposition, or Democrats voting against it in the Senate. Therefore, advertising runs the risk of unnecessarily antagonizing the government. In the interim, the industry should continue its negotiations with the government in order to gain the best possible legislation.

On the basis of the committee's discussion of the pros and cons of launching an advertising campaign, it recommended against it, at least for the time being. Committee members felt that the possible improvements in the legislation offered by the Prime Minister on 4 June 1985 made it inadvisable to advertise while these gains were being established. The committee noted in this regard that the federal government's entire approach to land rights legislation was under review.

The Aboriginal affairs committee recommended, therefore, that AMIC keep its options open. AMIC should continue discussions to improve the model, but should not back away from its opposition to national legislation. However, AMIC should not launch a 'state-based advertising campaign' against national legislation at this time. Nevertheless, it should prepare to inaugurate such a campaign in the event that talks with the government breakdown, or the results of the talks are unsatisfactory from the industry point of view. The committee concluded that if negotiations with the government fail, AMIC should run a campaign based upon state opposition to national legislation. This should be done by farming out AMIC funds and prepared advertising to be used by the Chamber of Mines in each state.

Government Concessions to Australian Mining Industry Council

In a letter dated 12 June 1985 from Senator Gareth Evans to Sir Bruce Watson, President of AMIC, the federal government outlined the concessions in the preferred model which they were prepared to make to the industry. Evans explained that the purpose of the letter was to clarify the government's position in the light of Watson's letter to Prime Minister Hawke dated 4 June, and the meeting between AMIC representatives and Hawke and Evans on the same day. Senator Evans explained that he was writing the letter in the absence of Hawke, who was on leave, and that Holding had seen and endorsed the text of the letter.

Gareth Evans indicated that his letter addressed the three major areas of industry dissatisfaction with the preferred model—access to Aboriginal land, compensation, and existing mining interests (Evans, 1985). With respect to access to Aboriginal land, the Minister said the Prime Minister took the position that 'no one group within the community should have the right to veto the development of national resources'. Evans noted that the Prime Minister had re-stated that position at their 4 June meeting. However, the government did support the rights of Aboriginal traditional owners to object to proposed exploration or mining on their land. In the event that there were objections which could not be resolved between the parties through negotiation, they would be heard and assessed by an independent tribunal. The tribunal would, in turn, make recommendations to the government for final determination.

The government did not think that this process would constitute a *de facto* veto insofar as specific time limits would be imposed governing both the preliminary negotiating stage and the subsequent tribunal stage for resolving potential conflict. The government felt that this proposal in no way resembled the right of Aboriginal traditional owners of land in the Northern Territory to refuse to consent under section 40 of the Northern Territory Aboriginal Land Rights Act (1976). The Minister stressed that what the government had in mind in the preferred model was an objection procedure with a mechanism for resolution of conflict, not what the miners referred to as a 'presumptive right to veto which has then to be reversed'.

On the issue of compensation, Evans stated that the government's intention was to institute an 'ordinary damage-based compensation regime'. That is to say, the government sought to ensure that compensation was based upon actual damage or disturbance to the land in question, not a generalized extension of the 'sacred sites' concept. However, he noted that Aborigines' relationship with the land had a 'specially sensitive character', and this could not be ignored in assessing mining compensation in the same way that other specially sensitive land use could not be ignored in a non-Aboriginal context.

With respect to miners' existing interests in land, Evans said that the government could not accept that the mere existence of a prior exploration title should in itself guarantee follow-on development without further opportunity for negotiation and tribunal considerations. Nevertheless, it did recognize the validity of AMIC's argument that special regard should be given to an existing title-holder who had spent substantial capital in exploring and proving-up a development project. This special regard for existing title-holders could be built into the criteria used by the tribunal in formulating its recommendations in the event of a dispute.

Evans concluded by saying that the preferred model did not represent a final government view. It was the basis for further discussion and consultation, and AMIC's input in this regard would continue to play an important role in the government's formulation of Aboriginal land rights.

Australian Mining Industry Council's Policy Implementation Plan

While AMIC regarded the 4 June meeting with Prime Minister Hawke, and the subsequent letter of 12 June from Gareth Evans, as a political victory for the industry, it continued to plan for an advertising campaign against national legislation. The industry undoubtedly wanted to keep up the pressure on the federal government to either drop the proposed legislation or to more fully accommodate AMIC's concerns regarding the preferred model. For example, AMIC officials met with Minister Holding on 8 October 1985 to explain their advertising campaign.[4] During the meeting, Strong emphasized that the industry would be taking every opportunity to speak on the issue of access to Aboriginal land, but that their decision to mount a 'high profile campaign' would remain frozen for the time being. After the meeting with Holding, AMIC representatives noted that there were no revelations. However, they made the observation that Holding seemed acutely concerned about the possibility of the industry conducting a major national television and newspaper campaign against the federal legislation which would be comparable to the one carried out in Western Australia.

Indeed, AMIC actually designed its policy implementation plan based upon the Western Australian campaign. In this regard, AMIC requested Duncan Bell, the chief strategist for the campaign in Western Australia, to be assigned to it in Canberra in the event that the national campaign was fully implemented. Within six months of AMIC's appeal to its member companies in March 1985 for campaign funds, it had collected over $500,000 for the advertising program. Only four small companies declined, on grounds of economic hardship, to contribute to the campaign. The policy implementation plan was inaugurated on 4 November 1985.

The policy promotion program was designed to be a grass-roots campaign with material distributed widely to politicians, the media, government departments and community groups. AMIC prepared glossy public relations folders entitled 'Mining and Access to Aboriginal Land: an Issue of National Importance'. The folders contained brochures stressing the importance of the industry's access to Aboriginal land, the importance of mining to Australia, and the disastrous consequences of national legislation. They also included tables, diagrams and maps of Australia before and after the introduction of the proposed federal land rights legislation (see Map 4), a map of Western Australia purporting to show the land available for Aboriginal land under the preferred model (Map 5), and a similar map for the Northern Territory (Map 6).

The campaign was to include speakers from the industry who were to use every opportunity available to speak to business and Aboriginal groups, clubs, and 'anyone who will listen' about the 'disastrous' consequences of national land rights legislation. Advertisements were scheduled to appear in newspapers such as *The Australian*, *The Australian Financial Review*, the *Sydney Morning Herald*, *The Age*, the *West Australian*, the *Courier Mail*, the *Adelaide Advertiser*, the *Northern Territory News*, the *Canberra Times*, and the *Hobart Mercury*. Each state and territory Chamber of Mines was to place the advertisements in its name. The maps, in particular, proved an effective advertising device. Many newspapers and magazines, for example, ran the maps on their front pages, along with a story, at no cost. This was a major source of free publicity for AMIC.

AMIC's policy implementation plan was never fully carried out, however. This was due largely to the fact that, by late 1985, the industry began receiving reports from usually reliable government sources that the proposed national legislation would be dropped. This led AMIC to adopt a low-profile 'wait and see' attitude toward launching a full-blown campaign against legislation which might well be doomed without its expending large-scale economic and political capital.

AMIC's low-profile strategy was vindicated when the federal government withdrew its proposed national legislation. However, this was not due to the policy promotion program conducted by the industry. Rather it was due to the compromise agreement reached between Burke and Hawke after the Western Australian state elections in February 1986. In other words, an intra-party compromise deal, designed to avert a factional 'bloodbath' at the national party conference scheduled for July 1986, achieved AMIC's principal policy objective on the land rights issue.

Removal of the Aboriginal Veto

The first tangible indication that AMIC's strategy was having an impact upon the federal government's land rights policy came in early November 1985 with the release of the proposed amendments to the Northern Territory Aboriginal Land Rights Act. In a letter accompanying the proposals, Holding described the amendments as a 'package' that achieves a 'balance of competing interests' while maintaining the government's overall land rights policy (Holding, 1985). The Minister proposed introducing the amending legislation in the 1986 autumn session of Parliament.

From the point of view of the government and the proponents of land rights, the amendments represented a major concession to the mining industry. The proposed amendments removed the Aboriginal power of the veto and replaced it with a tribunal. Under the existing Northern Territory Act, an exploration or mining interest on Aboriginal land could only be granted if the traditional Aboriginal owners consented to it. Their consent was also required for each follow-on title on any additional project (sections 40(1), 48).

However, under Holding's proposed amendment, if the land council with jurisdiction over Aboriginal land objected to the granting of an exploration license to a mining company, then the issue would be referred to a tribunal. The tribunal made its recommendation on the application (including the terms and conditions for the license and compensation) to the federal Minister for Aboriginal Affairs who, in consultation with the Minister for Resources and Energy, made the final decision (section 40(5.1-5.3). A similar tribunal procedure was proposed for Aboriginal objections to applications for a mining or development title on Aboriginal land (section 40(7.1-7.16).

The mining industry recognized the significance of the government's concession by indicating that this was an improvement over the existing Act insofar as a tribunal would replace the Aboriginal power of veto over mining and exploration. However, AMIC continued to press for additional concessions. It argued, for example, that the Aboriginal veto power was now replaced by a cumbersome, time-consuming, and costly tribunal system which, cumulatively, amounted to a *de facto* veto over mining. AMIC re-stated its position that, under such an arrangement, exploration and mining would continue to suffer. AMIC argued that if the Northern Territory Land Rights Act was to embody the principles 'now preferred by the federal government', then the amendments should reflect the views of government as expressed to the industry in Senator Evans' letter of 12 June 1985 (AMIC, 1985*a*).

MAP 4
FEDERAL LAND RIGHTS PROPOSAL

Extent of land where access for exploration and mining could be affected

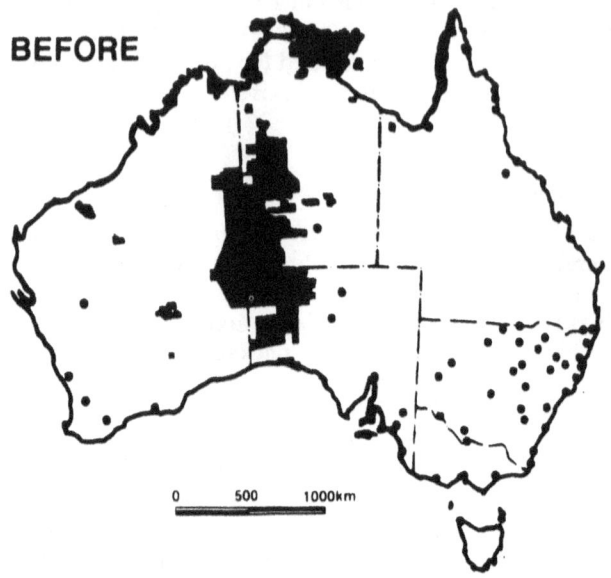

BEFORE

■ THIS IS ABORIGINAL LAND IN AUSTRALIA TODAY

• Reserves too small to be shown in detail at this scale

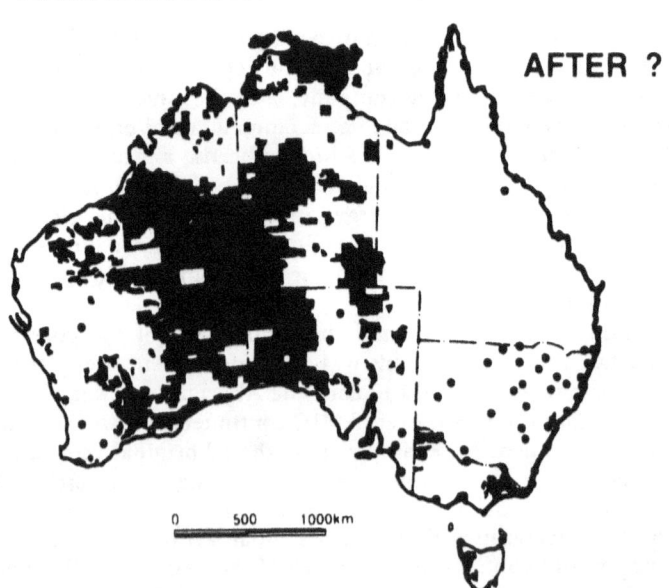

AFTER ?

■ IF THE FEDERAL GOVERNMENT'S PREFERRED LAND RIGHTS MODEL BECOMES LAW THIS IS THE LAND THAT WILL BE CLAIMABLE

• Reserves too small to be shown in detail at this scale

MAP 5
FEDERAL LAND RIGHTS PROPOSAL
FOR WESTERN AUSTRALIA

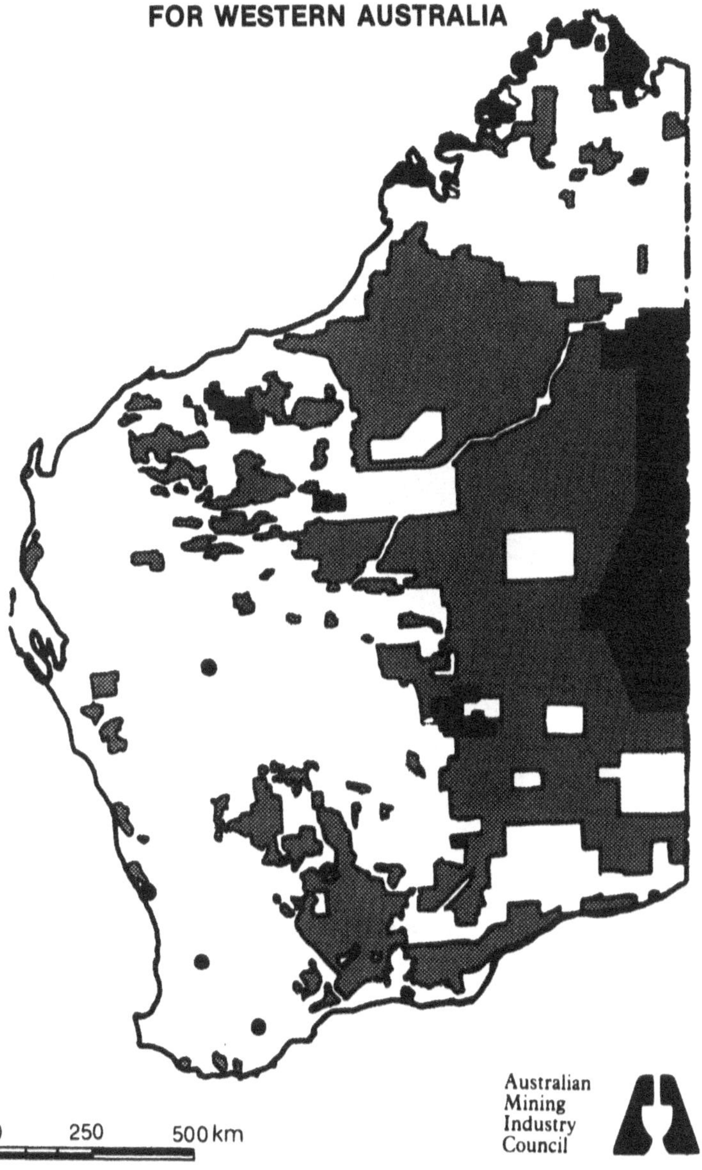

CURRENT ABORIGINAL LAND (includes land already granted; reserves, mission lands etc.)

LAND PROPOSED TO BE MADE AVAILABLE FOR CLAIM

LAND NOT AVAILABLE FOR CLAIM

MAP 6
FEDERAL LAND RIGHTS PROPOSAL
FOR THE NORTHERN TERRITORY

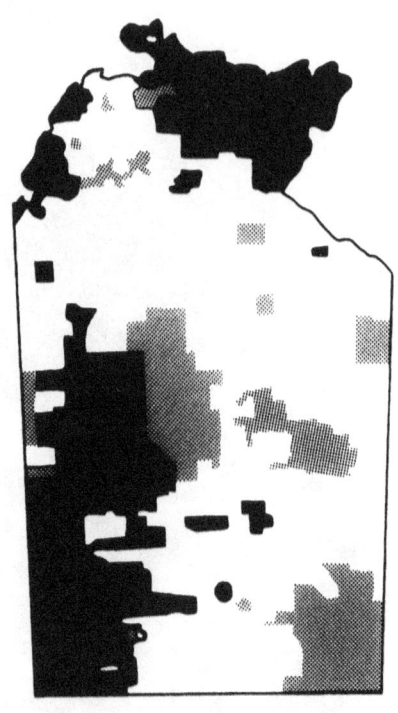

 CURRENT ABORIGINAL LAND (includes land already granted; reserves, mission lands etc.)

 LAND PROPOSED TO BE MADE AVAILABLE FOR CLAIM

 LAND NOT AVAILABLE FOR CLAIM

 Australian Mining Industry Council

THE ABORIGINAL COUNTER-OFFENSIVE

The Northern Territory land councils (the Northern Land Council, the Central Land Council and the Tiwi Land Council) opposed the removal of the mining veto from the Northern Territory Land Rights Act ever since the Prime Minister announced that Aborigines should not be able to block exploration and mining on their land. The Prime Minister first made this declaration at a full meeting of the Northern Land Council in Darwin, in the Northern Territory on 16 October 1984 (a few days before his campaign statement in Western Australia.)

Bob Hawke told the Northern Land Council gathering that he did not believe that Aboriginal people should be able to say no to exploration and mining, and he announced the idea of a tribunal in place of the veto (NLC, 1984). After the meeting, the Northern Territory land councils did everything in their power to persuade the government against making such changes to the Northern Territory Land Rights Act.

For example, on 16 October 1984, the chairman and assembled members of the NLC presented a letter of protest to the Prime Minister. On 7 February 1985, the central and northern land councils declared their refusal to attend a steering committee meeting on national land rights called by Minister Holding for 13 February. They also boycotted a meeting with the ALP Aboriginal Affairs Caucus Committee scheduled for the same day. The land councils refused to attend these meetings on the grounds that they were designed to give Aboriginal endorsement to the federal government's proposed national land rights legislation. They took the position that the pressure by the Western Australian government upon the federal government had created an 'unholy rush' toward 'hastily conceived Cabinet policy'. John Ah Kit, director of the NLC, said that, given the pressure of the Western Australian situation, no advance toward meaningful national land rights could be made (Central and Northern Land Councils, 1985).

On 11 February 1985 and on 22 March 1985, the chairmen of the Northern Territory land councils appealed to the 'Government of Australia' not to withdraw the Aboriginal power to veto exploration and mining (Northern Territory Land Councils, 1985). They also wrote to all ALP caucus members expressing their opposition to the proposals in the preferred national model which would weaken Aboriginal control over exploration and mining on their land by removing the mining veto (Northern Territory Land Councils, 1985a). In the land councils' letter to the ALP caucus they made the following statement:

> We are now being told by the Minister for Aboriginal Affairs that these words (*the 1984 ALP platform on land rights*) don't mean what they say. He is now telling us that we can refuse permission for mining but that whether or not that refusal will be allowed will depend upon the whim of the Minister after debate over the refusal has been masked by the charade of a Tribunal hearing.

The land councils' lobbying efforts consisted primarily of petitioning parliament and distributing information to support groups such as the churches, unions and academics. They also urged party branches to uphold the ALP platform on Aboriginal land rights.

In March 1985, the chairmen of the three Northern Territory land councils travelled widely throughout the territory, consulting Aboriginal communities about the government's preferred national model. On the basis of these consultations, the chairmen concluded that Aborigines in the Northern Territory overwhelmingly rejected the proposed changes to the mining provisions of the Northern Territory Land Rights Act. To support their contention, the land councils produced a record of their consultations in a video film entitled 'Our Land Is Our Life'. Another video of the consultations was made and circulated to ALP caucus members under the title 'Still you keep asking, asking'.

From 22 to 29 March 1985, the land councils had a delegation in Canberra to persuade the federal government and members of parliament not to change the mining provisions of the Northern Territory Act. Failing in this effort, however, a large number of Aborigines travelled from the Northern Territory to Parliament House in Canberra in May 1985 to publicly protest any changes in the Northern Territory Land Rights Act.

Despite these efforts, however, Minister Holding proposed the amendments to the Northern Territory Land Rights Act in November 1985. The land councils were so enraged by the government's decision to withdraw the mining veto from the Northern Territory Act, that they refused to even discuss the proposed amendments. They simply re-stated their position that any changes to the mining provisions of the Act were 'totally unacceptable'.

The Land Councils' Campaign

From October 1984 until January 1986, the Northern Territory land councils' lobbying to prevent the removal of the mining veto from the Northern Territory Aboriginal Land Rights Act appeared to have little success. However, in February 1986, the land councils' launched a new campaign which proved to be successful. While amendments to the Northern Territory Act were enacted, and while the land councils were adamantly opposed to any changes of the mining provisions of the Act, they did manage to restore the mining veto to the proposed amendments of the legislation.

There was nothing new, however, in the land councils' campaign in February 1986. For example, they sought to mobilize support primarily from among ALP caucus members and from among support groups who were traditional ALP supporters. Their lobbying efforts within the ALP caucus also did not change. For example, after the announcement of Holding's preferred model in February 1985, CLC (Central Land Council of the Northern Territory) officials representing the Federation of Land Councils co-ordinated their lobbying with Gerry Hand, convenor of the Socialist Left. In fact, Pat Dodson, Warren Snowdon, and others representing the land councils, operated out of Hand's office in Parliament House when lobbying ALP caucus members (interview with Jerry Hand, 24 September 1986). This relationship did not change after February 1986.

For example, Gerry Hand relied heavily upon the land councils for documentation and information to argue his case within the ALP caucus. In two discussion papers which were circulated by Hand to caucus members in July 1985 and in February 1986, the land councils provided background material and documentation to support Hand's argument for land rights.

In the paper circulated among ALP caucus members on 9 February 1986, Hand presented data which the land councils had generated in their earlier lobbying efforts to prevent the removal of the mining veto from the Northern Territory Act. Hand argued, for example, that, contrary to the mining industry's claims, the decline in mineral exploration activity in the Northern Territory had not fallen below the average for Australia as a whole. He pointed out that private capital expenditure on exploration for minerals (excluding petroleum or oil shale) in the Northern Territory in 1982 was $32 million. In 1984 the expenditure declined by 20 per cent to $25 million. By contrast, capital expenditure on exploration in Australia as a whole decreased from $575.6 million in 1982 to $437.9 million in 1983 which was a decline of 24 per cent. Therefore, the percentage decline in exploration expenditure in the Northern Territory during this period was less than the percentage decline for all of Australia.

Furthermore, the decline in the expenditure for mineral exploration in the Northern Territory was largely due to the fall in the international price of minerals, the poor profitability of the industry, and the federal government's policy of discouraging uranium mining (i.e. the 'three mines policy' of the ALP).

The dramatic decline in uranium exploration in the Northern Territory was given as the underlying cause of the fall in exploration activity in the territory. Table XVII contains data comparing expenditures on exploration by mineral in the Northern Territory for 1983 and 1984. The table shows the dominance of uranium in terms of exploration activity in the Northern Territory. Expenditure for uranium exploration in the Northern Territory declined from 50.4 per cent of total exploration expenditure in 1983, to only 9.3 per cent of the total expenditure in 1984. According to Hand, this largely explained the overall fall in exploration expenditure in the Northern Territory. Contrary to mining industry claims, therefore, commercial mining factors, plus the government's uranium policy, explained the fall in mineral exploration in the territory.

TABLE XVII

SHARES OF EXPENDITURE ON EXPLORATION FOR
DIFFERENT MINERALS AND GROUPS OF MINERALS
1982-1983 AND 1983-1984

(Northern Territory)

Minerals	1982-83	1983-84
	(%)	(%)
Copper, lead, zinc, silver, nickel cobalt	3.0	1.2
Gold	3.7	3.6
Uranium	50.4	9.3
All other metals	3.4	3.2
Total non-metallic minerals (including diamonds)	3.3	2.7

Hand also argued that an additional reason for the decline in mineral exploration in the Northern Territory was that the mining companies failed to pursue exploration license applications once they were granted. Evidence to support this contention emerged during a so-called breakthrough in the negotiation of a mining exploration licence agreement between Uranerz Australia Pty Ltd and the Northern Land Council in June 1986. The agreement provided for mineral exploration and mining activities to take place in Western Arnhem Land. This was the first such agreement concluded under the terms of the Northern Territory Aboriginal Land Rights Act since it was enacted in 1976. The only exception to this was the Ranger agreement which the NLC claimed was negotiated under federal duress.

The industry's reaction to the Uranerz agreement lent support to Hand's claim. The General Manager of Queensland Mines Ltd, John Lawler, urgently requested an opportunity to address the executive members of the Northern Territory Chamber of Mines in March 1986 to discuss the issue. In making this request, Lawler offered the following explanation for his concern:

> For the last five years, the Chamber has been advocating a united front by its members in negotiating exploration and development agreements with the two councils on terms and conditions acceptable to the industry as a whole. To this end QML, at a cost of goodwill with the NLC, has steadfastly refused to offer any exotic form of financial inducement for mineral rights. I think it is quite wrong for some members of the Chamber to now be departing from the chosen direction without the Chamber, as a whole, expressing a view (Lawler, 1986).[5]

The reason for the urgency of Lawler's request to address the executive directors of the Chamber was that the federal government had recently announced its intentions to amend the Northern Territory Land Rights Act. The fear was that the land councils would use the Uranerz agreement to advance their case that amendments to the mining provisions of the Act were not necessary. Indeed, this is precisely what the land councils did. However, it did not appear to have much of an impact on the government because of the existing 102 exploration applications which had not been negotiated.

The land councils also appealed to their support groups (e.g. the Catholic Church, the ACTU), and prominent academics such as Dr Coombs, who were traditional supporters of the Labor Party, to exert pressure upon the government to overturn the Prime Minister's decision to remove the veto from the Northern Territory Act. The land councils placed newspaper advertisements and circulated materials to these groups to support their position. For example, they circulated 2,000 copies of a high-quality glossy folder with brochures, tables and maps (Northern Territory Land Councils, 1986). Ironically, the land councils' folder and the format of its contents was remarkably similar to AMIC's folder and format. However, they continued to use the same documentation, data and argumentation they had been using from the beginning of their lobbying efforts in October 1984.

Cross-Factional Australian Labor Party Support

The land councils' campaign from October 1984 until January 1986 was largely ineffectual, however, in terms of influencing the government's land rights policy. The leadership of the left wing of the ALP was equally unsuccessful in influencing the government's land rights policy during this period. For example, Gerry Hand was refused, by Minister Holding's office, a copy of the proposed amendments to the Northern Territory Act. This was despite the fact that Hand was a senior member of the ALP Aboriginal Affairs Caucus Committee which was scheduled to discuss the amendments. In fact, the caucus committee chairman, John Gayler, complained that he had received a copy of the proposed amendments to the Northern Territory Act only two days before the committee was scheduled to discuss them (*West Australian*, 11 November 1985).

This situation changed dramatically, however, in February 1986. The reason for the change was that a cross-factional revolt against Hawke's land rights policy threatened to emerge within the ALP parliamentary caucus. The incident which triggered this cross-factional opposition was a campaign statement issued by Bob Hawke in Perth the weekend before the 8 February state election in Western Australia.

In response to questions from the press about the existence of conflict between the Burke and Hawke Governments' on land rights, Hawke stated that 'I have no problems living with Mr. Burke's position on the matter' (*Adelaide Advertiser*, 1 January 1986). In the light of the fact that Premier Burke was on record as saying that he would resign if land rights were forced on his state, Hawke's campaign statement alarmed members of the ALP caucus.

There had been growing frustration in caucus over the federal government's indecisiveness on the land rights issue, and anger over Burke's challenge to federal legislation. This frustration crystallized after the Prime Minister's campaign statement, and was manifest in cross-factional opposition to the government's position on land rights.

In this changed political environment, Gerry Hand and the land councils were able to effectively lobby the right-wing and Centre Left factions of the ALP caucus to challenge the government's land rights policy. For example, Hand circulated his discussion paper on land rights among his ALP colleagues on 9 February, immediately after the Western Australian election and just before federal parliament resumed meeting the week beginning 11 February.

In the paper Hand appealed for 'land rights solidarity'. He argued against the government's 'state-by-state' approach to land rights in place of national land rights legislation, on the grounds that state governments would capitulate to vested interests (i.e. miners and pastoralists) if land rights were left to them. He also argued against the federal government's plan to amend the Northern Territory Land Rights Act by removing the Aboriginal veto over mining on Aboriginal land. Hand maintained that, while the Northern Territory Land Rights Act was not perfect, it was a fundamental piece of social reform which had to be strengthened and its principles extended to Aboriginal people throughout Australia. This theme was also elaborated by representatives of the land councils in their lobbying efforts in Canberra.

The new-found success of the land councils' campaign was evident in a resolution passed on 12 February by the ten-member federal Labor Caucus Committee on Aboriginal Affairs opposing government policy on land rights. The committee, which included members from all factions of the ALP, passed a unanimous resolution calling for urgent consideration of the issue by the government. The resolution called for uniform national land rights legislation based upon Holding's five principles, to be introduced during the current session of parliament. Included in the resolution was the committee's opposition to any weakening of existing land rights legislation, such as the proposed amendments to the Northern Territory Act.

An indication of the cross-factional ALP opposition to the government's land rights policy was a statement made by the chairman of the caucus committee, John Gayler — a member of the right wing. Gayler made the following statement:

> I think there is strong feeling in Caucus that it [land rights] is a deeply moral issue, one that transcends factions. There is widespread support for it from all sections of the Government. We know some people are opposed to it, particularly the Western Australian Premier, but it is not about factions, it is only the issue that counts. (*Sydney Morning Herald*, 13 February 1986.)

Holding was able to use this support from the ALP caucus to persuade his cabinet colleagues to shift their position on the issue.

Concessions to the Land Councils

Armed with cross-factional support from government backbenchers, Holding made a final presentation to the cabinet on the proposed land rights legislation. At a cabinet meeting held on 3 March 1986, Holding made a detailed presentation. Holding followed a two-fold strategy.

His first approach, which he doubted would succeed because of the pressure from Brian Burke, was to persuade cabinet to endorse his preferred model for national land rights legislation. Secondly, if that failed, the Minister had a fall-back position. He would argue that the veto provisions of the Northern Territory Act should be retained in exchange for dropping the preferred model and taking a softer approach on state land rights policy.

As expected, Cabinet rejected the national legislation. However, Holding was successful in persuading cabinet to accept the retention of a modified veto in the Northern Territory Act. The feeling among ministers was that, in the light of the weakening of the federal stance on state land rights policy, by abandoning national legislation, they had to alter the amendments to the Northern Teritory Act to strengthen the rights of Aborigines to veto proposed exploration and mining on their land.

To do any less would be certain to invite bitter factional conflict at the Labor Party's national conference scheduled for July 1986. While cabinet's compromise decision averted a divisive controversy at the conference, Aboriginal groups throughout Australia declared their intention to disrupt the America's Cup races in Fremantle, and the bicentennial celebrations, to draw international attention to their demands for land rights justice. Aboriginal spokesmen also called for Aboriginal rights to be recognized in a national treaty, or in the Constitution.

The federal Labor Caucus Aboriginal Affairs Committee continued to put pressure on cabinet to accommodate the demands of the land councils. This included the caucus committee's condemnation of the 3 March cabinet decision for failing to consider the committee's resolutions calling for uniform national land rights legislation. On 10 March the committee requested and was granted a postponement of the cabinet decision of 3 March until the committee members had an opportunity to hold 'fresh talks' with the parties involved. The chairman of the committee threatened to take the issue to the full ALP caucus if cabinet did not agree to the committee's request.

The caucus committee worked in tandem with the land councils to press cabinet for further concessions to the councils' demands. The major achievement of the committee's support for the land councils' was the retention of the veto in the Northern Territory Act, and the allowance of 'spiritual' or social disruption as a basis of compensation for mining Aboriginal land.

The final agreement over amendments to the mining provisions of the Northern Territory Land Rights Act was reached at a joint meeting of the Northern Territory land councils in Lake Bennett on 6 May 1987. Ministers Evans and Holding (under instructions from Prime Minister Hawke) finalized an agreement on the mining provisions of the Northern Territory Land Rights Act (1976). Neither the mining industry nor the Northern Territory government, however, was consulted about the final agreement. In fact, the mining industry did not even have a copy of the final amendments before they were approved by the land councils at Lake Bennett. The agreement on the mining amendments was concluded just in time for the legislation to be put through the Senate on 7 May 1987.

There were four major elements of the agreement:

1. Veto powers over exploration remained, but new negotiations with Aboriginal land owners were possible after five years;
2. If consent were given, but there was no agreement on the terms and conditions of the consent, then the matter would be referred to a tribunal;
3. There would be no veto at the mining stage, but compensation would be freely negotiated between miners and traditional owners through their respective land councils;
4. If the nature of the proposed mining development changed (i.e. from copper to gold, or from under-ground to open-cut), then the former agreement was null and void and new negotiations would be required.

While the land councils opposed any change to the mining provisions of the Northern Territory Act as a matter of principle, Pat Dodson, director of the CLC (Central Land Council of the Northern Territory) at least gave qualified praise to the agreement calling it a 'brilliant compromise' (*Northern Territory News*, 7 May 1987).

Within twenty-four hours of the agreement with the land councils,

Gareth Evans addressed AMIC at its annual mining seminar. He informed the miners that the agreement represented a 'balanced' compromise. He said that it recognized Aborigines' rights to 'retain their traditional way of life' (referring to the retention of the veto powers). And, on the other hand, if the veto were not invoked, it could not be used as a 'bargaining tool' to extract financial advantages from the companies. However, the mining industry was not as sanguine as the Minister about the retention of the veto in the Northern Territory Act.

For example, immediately after the 3 March cabinet decision to retain the veto in the Act, AMIC expressed the view that 'the retention of the veto was a major blow and it was a reversal of a publicly stated undertaking that federal legislation would not include a veto' (AMIC, 1986). AMIC later informed the Northern Territory Chamber of Mines that Senator Evans had indicated the veto provision, plus 'open-ended' claims for compensation at the mining stage in the amendments to the Northern Territory Act, were 'non-negotiable'. AMIC took the view that the amendments were 'the best industry could hope for' in the circumstances. AMIC also warned the Northern Territory Chamber that if the industry continued to press for further changes to the Act, it might lose the limited gains they made in the amendments (Challen, 1986).

Conclusion

This study of the political influence of the mining industry in Australia departs from conventional treatments of the subject in several respects. First, it examines the political strategies of the mineral industry from the point of view of the industry itself. This provides insights into the miners' political motives and efforts to influence government policy. It is the first major study of the industry's influence on government policy which has had the benefit of unrestricted access to industry sources and documentation. Previous studies have been based upon secondary, non-industry sources. For the most part, they have been forced to rely upon informed speculation about the industry's actions.

Secondly, the study places the miners' attempt to influence government policy into an over-arching political context that shaped and determined their influence. That context was the internal politics of the political party in power—the ALP (Australian Labor Party). During the period under investigation, ALP factional politics created the framework or arena in which the mining industry competed for influence over government policy. While the industry, indeed, exerted political influence on government policy, that influence was subordinated to the over-riding nature of ALP factional politics. In fact, the mineral industry, as well as other groups, elaborated their strategies to influence government policy based in part, at least, upon the opportunities and constraints presented by factional divisions within the ALP. When internal conflict within the party was attenuated, the industry's influence on government policy tended to increase. However, when the factional divisions diminished, the industry's ability to influence policy declined.

Conventional Approaches

The approach adopted in this study differs from conventional treatments of the subject. For example, dependency is one major approach to understanding the political influence of industry groups in Australia. Dependency theory assumes that capitalist classes (ruling or 'dependent') are politically dominant and are rational in terms of designing political strategies to achieve their objectives. The economic importance of major industries is assumed to automatically give them preponderant political power. In addition, it is assumed that a capitalist class (or fraction of capital) automatically devises strategies which ensure their security and economic surplus. In the case of Australia, it is assumed that foreign subsidiaries of international corporations possess political power by virtue of their importance to the national economy. Little if any effort is made to establish the empirical validity of these assumptions.

The present study examines a major Australian industry with a view toward establishing whether, in fact, it enjoys preponderant influence in national politics, as dependency theory predicts. The study also seeks to determine the extent to which the industry is rational in terms of following policies which maximize its influence in national politics.

The mining industry was selected for study because of its traditional importance to the national economy — in terms of foreign-exchange earnings (roughly 40 per cent of exports), its contribution to the economy's gross domestic product (8 per cent), and its contribution to total private new fixed capital expenditure (over 30 per cent).

The second major approach to understanding industry politics is interest-group theory of capitalist democracies. Writers in this genre have tended to examine the relationship between industry-lobbying organizations and the process of democratic policy making. The emphasis in this approach is upon how these organizations, or pressure groups, influence the making or administration of public policy. However, the approach begs an important question. That is to say, how dominant is any industry or business class in national politics? The tendency is to assume that competing interest-groups, such as pro-Aboriginal organizations, churches and trade unions, cannot offset the political influence of large corporations. In the case of Australia, at least, no serious attempt has yet been made by students of pressure groups to subject this *a priori* assumption to critical scrutiny.

In order to evaluate the political power of the mining industry in Australia, the study has focused upon the objectives and strategies of the industry in national politics. Despite the fact that the mining industry has been active in Australia for over a hundred years, the industry only recently mounted a national political campaign. Its first political campaign was inaugurated in 1984 and was designed to defeat national Aboriginal land rights legislation. This policy was initiated by the newly elected Australian Labor Party government of Bob Hawke. The ALP's land rights policy was perceived by the industry to be a major threat to its guaranteed access to land for the purpose of exploration and mining.

The mining industry's campaign went beyond standard business advertising, and beyond the conventional lobbying efforts of pressure groups based in Canberra. The miners carried out a grass-roots public affairs campaign designed to mobilize the community against the government's efforts to implement land rights legislation. Over a million dollars was spent in this undertaking, with more funds available if needed. The campaign involved the heavy use of public advocacy advertising on television. This was unprecedented in Australia at the time.

The dependency and traditional interest-group approaches to understanding the political influence of the industry's campaign against land rights legislation lead to predictions of the industry's success. In the case of dependency theory, for example, the industry's defeat of land rights legislation would be asserted on the basis of its control of vast economic wealth. In the case of interest-group theory, it would be assumed that, without the countervailing influence of an equally dominant competing pressure group, the mining industry's political victory over land rights legislation was inevitable. Lindblom (1977:198) argues in this regard that labor unions, for example, do not enjoy the same privileged position in government and politics that business does. The reason given for this is that government depends upon corporations for production, employment and economic growth. Both approaches lead to exaggerated conclusions about the ability of the mining industry to influence government policy.

Approach Adopted in the Study

Conventional approaches to understanding the political power of the mining industry in Australia do not adequately explain the outcome of the national land rights issue. The present study leads to very different interpretations of the issue. For example, the mining industry's campaign against land rights legislation was not the principal reason for its defeat. In fact, the federal government abandoned national land rights legislation primarily to avoid self-destructive divisiveness within the governing Labor Party. Major factional conflict within the ALP was threatened by the Western Australian Labor government's opposition to federal land rights policy. While the mining industry sought to influence federal policy, the industry was not the principal reason for the government's decision to abandon national legislation.

This is not to deny, however, that the mining industry had a political strategy for defeating national legislation, and that it had an important role to play in events leading to its defeat. Nevertheless, the industry's role was subordinated to factors beyond its control. The existence of an overarching political framework, or context in which the government's land rights policy was formulated, dictated the outcome of the land rights controversy. That political context or framework was internal factional conflict within the governing Australian Labor Party.

The industry's political strategies (as well as the strategies of other groups) for influencing the government's land rights policy was formulated within the context of ALP politics. The reason for this was that the federal government's land rights policy was largely determined by the interplay of ALP factional politics. As a highly decentralized party dominated by ideosyncratic factors such as political leadership, favoritism, ideology, and sectarianism, major national policy issues were frequently accompanied by strenuously contested factional in-fighting. In fact, this is one of the major reasons that the Labor Party has historically done poorly in contesting national elections.

INDUSTRY STRATEGY AND INFLUENCE

The mining industry's efforts to influence the government's land rights policy was inextricably bound-up with ALP factional politics. The industry's ability to influence the government's land rights policy, in fact, changed as shifts occurred in the party's factional alignments. During the government's efforts to implement its national Aboriginal land rights policy, from 1983 to 1987, there were at least three distinct stages of ALP factional politics. The mining industry adjusted its political strategies to maximize its influence on government policy during each stage. However, the various stages of ALP factional politics had a determining influence on the industry's ability to influence the government's land rights policy. In other words, ALP politics rather than the mining industry's campaigns, determined the government's land rights policy. The three stages of ALP factional politics were: (1) party consensus; (2) factional conflict; and (3) party compromise.

Party Consensus

During the first stage of ALP factional politics, from the date the Hawke Government assumed office in March 1983 until the middle of 1984, the party was in a consensus mode on national land rights policy. The ALP's policy had yet to be implemented and, therefore, there was widespread consensus on its land rights policy as reflected in the party platform. The party's Aboriginal land rights policy was largely symbolic, and all major factions of the party subscribed to it.

During this period, the mining industry's influence over the government's land rights policy was minimal. In fact, the miners were not even consulted by the federal government on its land rights policy. In contrast, Aboriginal groups were given the exclusive prerogative to formulate national land rights legislation in concert with the Minister for Aboriginal Affairs. Furthermore, Aboriginal groups were promised by the federal government that they would have the power to veto any proposed land rights legislation of which they disapproved.

The mining industry was effectively denied any input into the determination of the government's Aboriginal land rights legislation. Faced with the threat of legislation which it feared could jeopardize their access to Aboriginal land, the industry designed a grass-roots political campaign to mobilize public opinion against national legislation. The campaign was launched first in Western Australia because the state Labor government of Brian Burke had taken the lead nationally in formulating land rights legislation under the federal Labor Party government.

The mining campaign against land rights legislation in Western Australia was carried out by the Chamber of Mines of Western Australia. The campaign was inaugurated in May 1984 and continued until the middle of September 1984. Despite the industry's claims for its success, the campaign represents the political impotence of the industry rather than its dominance. The miners were fearful of the ALP's land rights policy. The release of the Seaman inquiry's preliminary discussion paper in January 1984 shocked the industry into taking drastic action to counteract government policy.

During this period, the mining industry was not only not consulted about the ALP's proposed national land rights legislation, but it did not have access to key government policy-makers. In this threatening political environment, the industry devised a grass-roots public relations campaign designed to influence public opinion. Since the government would not listen to the industry's concerns, the industry felt it had to force the government to listen by mobilizing public opinion against its land rights policy.

The mining industry's campaign in Western Australia was successful in mobilizing public opinion against Aboriginal land rights. However, the campaign itself did not significantly alter public opinion. Aboriginal land rights legislation was an unpopular, albeit a minor political issue, during the 1983 elections. What the campaign did, however, was to transform an unpopular issue with a low public profile into an unpopular issue with a high public profile.

This had the effect of making Aboriginal land rights a high-profile public issue which the Opposition Liberal Party could turn into a damaging campaign issue against the Burke Government in elections. Much of the ALP's factional conflict over land rights legislation, in fact, can be explained in terms of the Burke Government's efforts to cope with the Liberal Party's election campaign against the ALP's platform policy on land rights. For example, in response to Liberal Party attacks, the Burke Government repudiated the ALP's national land rights policy and even threatened to resign if Burke was forced by the party to implement land rights legislation. However, the actions of the Burke Government triggered a bitter factional conflict within the ALP, between the Western Australian ALP backed by the Prime Minister and the right wing of the party, and the Victorian Socialist Left backed by the national left wing and some members of the Centre Left faction.

Factional Conflict

This phase of ALP politics occurred from late 1984 until March 1986. It was characterized by a bitter and divisive conflict over the implementation of the party's land rights policy. During this period there was a stalemate between the Western Australian and federal governments over land rights policy. The Burke Government refused to accept over-riding federal land rights legislation, and the federal government refused to abandon its national land rights policy without assurances that Western Australia would come up to certain national standards for land rights as determined by the federal government.

During this period the mining industry enjoyed its greatest influence over the government's land rights policy. For example, the Chamber of Mines of Western Australia as well as the Australian Mining Industry Council, participated on the Western Australian drafting committee for a state Aboriginal Land Bill. Most of the industry's concerns were accommodated in the resulting draft legislation.

Beginning in mid-September 1984, and continuing until June 1985, AMIC consulted with Prime Minister Hawke and Senator Evans, Minister for Resources and Energy, in order to accommodate the industry's interests in the proposed national legislation. Several of the miners' major concerns, such as removing the Aboriginal mining veto, and limiting Aboriginal compensation for damage to their land (as opposed to 'spiritual' and social damage) due to mining, were conceded by the Hawke Government. The industry was also able to persuade the government to remove the mining veto from the Northern Territory Land Rights Act (1976). This was evident in the government's November 1985 proposals to amend that Act.

For as long as the Western Australian government refused to accept national land rights legislation and, indeed, supported draft legislation that accommodated the miners' interests, the industry was able to effectively lobby the federal government to accommodate its interests. The miners also conducted a low-profile advertising campaign against national legislation in order to maintain pressure upon the federal government to accommodate their interests in the proposed legislation.

However, once the conflict between the Western Australian and federal governments was resolved, and a compromise position on land rights policy reached, the mining industry's ability to influence government policy significantly declined. It was faced with the prospect of conceding to the government's decision as a *fait accompli* or mounting a national publicity campaign against an ALP policy which had support from all major factions of the party.

Party Compromise

This period of ALP factional politics occurred following the 8 February 1986 state election in Western Australia and continued until the amending legislation to the Northern Territory Land Rights Act was introduced into the Senate in May 1987. This stage of ALP politics was characterized by two major compromise agreements between factions of the party. The first compromise was between the Western Australian and federal governments, the second was between the Hawke Government and backbench ALP Caucus members who were threatening to revolt against the Western Australian compromise. During this period the mining industry had virtually no input into government policy. While benefiting from the Western Australian government's defeat of national land rights legislation, the miners did not play a significant role in bringing that about. Likewise, the industry did not play a role in the compromise agreement with ALP backbenchers. Moreover, the federal government reneged on its promise to the industry to weaken the mining provisions of the Northern Territory Land Rights Act.

After the February 1986 state elections in Western Australia, which returned Brian Burke to power on a platform opposing any Aboriginal land rights legislation, the federal government negotiated a compromise agreement with his government. The compromise was motivated primarily by the Prime Minister's desire to avoid a factional 'bloodbath' at the upcoming ALP national conference in July 1986. The agreement which was negotiated by the Western Australian and federal Labor Party leadership involved a trade-off. The Hawke Government agreed to abandon its national land rights legislation in return for which the Burke Government agreed to grant Aboriginal rights in land through non-legislative means.

However, the Western Australia-federal compromise agreement triggered within the party another factional conflict over land rights. The backbenchers in the ALP parliamentary caucus threatened to mount a cross-factional revolt against the Hawke Government's concessions to Western Australia. Early in February 1986 the ALP caucus committee on Aboriginal Affairs voted unanimously to insist that the government implement the ALP policy of uniform national land rights legislation. It also rejected the government's efforts to weaken the Northern Territory Land Rights Act by removing the Aboriginal mining veto. The caucus committee threatened to take the issue to the full federal ALP Caucus to reject the government's actions if its views were not taken into account.

In order to contain this potential revolt by ALP backbenchers, the

Hawke Government made a further compromise agreement with the leaders of the cross-factional movement. Hawke agreed to retain the Aboriginal mining veto provisions in the Northern Territory Act, plus allow mining compensation claims for 'spiritual' and social disruption on Aboriginal land being mined. In return, the ALP caucus committee agreed not to insist upon national land rights legislation, provided that the states made progress in granting Aboriginal rights in land through non-legislative means.

As a result of these two compromise agreements, the mining industry gained a political victory but it also suffered a setback. In both cases, however, the industry itself had little influence on the outcome of the issues. The federal government's decision to abandon national land rights legislation was primarily due to the pressure on the Hawke Government to avoid a major factional conflict over the Western Australian government's challenge to ALP land rights policy. Likewise, the decision to allow the mining veto to remain in the Northern Territory Act was due to the pressure on the Hawke Government to avert a threatened ALP backbench revolt against federal concessions to the Western Australian government.

Innovation of the Approach

The approach to industry politics as outlined in this study challenges the dependency and interest-group theses of the privileged position of corporations in capitalist democracies. The findings of the study tend to support the counter-thesis advanced by Vogel (1987). He argues that corporations are not uniquely powerful, and that their political influence over the public agenda and the outcome of issues is relative. It varies according to the political issue, the historical timing, and the differences between capitalist democracies.

This case study of corporate power in Australia justifies Vogel's admonition that it is necessary to study history and comparative politics in order to understand the nature of corporate political power. The study illustrates the importance of corporate strategies designed to influence public policy, plus the over-riding importance of the political context in which these strategies are carried out. It suggests, for example, that the same strategy will not necessarily work, nor will it necessarily fail, in different political contexts and historical situations. The study also underscores the fact that an industry's possession of great economic wealth, or its importance to the economy, does not in itself bestow political power. Factors such as political strategy, timing and, above all, political context also play a role in determining the extent of corporate political power in capitalist democracies.

Epilogue

Since the re-election of the federal ALP government of Bob Hawke in July 1987, and the appointment of Gerry Hand as the new Minister for Aboriginal Affairs, there has been a shift in the tone of the Aboriginal land rights debate. The Hand ministry has revived the concept of the Makarrata, or compact, between Aboriginal and non-Aboriginal people. He has proposed that the Constitution be amended to ensure that Aborigines are guaranteed land under 'secure long term tenure' and, wherever possible, in the form of 'inalienable communal freehold title' (Hand, 1987: 12).

Consistent with this proposal, the Minister has proposed the complete reorganization of the federal Aboriginal affairs bureaucracy, including the creation of an Aboriginal and Torres Strait Islander Commission to replace the National Aboriginal Conference. The Commission would take over the functions of the Department of Aboriginal Affairs, the Aboriginal Development Commission, Aboriginal Hostels Limited, and the Australian Institute of Aboriginal Studies. Since the Commission would be based upon twenty-eight Regional Councils, it represents an effort to decentralize federal Aboriginal affairs and create a democratically representative national body to formulate federal Aboriginal policy.

While these proposals are not entirely new, they do reflect the lessons learned by the ALP from its efforts to legislate national Aboriginal land rights under the Holding ministry. First, they recognize the necessity of having united Aboriginal support for federal initiatives. Secondly, they show that the Labor government understands the importance of having national political support from non-Aboriginals to carry out its Aboriginal policies. And, finally, they accept as a point of departure, the existence of multiple state, territory and federal jurisdiction over Aboriginal land, and the existence of a variety of land tenure systems. In other words, the Hand approach recognizes the necessity of having the support of state and territorial governments before embarking upon an ambitious program of Aboriginal land reform.

Nevertheless, there are certain dangers in pursuing this approach. Unlike the public attitudes toward Aborigines in 1967, the present political climate in the country may not be sympathetic to such a recommendation. If the proposal to amend the Constitution were rejected, it could be interpreted as a loss of public support for the not inconsiderable gains that Aborigines have made in acquiring land since 1976.

A public or symbolic display of support for pro-Aboriginal policies is critical for any significant improvement in existing land rights legislation.

Epilogue 155

The reason for this is that Aboriginal land rights in Australia are a vast patchwork of laws and administrative regulations which differs from state to state and territory. Furthermore, the legislation and administration of Aboriginal land is subject to political pressures which are animated by state or territorial politics. For example, the Greiner Government is currently attempting to weaken the New South Wales Aboriginal Land Rights Act. Likewise, the pastoralists, miners, and the Northern Territory government are bitterly protesting rulings of the High Court which could increase the amount of Aboriginal land in the territory from roughly one-third of the total area at present to an area of 45 per cent of the Northern Territory. And in Tasmania, the government still refuses to transfer land for the exclusive use of Aborigines (see Edmunds, 1988; O'Faircheallaigh, 1988).

If Hand's faith in the Australian community's sense of historic justice is vindicated, and his proposal to amend the federal Constitution is accepted, it would undoubtedly enhance the political climate for increased ownership and control of traditional Aboriginal land. On the other hand, if Hand's compact fails, or if the opposition comes to power, any negative change in public opinion toward Aboriginal land rights would have an adverse affect upon existing legislation. In either case, it is almost certain that the issue of Aboriginal land rights will continue to be a contentious one for some time to come.

NOTES

Introduction

1. In 1986, for example, mineral and metal production contributed 8 per cent of Australia's Gross Domestic Product and was directly or indirectly responsible for 450,000 jobs, or about 6 per cent of total employment. In 1987/88, mineral exports constituted more than 40 per cent of total Australian merchandise exports, and the industry paid about $3.8 billion to governments. AMIC estimates that during the past ten years the mineral industry has paid $25 billion in taxes or fees for services to governments in Australia, and provided about 20 per cent of total new investment (AMIC, 1986: 3; and private communication from AMIC, 17 January 1989).
2. The only major exception to this line of argumentation is Tsokhas (1986). He argues that the four major Australian mining companies he examined have not been subordinated by foreign corporations, nor have their joint ventures come under foreign control. The current interest among Australian political scientists is the core-periphery dependency thesis applied to federal-state relationships. See, for example, Head, 1984, 1986; Harman and Head, 1981; and Stevenson, 1976.
3. The only recent change in the emphasis that Australian scholars' have given to pluralist, interest-group politics is a questioning of whether Australia is a liberal democratic, or a corporatist state. For an exchange of views on this issue, see McEachern, 1986; Gerritsen, 1986; Stewart, 1985; Loveday, 1984; and West, 1984.
4. Examples of this literature are Jennett, 1983, 1985; Nettheim, 1986; and Drakakis-Smith, 1983. Peterson (1985: 95) takes a similar, albeit more nuanced, position. He argues that trans-national capital was the major force behind Aboriginal land claims in Australia, Canada and the United States. However, the state, and particular historical circumstances, determined the outcome of the settlements. It is interesting to note that representatives of Aboriginal land councils do not necessarily see the relationship between miners and Aborigines on the issue of land rights in such stark terms. For example, Vachon and Toyne (1983: 324) argue that satisfactory negotiations between Aborigines and corporations on land rights issues depend critically upon having unified Aboriginal support in order to counter the undue influence of mining companies.

Chapter One
FACTIONAL POLITICS AND LAND RIGHTS IDEOLOGY

1. The ALP was founded during the 1890-1891 period in New South Wales. However, during the Party's roughly one-hundred-year history, it has held national power for only brief periods. For example, the ALP was the party in power during 1929-1932, during 1941-1949, and between 1972 and 1975, before coming to office in 1983.
2. Parkin (1983: 18, 20) argues that the ALP is a 'labour party' and not just a Social Democratic Party, insofar as trade unions are directly affiliated with party branches, and provide the preponderance of party revenue.
3. Factions were artificially introduced into Western Australia as a result of a national ALP conference decision in 1984 that all ballots for national positions had to be conducted by proportional representation. Previously, Western Australia was regarded as a left-wing state. The requirements for pragmatic decisions following the election of Brian Burke in 1983 assisted in the assimilation of factions.

    Left-wing unions such as the Amalgamated Metal Workers Union, the Miscellaneous Workers' Union, the Electrical Trades Union, the Building Industry Employees' Union, and about 40 per cent of the party membership made up the left wing, which was the first official faction. The Centre Left was formed after the 1984 national conference. It comprised about 18 per cent of the state executive vote, and is mainly based on politicians and party members, including federal politicians Peter Cook and Peter Walsh. The Third Floor Alliance (named after the office floor representatives occupy in the Labor Centre which houses the state ALP headquarters in Perth) usually supports the Centre Left. It is made up of the Builders Labourers' Federation, the Transport Workers'

Union, the Plasterers and Decorators' Union. The right wing was the last faction to officially proclaim itself in Western Australia. It did so in response to pressure from the national right-wing faction at the 1986 national conference. It consisted of some large unions — the Australian Workers', the Shop Distributors and Allied Industries, Storemen and Packers, Liquor and Allied Trades — and politicians such as Kim Beazley and Brian Burke.

Another small faction was formed in Western Australia near the end of 1985. It was called the Independents and was made up of the Australian Society of Engineers and Moulders, and some left of center but right of the left-wing members of parliament. This faction eventually amalgamated with the Centre Left in 1987 and became known as the Independent Faction. The early Independents were formed mainly to give the present State Secretary, Stephen Smith, a power based from which to be elected, as the replacement for Michael Beahan.

4. The right wing of the ALP is known as Centre Unity in Victoria, and as Labor Unity in New South Wales, Western Australia, and Queensland (where it is divided into two subfactions — the 'old guard' and the 'AWU'). The right wing is also known nationally as Labor Unity.
5. The ideological position of the Victorian Socialist Left has never been clear. The only area in which there is consensus concerns the ALP's original socialist objective of state capitalism, and socialization of the means of production. For a discussion of the party's commitment to socialist ideology see, for example, the minutes of the ALP's 1978 Victorian annual conference, and the federal ALP's 1981 biennial party conference. At the 1978 conference, Senator Gareth Evans' effort to advance a 'reformist' doctrine in opposition to the traditional state capitalist concept was defeated.
6. The Centre Left was formed in 1984 essentially because moderate cabinet ministers saw the need to moderate the ultra-pragmatic influence of the right wing then being brought to bear on Hawke. Several key ministers including Bill Hayden, John Dawkins, Neal Blewett, Peter Walsh, Barry Jones and, later, John Button (Victorian Indpendents), joined the Centre left at this time. Peter Morris also caucussed nationally with the Centre Left.
7. For a discussion of the bitter animosity and conflict between Bob Hawke and the Victorian Socialist Left, see d'Alpuget, 1982: 34, 268, 292, 304, 335, 281-2.
8. For present purposes, Weber's (1930, 1964) conception of ideology as a 'neutral' belief structure in society has been adopted. This connotation of ideology does not question the validity of its basis. Hence no judgment is made of the truth or falsity of the ALP's Aboriginal land rights doctrine. Ideology, like other political resources, can be employed for the general legitimacy of institutions, or to legitimate specific policy objectives. For examples of this conception of ideology applied to international politics and to American politics respectively, see Johnson, 1975; and Edelman, 1977.
9. The principal difference between the bill sponsored by the Whitlam Government and the one adopted by the Fraser Government related to Aboriginal powers of consent to mining in areas where leases were applied for before the legislation was enacted. The Labor bill gave Aboriginals the power to veto the mining of petroleum and uranium on so-called 'Ranger Land', a mining enclave located inside the boundaries of the Kakadu National Park. In contrast, the bill which was passed by the Fraser government empowered the Minister for Aboriginal Affairs to negotiate mining agreements with interested companies if, in his opinion, Aborigines were being unreasonable.

Therefore, under the Liberal-National Country Party government's bill, Aborigines did not have the power to veto petroleum and uranium mining operations. Nevertheless, the companies were still legally obliged to negotiate with the representatives of the traditional Aboriginal owners of the land — i.e. regional land councils set up for that purpose: the Northern Land Council; the Central Land Council; the Tiwi Land Council environmental and financial terms for mining exploration and operations on pre-1977 leaseholds.
10. However, this is not to say that Hand's position was not amenable to compromise. For example, he did not take the more extreme position of Bill Hartley: at the 1982 biennial conference of the ALP in Canberra, Hartley and his deputy, Crawford, proposed an amendment to the party platform which would have granted Aboriginal people absolute ownership rights to minerals on their land. This proposed amendment was defeated, however, on the grounds that it would have required an amendment to the Australian Constitution. In opposing the amendment, the chair of the Aboriginal Affairs Platform Committee, Senator Susan Ryan, argued that the amendment would violate the consti-

tutional principle that mineral rights reside in the Crown. It was a principle to which both Europeans and Aborigines were subject. Ryan successfully argued for staying within the framework of the Woodward principles and granting to Aboriginals title to land that was as secure as possible (see ALP, 1982: 331-4). Hand's position on the land rights issue has been consistent with this rationale. Therefore, much of his political influence on the land rights issue has been directed at securing for Aborigines the most 'secure title' possible for their land. Hand did not challenge the existing constitutional framework for land rights.

11. Campbell stated that the other needs of tribal Aborigines could also be easily met with 'relatively modest amounts of money'. He noted, for example, that modest appropriations could meet their needs for improved health conditions, schooling, transport and communication, as well as coping with alcoholism. The problems of the urban Aboriginal, however, were said to be far more complex. In this regard, Campbell argued that their needs must be seen in socio-economic terms and not in cultural terms. By implication, urban Aborigines (who were more numerous than tribal Aboriginals) no longer had any 'spiritual connection' with the land. He stated that urban Aborigines did not represent the interests of tribal Aborigines. For example, the demands of urban Aboriginals for the use of Aboriginal languages and the acceptance of Aboriginal English as having equal status in schools, was not something that tribal Aborigines wanted. Campbell also asserted that urban Aborigines had a low level of political awareness and, therefore, unlike tribal Aborigines, were politically impotent.

Chapter Two
THE FEDERAL INITIATIVE

1. In September 1983, the following panel of lawyers representing the interested parties, but paid for by the federal government was agreed to: Jeff Sher, Q.C., Joe Lynch, and Heather Sculthorpe (National Aboriginal Conference), Phillip Toyne (Pitjantjatjara Land Council); John Coldrey (Central Land Council and the National Federation of Land Councils); Graham Neate (Department of Aboriginal Affairs), A. R. Castin, Q.C. (Minister's office); and Kim Wilson (Minister's private secretary).
2. This view of the NAC was also expressed by H. C. Coombs in his report to Clyde Holding on 'The Role of the National Aboriginal Conference' in April 1984. The federal Council for the Advancement of Aborigines and Torres Strait Islanders, of which Coombs was a member, expressed a similar view of NAC's predecessor, the National Aboriginal Consultative Committee. It took the position that, with the exception of 'urban activists', Aboriginal people were represented at local or at most regional levels. National Aboriginal organizations such as the federal Council were said to be 'alien' to tribal Aborigines and, therefore, did not represent their interests. For a discussion of the origin and history of the National Aboriginal Consultative Committee and the NAC, see Weaver, 1983, 1983a).
3. There was a strong preference among Aboriginal groups for a treaty of sovereignty comparable with the treaties between American Indians and the federal government in the United States. The reason for this was that Aborigines did not trust the state governments and, therefore, preferred to negotiate directly with the federal government for the return of their tribal land, and for compensation for the dispossession of their land.
4. At the ALP conference the steering committee argued for inalienable title to Aboriginal land. There was, however, a difference of opinion between tribal Aborigines and urban Aborigines over whether or not all of the land to be returned under the proposed land rights act should be held in inalienable title. Urban Aborigines preferred a lesser title to land which would enable them to mortgage the land. However, Ron Castan, Q.C., the Minister's nominated lawyer on the panel of lawyers, suggested, in a legal opinion he submitted to the steering committee, a way around this problem. Castin said that there were essentially four ways they could raise money for economic activities on inalienable Aboriginal land:
    1. Government guaranteed loan;
    2. Debenture secured by a floating charge;
    3. 'Chattel mortgage' or 'lease-back' where the goods of a business represent the security for the loan;
    4. Crop or stock 'liens' where it is the crop being grown or the stock of animals which represents the security.

Notes   159

   Castin concluded that inalienable title is not a barrier to development projects on Aboriginal land. He pointed out, however, that this form of title is still an obstacle for those who may wish to sell outright the land which is returned to them under a land rights act (NAC, 1984d).
5. While the Coombs' report was a damaging blow to the NAC's role of advising the Minister on national Aboriginal land rights legislation, the report in itself did not undermine the NAC's participation on the steering committee. In fact, after Coombs' submitted his report to the Minister in March 1984, the NAC continued to participate actively on the steering committee (albeit under a new national chairman, Rob Riley). Holding continued to seek the NAC's endorsement for his legislative initiatives.
   The Minister insisted upon changes in the NAC's accountability, and called for significant restructuring of the organization. However, unlike the Coombs report, he did not challenge the legitimacy of the NAC or its right to speak for Aboriginal people. Holding only endorsed Coombs scathing attack on the NAC after it openly condemned the Minister and the ALP, and threatened to run a national publicity campaign against the Hawke Government.
6. During August 1984, the Minister, in consultation with the DAA, produced a confidential paper entitled 'National Aboriginal Land Rights Steering Committee Discussion Paper'. The paper included an attachment which contained the major principles of the federal government's 'model' national land rights legislation.

Chapter Three
THE BREAKDOWN IN INITIATIVE

1. The Minister mistakenly attributed the television campaign to AMIC. In fact, the television advertisements, as well as an elaborate political campaign carried out in Western Australia in 1984, was conceived, financed, and implemented by the CMWA (Chamber of Mines of Western Australia). Furthermore, by one account, at least, by the time Holding and Hawke met with representatives of CMWA and AMIC in mid-September, the public advocacy advertisements on television were nearing their scheduled completion (interview with David Fardon, Executive Officer, CMWA, 25 February 1987). In other words, the television advertisements in Western Australia might have ended when they did, whether or not Holding and Hawke had met with industry representatives. Nevertheless, no further advertisements were shown on television after that meeting with the Prime Minister. For a discussion of the campaign and the meetings with the Prime Minister, see Chapters Five and Six.
2. Under South Australia's Pitjantjatjara legislation, disputes between Aboriginal land owners and miners concerning exploration and mining on their land is placed before a superior court judge. The judge must take into account the effect of mining on the way of life and culture of the Pitjantjatjara people, their interests and freedom of access, the suitability of the applicant, as well as the material, environmental, and economic significance of the proposed development to the state and to Australia as a whole. Although this arbitration system was held up by the federal government as a model for national land rights legislation, no dispute has ever been submitted to it for arbitration.
3. In this regard, the report noted the fact that the larger mining companies changed their approach from one of hostility toward the Northern Territory Land Rights Act to one of accommodating to it, and to Aboriginal interests in other states. The willingness of the companies to finance sacred site surveys prior to exploration and mining on Aboriginal land was mentioned as an indication of their changed attitude toward land rights. The document also mentioned the fact that, in land claim hearings, pastoralists have been willing to acknowledge the existence of 'mutually co-operative relations' with Aborigines which have been built up over decades.
4. The referendum was held on 27 May 1967. It proposed the following amendment to the Constitution:

   The first proposed alteration is to remove the words 'other than the Aboriginal race in any State' from paragraph (xxvi) of Section 51. Section 51 (xxvi) reads: The Parliament shall, subject to this Constitution have power to make laws for the peace, order, and good government of the commonwealth [of Australia] with respect to: (xxvi) The people of any race, other than the aboriginal race in any State, for whom it is deemed necessary to make special laws. (Quick and Garran, 1976: 508, 622, 623)

The principal purpose of the referendum was to make it possible for the federal Parliament to make special laws for the people of the Aboriginal race, wherever they lived, if Parliament considered it necessary.

Chapter Four

THE MINING INDUSTRY CAMPAIGN IN WESTERN AUSTRALIA

1. Individual mining companies have, however, previously conducted paid media campaigns. For example, 'The Big Australian' and 'The Quiet Achiever' were designed to tell the general public the importance of mining to the economic welfare of Australia. They also stressed that mining companies were good citizens of Australia. These company publicity campaigns were patterned after AMIC's first national public relations campaign — 'mining is the backbone of the country' — which was conducted in 1982. More recent efforts to influence government policy on mining-related issues have either not involved AMIC, or they were not major campaigns. For example, the gold tax campaign did not have AMIC involvement. The Chamber of Mines of Western Australia contributed to the campaign, but it was only marginally involved. Likewise, the mining industry did not undertake a major public campaign against the fringe benefits tax. AMIC relied upon its more traditional style, lobbying the industry's bureaucratic contacts in government.
2. For a discussion of the origins and circumstances surrounding the formation of AMIC in 1967, see Tsokhas, 1984: 58–86.
3. For an elaboration on the theme of the mineral industry being a scapegoat for proponents of land rights and environmental issues see Morgan, 1984.
4. There are similar examples of the industry's political *naïvete*. For example, under Rex Connor, the government imposed a $6.00-per-ton coal export levy on the companies in 1976 without even consulting them. According to AMIC this was an effort by the government to cream profits 'off the top'. The industry simply acquiesced to the decision (interview with Murray Hohnen, 4 March 1987).

   Another example of the mineral industry's political *naïvete* occurred in 1979, under Malcolm Fraser's Liberal-National Country Coalition Government. In March 1979, AMIC made a public submission to the South Australian House of Assembly Select Committee on the Pitjantatjara Land Rights Bill. In the submission, AMIC made its first attempt to explain to the Australian public how the Northern Territory Land Rights Act (1976), and the proposed South Australian legislation, would adversely affect the community's standard of living.

   Since AMIC's submission was discussed in the South Australian House of Assembly, it became a public document. The document was written in layman's language, and for the first time, was picked-up by the media, and received much favorable comment. The newly appointed Minister for Aboriginal Affairs, Senator Fred Chaney, responded to this media attention by commissioning an independent legal expert, Mr Barry Rowland, Q.C., to review the Northern Territory Act. However, Chaney advised AMIC to suspend any efforts to publicize the issue while the review was under way. AMIC *naïvely* accepted Chaney's suggestion and remained silent on the land rights issue during the following year. In the meantime, the Rowland report came out without endorsing any of AMIC's proposed amendments. Hence AMIC not only failed to influence the Northern Territory Act, but it voluntarily gave up what it later recognized was the only means to that end, public advocacy, without getting anything in return.
5. It is also interesting to note that the official who planned the Western Australian mining industry campaign in 1984, Duncan Bell, was later hired by Western Mining Corporation to work at its corporate headquarters in Melbourne. And the solicitor representing the Chamber of Mines of Western Australia on the state land rights drafting committee which was convened by Premier Burke, J. D. Stewart, was also employed by the Western Mining Corporation.
6. Both the Western Australian and federal governments made similar criticisms of the Seaman inquiry, albeit for different reasons. The inquiry lasted for just over one year, from 9 September 1983 to 17 September 1984, the date the report was handed over to the Western Australian government. However, it was not officially released by the government until ten days later, on 27 September. Since the inquiry was conducted in communities throughout the state, and since it was held in public, a wide range of submissions was made — 233 written and 1,046 oral. The press was frequently in attendance. Its

attention tended to focus upon the more sensational evidence presented. The chairman of the inquiry, Paul Seaman, was also blamed for the controversy surrounding the inquiry. He followed the rules of law during the hearings, but tended to adopt the role of devil's advocate. This encouraged observers to place extreme interpretations upon the line of questioning he pursued at the hearings.

The Western Australian government, in particular, was distressed at the extended length of the hearings, and the growing controversy surrounding the inquiry in the media. Of course, this was precisely what Holding had warned Burke might happen if such an inquiry were held.

7. The same limitation probably would have applied to the recommended Australian National Opinion Polls public relations campaign to improve white Australians' image of Aborigines. In June 1985 there was speculation that three major advertising agencies were invited to submit bids for three alternative campaigns along the lines suggested by the 1984 ANOP report, which was commissioned by the Department of Aboriginal Affairs. The bids were reportedly for campaigns of $0.5 million, $1.0 million and $1.5 million. There were reports that a contract was awarded to one of the agencies. It was never finalized, however, and the federal government never ran a major pro-Aboriginal advertising campaign to counter the Western Australian campaign.

Chapter Five
THE LIBERAL PARTY CHALLENGE TO PREMIER BRIAN BURKE

1. Bill Hassell, the leader of the opposition Liberal Party at the time, disagrees with this interpretation. He tends to discount the role of Brian Burke and the Labor Party, and argues instead that the mining industry campaign, and especially the Liberal Party's campaign, was responsible for the defeat of national land rights (private communication, 28 March 1988).
2. For election purposes, Western Australia is divided into three zones: Metropolitan (including Perth and its suburbs); Agricultural, Mining and Pastoral; North-West Murchison-Eyre. Each zone is allocated a fixed number of electoral districts and electoral provinces. Members of the Legislative Assembly are elected from the districts, whereas members of the Legislative Council (the upper house) are elected from the provinces. In 1983, the districts were allocated by zone in the following way: metropolitan—thirty; agricultural, mining and pastoral—twenty-three; and North-West Murchison-Eyre—four; for a total of fifty-seven. By contrast, the provinces for the Legislative Council zones were allocated as follows: metropolitan—seven; agricultural, mining and pastoral—eight; and North-West Murchison-Eyre—two; for a total of seventeen. Since the bulk of the population is concentrated in the Perth metropolitan area, there is a strong rural-country bias in parliament. This is particularly the case with the Legislative Council, where rural provinces out number metropolitan provinces.
3. For a discussion of Rod Cameron's role as the ALP's chief pollster and campaign adviser, see Mills, 1986: 20-1. Cameron's role, however, has been severely criticized by the majority of the Victorian Socialist Left who blame him for the ALP's abandonment of the party's traditional policy positions. Cameron has advised the Party for years to focus upon the so-called 'selfish swinging voter' who is described as being apolitical and concerned primarily with maintaining their suburban middle-class living standards.
4. In January 1986, during the lead-up to the Western Australian state election, Hassell listed the Liberal Party's four major campaign issues. Aboriginal land rights was placed at the top of the list. He said that 'the public he believes has given the Liberals tremendous credit for their firmness against land rights' (*The Australian*, 13 January 1986).
5. The National Aboriginal Conference was represented on the drafting committee by Western Australian solicitor Philip Vincent. He was temporarily expelled from the committee on the grounds that the NAC had leaked confidential information about committee deliberations to the Melbourne newspaper, *The Age*. The information in question was reported in the 22 November 1984 issue. Informed speculation at the time was that the NAC leaked the information because it was adamantly opposed to Burke's statement of principles. NAC feared that the weakened Western Australian version of land rights legislation (at least compared to the Northern Territory Act and the South Australian legislation), would become the model legislation for other states. In the process, it would exert pressure to weaken existing land rights legislation. Therefore, the NAC's action was calculated to sabotage Burke's land rights legislation. The Premier subsequently re-

instated the NAC's observer status on the committee, and Vincent returned to the meetings in January 1985.
6. Bill Hassell has claimed that the differences between the non-Labor parties over the land rights issue during the campaign were relatively minor. Furthermore, he has argued that the alienation of the industry groups from the Liberal Party did not extend to the rank and file of these organizations, nor did it extend to the general public (private communication from Bill Hassell, 28 March 1988).
7. Nevertheless, Burke had been in parliament for four years when the Woodward Commission brought down its recommendations. In addition, these recommendations were included in the 1978 Western Australian state ALP platform and reconfirmed in 1980 and in 1982 when Brian Burke was the leader of the party. The state's land rights platform was altered in 1984 when Burke was Premier and Minister for Aboriginal Affairs.
8. An example of this was the ground-rules for handling disputes among participants on the committee. In cases where participants could not agree on a section of the draft legislation, the dissenting party or parties would submit to Burke personally a one-page statement outlining their position. The Premier would then act as an arbiter in settling the disputes.
9. The day before cabinet's decision, Burke criticized the federal cabinet for succumbing to factionalism. The Premier endorsed the Prime Minister's call for an end to factionalism, and added that if he had had that difficulty with his cabinet he would have fired 'three ministers'. Within twenty-four hours of Burke's statement, federal cabinet endorsed Holding's preferred model (*The Australian*, 17 August 1985).
10. The Labor Party did not, however, win control of the Legislative Council. With the National party, the Liberal Party retained a majority in the Council by a margin of two (eighteen to sixteen).

Chapter Six

AUSTRALIAN MINING INDUSTRY COUNCIL'S OFFENSIVE AND THE ABORIGINAL COUNTER-OFFENSIVE

1. The $11.8 million expenditure on mining exploration in the Northern Territory during the 1983-84 period was an erroneous figure reported by the ABS (Australian Bureau of Statistics). ABS subsequently revised this figure upward to $24 million. The revised estimate represents a 5 per cent decline in exploration expenditure compared with the previous year. This was consistent with the 5 per cent overall decline in exploration expenditure in Australia during the 1983-84 period. According to ABS, the under-reporting was a result of late returns made by the mining companies concerned. For a discussion of this anomaly see Macklin, 1986: 4002-4, and O'Faircheallaigh, 1988.
2. Strong was referring to a decision by a consortium comprising Broken Hill Proprietary Co. Ltd, Agex (the exploration arm of Australian Gas Light Co.) and Australian Occidental. In July 1984, the consortium announced its decision to withdraw from a $10 million petroleum exploration project in the state's far north. The reason it gave for this decision was that the Pitjantjatjara Aborigines demanded a 'totally unacceptable' $2 million compensation claim for disturbance to their lands. The Pitjantjatjara Council denounced the consortium for 'dishonesty' on the grounds that the council had never set a figure for the compensation to which it was entitled under the Pitjantjatjara Land Rights Act. The council's legal adviser, Phillip Toyne, accused the consortium of deliberately misrepresenting the council's position, and he implied that the companies were using this tactic to discredit the Pitjantjatjara Land Rights Act (*Adelaide Advertiser*, 12 July 1984).
3. AMIC's Aboriginal affairs committee was comprised of the representatives of major mining companies which had substantial interests in Aboriginal land, or in land that was likely to be effected by Aboriginal issues, including land rights legislation. In July 1986 there were eleven members of the committee. The members and the companies they represented were as follows: M. R. Rayner (Chairman), COMALCO; D. J. Barnett, Peko-Wallsend; D. Fardon, Chamber of Mines of Western Australia; R. H. Challen, MIM Holdings, and the Northern Territory Chamber of Mines; P. Crooke, CRA; J. Farthing, Energy Resources of Australia; I. Gunn, BHP; G. Heath, BHP; J. W. Lawler, Queensland Mines; A. McKenzie, CSR; J. A. Reynolds, Western Mining Corporation.
4. AMIC officials met with Minister Holding on 8 October 1985 to explain the industry's advertising campaign. Strong stressed that the industry would take every opportunity to

speak on the issue of access to Aboriginal Land. However, they indicated that AMIC would place its high-profile campaign against national land rights 'on hold' for the time being.
5. Lawler also noted the fact that, until recently, the Northern Territory government directed companies which were seeking exploration and development agreements with the NLC not to offer any form of payment such as royalties, profit-sharing, or equity. The Northern Territory government was opposed to any offers of royalties or equity on the grounds that that would imply ownership of minerals by the Aborigines (Lawler, 1986).

REFERENCES

Aboriginal Land Inquiry (Seaman Report) 1984. Discussion Paper. January.
Adelaide Advertiser, 1 January, 1986.
Adelaide Advertiser, 12 July 1984.
The Age, 1 February 1986.
The Age, 8 November 1985.
The Age, 25 September 1984.
Almond, G. A. and Powell, G. B. 1966. *Comparative Politics: A Developmental Approach*. Little Brown, Boston.
Altman, Jon C., and Nieuwenhuysen, J. 1979. *The Economic Status of Australian Aborigines*. Cambridge University Press, Cambridge.
Transcript from 'A.M.' radio program, 24 January 1985.
Australian Mining Industry Council (AMIC) 1986. 'Submission on Broad Budget Strategy for 1986-1987'. April.
——— 1986a. 'AMIC's Comments on Federal Land Rights Proposals'. 6 March.
——— 1985. Letter from Murray Hohnen, Assistant Director of Australian Mining Industry Council to the Honourable Clyde Holding, Minister for Aboriginal Affairs. 23 December.
——— 1985a. Aboriginal Affairs, Executive Committee Meeting. Recommended Approach. 12 June.
——— 1985b. Comments on the Commonwealth Government 'Preferred National Land Rights Model'. 7 May.
——— 1985c. Notes of Meeting held at Parliament House between Minister Holding, Senator Evans and AMIC. Wednesday 17 April.
——— 1985d. Release of 'Preferred National Land Rights Model'. Media Release MR-2-85/21. 21 February.
——— 1973. Letter from G. Paul Phillips, Executive Director, to the Hon. E. G. Whitlam, Q.C., M.P., dated 8 February. *Aboriginal Land Rights: A Selection of AMIC Submissions and Discussion Papers 1973-84*, Vol. 1 of 2 volumes.
Australian National Opinion Polls (ANOP) Market Research 1985. *Land Rights: Winning Middle Australia—an Attitude and Communications Research Study*. Presented to the Department of Aboriginals Affairs. January.
The Australian, 'Don't Write off Bill Hassell in the West', 13 January 1986.
The Australian, 1 January 1986.
The Australian, 17 August 1985.
The Australian, 1 February 1985.
The Australian, 30 January 1985.
The Australian, 24 January 1985.
Australian Government 1974. *Aboriginal Land Rights Commission*. Second Report (April). Government Publishing Service, Canberra.
Australian Labor Party 1986. Transcript of 37th Biennial National Conference. Hobart, Tasmania. 7 July.
——— 1984. Transcript of 36th Biennial National Conference. Canberra. 9 July.
——— 1984a. 'Australian Labor Party Platform, Constitution and Rules as approved by the 36th National Conference. Canberra.
——— 1983. 'Aboriginal Affairs Policy 1983: Labor's Programme for Self-Determination'.
——— 1982. Transcript of 35th Biennial National Conference. Canberra. July.
Bailey, Stephen K. 1950. *Congress Makes a Law: The Story Behind the Employment Act of 1946*. Columbia University Press, New York.
Bell, D. R. 1984. 'Public Opinion—A Vital Factor'. Unpublished paper presented to a joint Australian Mining Industry Council and the Chamber of Mines of

Western Australia (incorporated) Conference on Aboriginal Land Legislation. 8-9 February.

―――― 1984a. Memo from D. R. Bell to J. E. L. Manners, the Chief Executive Officer of the Chamber of Mines of Western Australia on the subject of Aboriginal Affairs Policy Promotion Programme Meeting with Premier. 30 April.

Bennett, Robert, and Joseph Poprzeczny 1986. 'Jobs for the Boys: Burke's Pillars', in Patrick O'Brien (ed.), *The Burke Ambush*. Apollo Press, Perth.

Bozzoli, Belinda 1981. *The Political Nature of a Ruling Class: Capital and Ideology in South Africa, 1890-1933*. Routledge & Keagan Paul, London.

Bryan, Richard Howard 1984. 'The State and the Internationalisation of Capital in the Australian Mining Industry, 1965 to 1980'. Ph.D. Thesis, Institute of Development Studies, University of Sussex, January.

The Bulletin 1985. 17 December.

The Bulletin 1985a. 10 September.

Burke, Brian 1985. Media Statement of the Premier of Western Australia. 13 August.

―――― 1984. 'Reform in Hard Times: Burden of Dreams'. Unpublished paper originally scheduled to appear in K. Thomson (*et al.*), *Labor Essays*.

―――― 1984. Letter to the President of the Chamber of Mines of Western Australia. 24 September.

Campbell, Graeme 1984. Letter circulated to the ALP Parliamentary Caucus. 28 March.

Canberra Times, 24 January 1985.

Central and Northern Land Councils 1985. Press Release: Central and Northern Land Councils on Refusal to Attend National Steering Committee. 7 February.

Challen, R. H. 1986. Minutes of the Aboriginal Affairs Committee of the Northern Territory Chamber of Mines. 8 September.

Commonwealth Record 1984. 15-21 October.

Coombs, H. C. 1984. *The Role of the National Aboriginal Conference*. Report to the Hon. Clyde Holding, Minister for Aboriginal Affairs (April). Australian Government Publishing Service, Canberra.

Corrighan, Tony 1984. 'The Political Economy of Minerals'. *Bowyang*, No. 2. September.

Cousins, David and John Nieuwenhuysen 1984. *Aboriginals and the Mining Industry*. George Allen & Unwin, Sydney.

Crisp, L. F. 1955. *The Australian Federal Labor Party 1901-1951*. Longmans, Green & Co., London.

Crough, Greg and Ted Wheelwright 1982. *Australia: A Client State*. Penguin Books, Victoria.

Dahl, Robert and Charles Lindblom 1976. *Politics, Economics and Welfare*. University of Chicago Press, Chicago.

D'Alpuget, Blanche 1982. *Robert J. Hawke: A Biography*. Schwartz Penguin Books, Victoria.

Davis, G., J. Wanna, J. Warhurst, and P. Weller 1988. *Public Policy in Australia*. Allen and Unwin, Sydney.

Dodson, Pat 1983. Telex from Pat Dodson. National Co-ordinator, National Federation of Lands Council to Clyde Holding, Minister for Aboriginal Affairs, Canberra. 17 October.

Drakakis-Smith, David 1983. 'Advance Australia Fair: Internal Colonialism in the Antipodes', in David Drakakis-Smith and Stephen Wyn Williams (eds), *Internal Colonialism: Essays Around a Theme*. University of Edinburgh, Edinburgh.

Duncan, Tim 1985. 'The State of the Debate', in Ken Baker (ed.), *The Land Rights Debate: Selected Documents*. Institute of Public Affairs, Sydney.

―――― 1985a. 'Western Mining's Messiahs of the New Right'. *The Bulletin*. 2 July.

Edelman, Murray 1977. *Political Language: Words that Succeed and Policies that Fail*. Academic Press Inc., London.

Edmunds, Mary 1988. 'Challenges for the Treaty'. *Australian Society*. July.
Evans, Gareth 1985. Letter from Senator the Hon. Gareth Evans, Q.C., Minister for Resources and Energy, to Mr B. D. Watson, President, Australian Mining Industry Council. 12 June.
Fitzgerald, T. M. 1974. *The Contribution of the Mineral Industry to Australian Welfare*. Report to the Minister for Minerals and Energy, the Hon. R. F. X. Connor, M.P. Australian Government Publishing Service, Canberra. April.
Gallop, Geoff 1983. 'Labor to Power: The Western Australian State Election 1983'. Discussion Papers in Public Policy No. 3. Murdoch University, Perth.
Gerritsen, Rolf 1986. 'The Necessity of 'Corporatism': The Case of the Hawke Labor Government'. *Politics*, Vol. 21, No. 1 (May).
Giddens, Anthony, and Held, David 1982. *Classes, Power & Conflict: Classical & Contemporary Debates*. University of California Press, Berkeley.
Giddens, Anthony 1977. *States in Social & Political Theory*. Basic Books, New York.
────── 1971. *Capitalism & Modern Social Theory: An Analysis of the Writing of Marx, Durkheim & Max Weber*. Cambridge University Press, Cambridge.
Gramsci, Antonio 1973. *Letter from Prison*. Harper & Row, New York.
────── 1968. *The Modern Prince, and Other Writings*. International Publishers, New York.
Hand, Gerry 1987. 'Foundations for the Future'. Policy Statement. Australian Government Publishing Service, Canberra. December.
────── 1986. 'Land Rights – A Question of Social Justice'. An unpublished paper circulated to the ALP Federal Parliamentary Caucus. 9 February.
────── 1985. 'Aboriginal Land Rights – A Discussion Paper'. An unpublished paper circulated to the ALP Federal Parliamentary Caucus. 12 July.
Harman, Elizabeth J., and Brian W. Head 1981. *State, Capital and Resources in the North and West of Australia*. University of Western Australia Press, Nedlands.
Hartley, P. R. 1984. 'Foreign ownership and the Australian Mining Industry', in L. H. Cook and M. G. Porter (eds), *The Minerals Sector and the Australian Economy*. George Allen & Unwin, Sydney.
Hassell, W. R. B. (Bill) 1986. Letter to Hon. A. C. Holding, M.P. 20 March.
────── 1985. 'Speech in Opposition to the Aboriginal Land Bill 1985'. Parliament of Western Australia, Perth. 26 March.
Head, Brian 1986. *The Politics of Development in Australia*, Allen & Unwin, Sydney.
────── 1984. 'Australian Resource Development and the National Fragmentation Thesis'. *ANZJ*, Vol. 20, No. 3. November.
The High Court of Australia (Darwin) 1985. 'Statement of Claim between Northern Land Council (Plaintiff) and Commonwealth of Australia and Energy Resources of Australia Limited (Defendants)'.
Holding, Clyde 1985. Letter to M. Gamble, Executive Officer of the Northern Territory Chamber of Mines. 4 November.
────── 1985a. Telex message from Clyde Holding, Minister for Aboriginal Affairs, to Rob Riley, Chairman of the National Aboriginal Conference, Pat Dodson, Central Land Council of the Northern Territory and John Ah Kit, National Land Council of the Northern Territory. 11 February.
────── 1984. 'The Racism that Bedevils Society ... The Rights of Indigenous People'. 23 August.
────── 1983. 'Aboriginal Past: Australia's Future'. Speech by the Minister for Aboriginal Affairs, Hon. Clyde Holding, M.P., moving a resolution in the Parliament. 8 December.
Jacks, Harvey 1983. Letter from the Acting Secretary of the Department of Aboriginal Affairs to R. Nichols, Chairman of the National Aboriginal Conference. 23 May.

Jennett, Christine 1985/86. 'The Great Australian Backlash: Growing Opposition to Land Rights'. *National Outlook*, Vol. 7, No. 11.
—————— 1985. 'The Hawke Government and Aboriginal Affairs—Past, Present, Future'. Proceedings of the 27th Annual Conference of the Australasian Political Studies Association, Vol. 1.
—————— 1983. 'Aborigines, Land Rights and Mining', in *Essays in the Political Economy of Australian Capitalism*, Vol. 5. ANZ Press, Sydney.
Johnson, James T. 1975. *Ideology, Reason, and the Limitation of War: Religious and Secular Concepts 1200-1740*. Princeton University Press, Princeton.
Kennedy, Peter 1978. 'Why Labor got only a third of the vote in W.A.'. *The National Times*. 16-21 January.
Kolig, Erich 1988. *The Noonkanbah Story*. University of Otago Press, Dunedin.
Land Rights News. Bureau of the Northern Land Council. Darwin. September 1985.
Lang, A. G., and M. Crommelin, 1979. *Australian Mining and Petroleum Laws*. Butterworths, Sydney.
Lawler, John 1986. Telex to M. Gamble and R. Adams, Northern Territory Chamber of Mines. 7 March.
Liberal Party of Australia 1983. *Policy on Aboriginal Affairs*.
Lindblom, Charles E. 1977. *Politics and Markets*. Basic Books, Inc., New York.
Lloyd, P. J. 1984. 'Introduction to Part 2', in P. J. Lloyd (ed.), *Mineral Economics in Australia*. Allen & Unwin, Sydney.
Loveday, P. 1984. 'Corporatist Trends in Australia?'. *Politics* 19. 1 May.
—————— 1982. *Promoting Industry*. University of Queensland Press, St Lucia.
—————— 1970. 'Pressure Groups', in V. G. Venturini (ed.), *Australia: A Survey*. Wiesbaden, Harrassowitz.
Loveday, P. 1962. 'Group Theory and its Critics', in *Groups in Theory and Practice*. Sydney. Studies in Politics, I.
Lunch, William M. 1987. *The Nationalization of American Politics*. University of California Press, Berkeley.
Macklin, Michael 1986. *Hansard Senate Debates*. 13 June.
Malezer, Les 1983. Letter from the Director of Research of the National Aboriginal Conference to members of the National Aboriginal Conference Subcommittee on Land Rights. September.
Manners, Jack 1985. Telex from J. E. L. Manners, Chief Executive Officer of Chamber of Mines of Western Australia, to J. A. Strong. Subject: Aboriginal Land Rights—National Policy Promotion Programme. 11 June.
—————— 1985a. Letter to W. R. B. (Bill) Hassell, M.L.A. 25 March.
Marketing Centre Research Pty Ltd 1984. *Aboriginal Land Rights Issue: Evaluating the Impact of the Recent Chamber of Mines Advertising Campaign*. May.
Matthews, Trevor 1980. 'Australian Pressure Groups', in Henry Mayer and Helen Nelson (eds), *Australian Politics: a Fifth Reader*. Longman Cheshire, Melbourne.
McEachern, Doug 1986. 'Corporatism and Business: Responses to the Hawke Government'. *Politics*, Vol. 21, No. 1. May.
McGill, Stuart, and Crough, G. J. 1986. *Indigenous Resource Rights and Mining Companies in North America and Australia*. Australian Government Publishing Service, Canberra.
Mills, Charles Wright 1957. *The Power Elite*. Oxford University Press, New York.
Mills, Stephen 1986. *The New Machine Men*. Penguin Books, Victoria, Australia.
Mitchell, Douglas 1983. 'Western Australia: The Struggle to Adapt', in Andrew Parkin and John Warhurst (eds), *Machine Politics in the Australia Labor Party*. George Allen & Unwin, Sydney.
Moore, Norman, M.L.C., 1985. Letter to Mr Colin Pearse, C.B.E., Chairman, Pastoral Division, Pastoralists & Graziers Association. 18 February.

Morgan, Hugh M. 1984. 'Aboriginal Land Rights—A View', in *Minerals Outlook Seminar—1984*. Proceedings published by the Australian Mining Industry Council. May.

National Aboriginal Conference (NAC) and National Federation of Land Councils (NFLC) 1985. Press Release from Joint Meeting. Canberra. 13 February.

National Aboriginal Conference (NAC) 1985a. Meeting of State Chairpersons and Land Councils. Canberra. 12-13 February.

―――― 1985b. Land Rights: Minimum Expectations of National Land Rights Legislation as prepared by the National Aboriginal Conference. February.

―――― 1985c. Letter from Rob Riley, National Chairman, to the Honourable R.J. Hawke, Prime Minister. 29 January.

―――― 1985d. Briefing paper to the National Federation of Land Councils (NFLC) on the National Aboriginal Conference position toward National Aboriginal Land Rights. 25 January.

―――― 1984. Land Rights Sub-Committee Meeting. Canberra. 23-24 July.

―――― 1984a. The Proposed Aboriginal Land Rights Platform for the Australian Labor Party (ALP) for resolution at their national policy conference. Canberra. 9-13 July.

―――― 1984b. 'Report on Developments on National Aboriginal Land Rights and Cultural Heritage Legislation'. April.

―――― 1984c. 'National Aboriginal Land Rights Legislation: Discussion Paper'. February.

National Aboriginal Conference Secretariat (NAC) 1984. Letter from Heather Sculthorpe, Senior Research Officer, to NAC members and State Secretariats. 29 May.

National Party of Western Australia 1983. *Objects and Draft Platform*.

Neate, Graeme 1983. Letter from the Department of Aboriginal Affairs to R. Nichols, Chairman, National Aboriginal Conference, confirming an agreement stemming from a meeting between the Minister and Roy Nichols on 17 June 1983. 28 June.

Nettheim, Garth 1986. 'Justice or Handouts? Aborigines, Law and Policy'. *The Australian Quarterly* 3. Autumn.

Northern Land Council (NLC) 1984. Transcript of meeting of Prime Minister and Northern Land Council. Tuesday 16 October.

Northern Territory News, 7 May 1987.

Northern Territory Land Councils 1986. 'Land Rights: An Act of Justice and Social Reform. 21 February.

―――― 1985. 'An Open Letter to ALP Caucus Members'. 22 March.

―――― 1985a. 'Appeal to the Government of Australia'. 22 February.

O'Brien, Patrick 1986. *The Burke Ambush: Corporatism and Society in Western Australia*. Apollo Press, Nedlands.

O'Faircheallaigh, Ciaran 1988. 'Land Rights and Mineral Exploration: The Northern Territory Experience'. *Australian Quarterly*, Vol. 60. Autumn.

Panel of Lawyers Meeting 1983. Meeting with the National Aboriginal Conference and Aboriginal Land Councils. 23-25 November.

Parkin, Andrew and John Warhurst 1983. *Machine Politics in the Australia Labor Party*, George Allen & Unwin, Sydney.

The Pastoralists and Graziers Association of Western Australia (PGA) 1985. An Open Letter to the Members of the Western Australian Legislative Assembly and Legislative Council—on the Question of the Aboriginal Land Bill—1985. 20 March.

Peterson, Nicolas 1985. 'Capitalism, Culture and Land Rights: Aborigines and the State in the Northern Territory'. *Social Analysis*, No. 18.

Pervan, R., and D. Mitchell 1979. 'The Changing Nature of the Australian Labor Party', in R. Pervan and C. Sharman (eds), *Essays on Western Australian Politics*. University of Western Australia Press, Nedlands.

Preferred National Land Rights Model 1985. Distributed by the Commonwealth Government for Discussion. 20 February.

Quick, John, and Robert Randolph Garran 1976. *The Annotated Constitution of the Australian Commonwealth*. Legal Books, Sydney.

Redford, Emmettee S. 1952. *Administrataion of National Economic Control*. MacMillan, New York.

Redhorse, D., and T. Reynolds Smith 1982. 'American Indian Tribal Taxation of Energy Resources'. *Natural Resources Journal*, Vol. 22. July.

Reece, Bob 1980. 'Two Kinds of Dreaming: Sir Charles Court and the Sacred Goannas of Noonkanbah'. Unpublished paper presented at the Australasian Political Studies Association 22nd Annual Conference, at the Australian National University. 27-29 August.

Riley, Rob, Margaret Mallard, Darryl Kickett 1984. Telex to Hon. A. C. Holding, re: Steering Committee National Land Rights. 26 September.

Ryan, Hiram 1985. Briefing paper entitled 'Government Back Down: Four of the Five Policy Principles'. 29 January.

——— 1984. Report from the Land Rights Section of the National Aboriginal Conference to all NAC members and state secretaries. 17 December.

Scrutton, Stan 1984. Telex sent to the Hon. Clyde Holding on Control over Mining and Exploration on Aboriginal Land. 26 September.

Seven Years On 1983. Report by Mr Justice Toohey to the Minister for Aboriginal Affairs on the Aboriginal Land Rights (Northern Territory) Act 1976 and Related Matters (December). Australian Government Publishing House, Canberra.

Skocpol, Theda 1979. *States and Social Revolutions: A Comparative Analysis of France, Russia, and China*, Cambridge University Press, Cambridge.

South West Development Authority 1983. *Bunbury 2000: Policy Document*. Office of the Premier. December.

Stevenson, Garth 1976. *Mineral Resources and Australian Federalism*. Centre for Research on Federal Financial Relations, Canberra. Research Monograph No. 17.

The Steering Committee on National Land Rights 1984. Minutes of a Joint Meeting of National Aboriginal Conference and Land Councils with the Minister for Aboriginal Affairs, Canberra. 4 October.

——— 1984a. Minutes of Meeting of Aboriginal Steering Committee on National Land Rights, Canberra. 24 August.

——— 1984b. Minutes of Model Land Rights Legislation Discussion, Canberra. 4 April.

The Steering Committee on National Land Rights 1984c. Minutes of Meeting held at Treasury Place, Melbourne. 21 February.

——— 1984d. Minutes of Discussion on National Land Rights Legislation, Melbourne. 20-23 February.

Stewart, Randal G. 1985. 'The Politics of the Accord: Does Corporatism Explain It?'. *Politics* 20, 1.

Stokes, Geoff 1986. 'Mining Corporations and Aboriginal Land Rights in Australia: A Critique and Proposal'. Unpublished paper presented at the Native Peoples Section of the Biennial conference of the Association for Canadian Studies in Australia and New Zealand. Brisbane, 14-16 May. Subsequently published in *Australian Quarterly*, Vol. 59, No. 4. Winter 1987.

Strong, James 1985. 'The Realities of Aboriginal Land Rights and Mining: Government Policies (and the Future of Australian Mining) at the Crossroads'. Unpublished paper presented at the Australian Mining Industry Council Mining Industry Seminar, Canberra. 2 May.

Sydney Morning Herald. 13 February 1986.

Sydney Morning Herald. 'The Hassell Credo of Being Right All the Way, All the Time'. 24 January 1986.

Sydney Morning Herald. 25 January 1985.
Sydney Morning Herald. 25 September 1984.
Thompson, H., M., 'The Pyramid of Power: Transnational Corporations in the Pilbara', in E. L. Wheelwright and Ken Buckley (eds), *Essays in the Political Economy of Australian Capitalism*. Australia and New Zealand Book Company, Sydney.
Tsokhas, Kosmas 1986. *Beyond Dependence: Companies, Labour Processes and Australian Mining*. Oxford University Press, Melbourne.
────── 1984. *A Class Apart?* Oxford University Press, Melbourne.
Vachon, Daniel, and Phillip Toyne 1983. 'Mining and the Challenge of Aboriginal Land Rights', in N. Peterson and M. Langton (eds), *Aborigines, Land and Land Rights*. Australian Institute of Aboriginal Studies, Canberra.
Vincent, Philip 1983. 'Noonkanbah', in N. Peterson and M. Langton (eds), *Aborigines, Land and Land Rights*. Australian Institute of Aboriginal Studies, Canberra.
Vogel, David 1987. 'Political Science and the Study of Corporate Power: A Dissent from the New Conventional Wisdom'. *British Journal of Political Science*, Vol. 17 (October).
Warhrust, J. 1982. *Jobs or Dogma?* University of Queensland Press, St Lucia.
Weaver, Sally M. 1983. 'Australian Aboriginal Policy: Aboriginal Pressure Groups or Government Advisory Bodies? *Oceania*, Vol. 54, No. 2. December.
────── 1983a. 'Australian Aboriginal Policy: Aboriginal Pressure Groups or Government Advisory Bodies? *Oceania*, Vol. 54, No. 1. September.
Weber, Max 1983. *Max Weber on Capitalism, Bureaucracy, and Religion: A Selection of Texts*, Stanislav Andreski (ed.). Allen & Unwin, Boston.
────── 1964. *The Sociology of Religion*. Beacon Press, Boston.
────── 1930. *The Protestant Ethic and the Spirit of Capitalism*. Allen & Unwin, London.
West, Katharine 1984. *The Revolution in Australian Politics*. Ringwood, Penguin.
West, Stewart 1980. 'Aboriginal Affairs: A Guideline to Labor Policies'. June.
West Australian, 14 January 1986.
West Australian. 'Hassell Attacks Fraser Legacy'. 18 November 1985.
West Australian, 15 August 1985.
West Australian, 18 June 1985.
Western Australian, 11 November 1985.
Western Australian Government 1985. *Parliamentary Debates of the Legislative Assembly*. 26 March.
────── 1984. *Parliamentary Debates of the Legislative Assembly*. 28 November.
────── 1984. *The Aboriginal Land Inquiry*. Report by Paul Seaman, Q.C. September.
Western Farmer, 28 March 1985.
Western Mail Weekend, 25-26 January 1986.
Whitlam, Gough 1986. *The Whitlam Government, 1972-1975*. Viking Penguin Books Australia Ltd, Victoria.
Office of Mick Young (Special Minister of State) 1984. Briefing paper on the 1984 federal election campaign entitled 'Aboriginal Land Rights — Current controversies'. Undated.

INDEX

Aboriginal Development Commission, 19; bicentennial program, 28 34; campaign against federal policy, 54

Aboriginal land councils, 22; rivalry, 23-4, 30, 35; veto over federal legislation, 40, 42

Aboriginal land rights, xxiii; U.S. and Canada compared, xxiii; miners versus Aborigines, xxv; national interest, 11-12; working-class backlash, 15-16; tokenism, 16; constitutional framework, 17; uniform national legislation, 19; absence of consensus, 23-6; reparation, 24; Aboriginal ownership of Australia, 28; losses in elections, 48; public opinion, 61; Aboriginal advertising, 80

Aboriginal population, xxiii; compared to U.S. and Canada, xxiii; prior owners, 13; urban/rural dichotomy, 24; privileged people, 49

Aboriginal sacred sites, 30

Aboriginal sovereignty, 28, 146, 158

Aboriginal and Torres Strait Islander Bill, 31, 34, 73

Ah Kit, John, 42; 'unholy rush' for land rights, 139

Australian Mining Industry Council (AMIC), xxi, 38-41, 46, 56-7; silenced by government, 57; defending the industry, 57-8; public relations committee, 57; backbone of the nation campaign, 57-8; importance of TV, 58; Morgan's leadership, 58-60, 62, 76, 81, 101, 109; campaign against land rights, 115-38; government reneging, 115; meetings with Hawke and Holding, 116; reaction to preferred model, 116-29; survey of N.T. companies, 118; W.A. approach, 119-20; federal versus W.A. approaches, 120; tribunal unworkable, 120; meetings with P.M., 120-1; Aboriginal veto power, 121-2; tribunal in preferred model, 122; de facto veto, 122, 126; compensation for access, 123; commercial legal power game 124; Aboriginal affairs strategy, 124; consultations with P.M., 126-9; decline in exploration, 127-8; Aborigines anti-mining, 128; Aboriginal affairs strategy, 129-32; Aboriginal and Democrats' opposition, 130; countervailing reaction to campaign, 130; arguments for and against advertising, 131; equal rights slogan, 132; states rights campaign, 132; federal concessions, 132-3; campaign against land rights, 133-5; W.A. campaign as AMIC model, 134; funds for national campaign, 134; anti-land rights campaign, 134-9; Hawke-Burke compromise and AMIC, 135; impact on federal government, 135; retention of N.T. veto, 146; public relations campaign, 160; origins of AMIC, 160; political naïvete, 160; membership of Aboriginal affairs committee, 162

Anti-land rights mining campaign, 28, 33, 39; newspaper and TV ads, 70-80; 'wall' TV ad, 80; success of campaign, 69-84; impact on Burke Government 69-73; policy promotion program 134-8

Arnhem Land, 42

Association of Mining and Exploration Companies (AMEC), 101, 109

Australian client state, xx

Australian Council of Trade Unions (ACTU), 6, 142

Australian Democrats, 73, 130

Australian Labor Party (ALP). 1, factionalism, xxii-xxiii, 1-8, 33; Anti-Hawke faction 6; relationship to trade unions, 1; Western Australia, 2-4; Victoria, 4-7; Aboriginal platform, 2, 7, 11-15, 32, 72, 86, 100, 103, 139; Aboriginal doctrine, 9; 1984 national conference, 12, 29, 32-4; parliamentary caucus, 12, 14-15, 87, 105, 152; 1986 national conference, 16, 86, 111; betrayal of Aborigines, 22; left wing, 37, 50, 86, 100; federal caucus, 37, 50; 1984 federal election campaign, 41; land rights as election liability, 47; factional compromise, 86; preferred model, 97; support for N.T. Act, 98; factionalism in federal government, 110-11; W.A.-federal compromise agreement, 114; Aboriginal protest to caucus, 139; three mines policy, 141; caucus division over land rights, 143; right wing, 143; stages of faction politics, 149-53; party consensus, 150-1; factional conflict, 151-2; W.A.-federal stalement, 151; party compromise, 152-3; factional 'bloodbath', 152; cross-factional movement, 153; history, 156; Australian Labor Party Committee on Aboriginal Affairs, 52-3; boycott. 139, 143; Hawke's campaign statement, 143-4; opposition to government policy, 144-5; pressure on cabinet, 145; coordination with land councils, 145; revolt against Hawke-Burke compromise, 152

Australian National Opinion Polls

(ANOP), 46, 84, 90, 161
Australian Petroleum Exploration Association (APEA), 101, 109
Ayers Rock, 16

Batchelor, Peter, 4
Beahan, Michael, 3, 114, 157
Beazley, Kim, 17-18, 37, 50, 110, 157
Bell, Duncan, 62-6, 69, 83, 134, 160
Bjelke-Petersen, Sir Joh, 16, 18
Bowen, Lionel, 50
Bryan, Richard, xx
Bryce, Mal, 2
Bunbury 2000 Development Strategy, 88-9
Burke, Brian, 1, 6-7, 14, 17-18, 27, 35, 37, 39-40, 43, 49, 50, 92, 96, 97, 99-100, 101; pragmatic leadership, 2-4; consensus building strategy, 4, 109; conflict with federal government, 50, 52, 55, 62, 67, 69, 72-5; wall ad, 76; elements of land rights proposal, 76-7; impact of mining campaign, 80-5; election strategy, 85-6; leadership style, 87-90; principles for land rights, 101; land rights drafting committee, 101, 103, 107-9; threat to resign, 103, 105, 113; response to Liberal campaign, 105-10; background in politics, 105; 1982 speech to Ngaanatjarra Aborigines, 105; 1983 campaign, 105-6; lack of understanding land rights, 106-7; land rights drafting committee, 107-9; defusion of land rights as an election issue, 107; isolating the political opposition, 108-9; miners concession to Burke, 108; support for the miners' position, 108-9; assurances against federal intervention, 109; Burke-Hawke campaign strategy, 110; Liberal Party pressure, 111-12; dispute with Holding, 112; reaction to cabinet adoption of preferred model, 113; altering federal Aboriginal ALP platform, 113; federal compromise, 114, 150; 1986 election victory, 152, 157; W.A. land rights platform, 162; criticism of federal cabinet, 162
Burke, Tom, 3

Cain, John, 4 5
Cameron, Max, 102
Cameron, Rod, 90; criticism from left wing of ALP, 161
Campbell, Graeme, 12, 15 16; one issue zealots, 15, 158
Catholic church, 142
Central Land Council (CLC), 12, 19, 24, 32, 36, 53, 139
Centre Left faction of ALP, 6 7, 33, 110, 143, 151, 157
Centre Unity faction of ALP, 7
Centre Unity faction of Victoria, 4, 6
Chamberlain, Joe, 3

Chamber of Mines of Western Australia (CMWA), 38, 59, 61-2, 65, 101-2, 109, 150, 159; 'terror campaign', 41; September 1984 poll, 66; equality in land rights, 66; public support, 72-6; opinion polls, 74-6; 12-point land rights proposal, 76, 79; land rights campaign, 77, 80-2; claims for success of campaign, 83-4, 86; equal rights slogan, 92-3; timing of national campaign 131
Chaney, Senator Fred, 73, 98, 109, 160
Collins, Les, 27
'Conservative States', 11
Connor, R. F. X., 56
Constitutional Referendum of 1967, 49, 159-60
Contribution of study, 147-9, 153; approach adopted, xxii, 149
Cook, Peter 156
Coombs Report, 33, 142, 158-9
Coopers & Lybrand, 57
Corporate power, xx-xxi
Corrighan, Tony, xix-xx
Court, Sir Charles, xxv, 3, 87, 96, 98-9
Crawford, George, 4, 157
Crisp, L. F., 1
Crough, Greg, xix-xx
Crown land. xxiii, xxvii, 2, 24, 81, 103, 108-9, 113, 121, 158; federal compensation, 18, 64-7, 75; crown lease 76
Cultural heritage legislation, 30-2, 38
Cruse, Ossie, 33

De facto veto, xxv; Aboriginal bargaining power, xxv
Dahl, Robert, xx
Davies, Ron, 2
Dawkins, John, 7, 37, 50
Denison Australia Pty Limited, 42
Department of Aboriginal Affairs (DAA), 9, 19, 23, 26, 34, 46, 53, 101
Dependency theory, xix-xx; applied to Aboriginal land rights, xx, xxv, xxvii; dominance of mining industry, xxvii, 147 8; core-periphery thesis, 156
Dodson, Pat, 19, 23, 41, 140, 145; criticism of NAC, 23, 27, 32
Drakakis-Smith, David, xx, 156
Duncan, Tim, 5, 59, 61

Elections, 30; federal, 42, 46 7; 1983 federal elections, 87; 1984 federal elections, 46, 48, 80; Aboriginal electorates, 47; 1986 W.A. state elections, 135
Evans, Senator Gareth, 5, 31, 37, 50, 86, 110, 115; Amendments to the N.T. Act, 117, 124 5; accommodating the miners, 125 6; diluting the N.T. Act, 125; precondition for amending the N.T. Act, 125; government deviation from ALP platform, 126; preferred model, 128 129, 133, 135; letter to Watson,

Index

132-3; no de facto veto, 133, compensation based on damage to land, 133; lands rights compromise, 145-6; consultations with AMIC, 151, 157
Everingham, Paul, 39, 45

Fardon, David, 83, 159
Federal ministerial committee on land rights, 50; membership, 50, 53, 112
Federation of Aboriginal land councils, 21, 26, 49, 52-3; challenge to the NAC, 23-4
Fitzgerald, Tom, 56-7
Fraser, Malcolm, 9, 11, 87, 98
Freehold title to land, xxiii

Gallop, Geoff, 3, 87, 89, 90
Galligan, Brian, xx
Gayley, John, 143-4
Grill, Julian, 105

Hand, Gerry, 1, 4-7, 12-14, 18, 37, 50; attack on Burke, 50, 86; coordinating lobbying with CLC, 140-2; decline in mining exploration in the N.T., 141; disputing AMIC's claims, 141, 143; opposition to state land rights legislation, 143, 157; constitutional principle, 158
Hartley, Bill, 4-5, 157
Hassell, Bill, 96-7; 'purist' leadership, 97-103; criticism of Burke, 103-4; criticism of Hawke and ALP left wing, 104; constitutionality of federal intervention, 104-5; criticism of Burke in parliament, 106-7; Burke 'cover-up', 107, 110-13; Hawke-Burke 'secret deal', 113, 161-162
Hawke, Bob, 2, 4-7, 14, 39, 50, 75-6, 80, 112-13, 148, 151; double-cross, 14, 36-7, 148; Hawke's law, 37-8; impact of CMWA campaign, 80-4, 86-7, 99; 1984 unilateral campaign statement, 109; 1986 campaign statement not to override W.A., 109-10, 112-13; compromise with W.A., 114; cross-factional opposition, 115; 1987 federal elections, 116; 1988 bicentennial celebrations, 116; promise to review N.T. Act in 1989, 116-17; assurances against de facto veto, 122, 126, 129, 133; pro-mining sentiment, 128-9; removal of mining veto, 139; cross-factional revolt, 143; land rights compromise, 145; consultations with AMIC, 151; avoiding factional 'bloodbath', 152
Hohnen, Murray, 55, 61, 160
Holding, Clyde, xxv, 5; United Nations speech, 13; five principles for land rights, 13, 17-18, 19, 21, 32-3, 35, 109-11, 130, 144, 158; initial strategy, 19-20; steering committee, 19-23, 26, 28-32, 36-7, 39, 40-1; panel of lawyers, 19-22, 30, 158; pressure from Hawke, 22; reversal of position, 22; subversion of Aboriginal consultation, 26-8; scenario for land rights policy, 26-7; claiming private land, 27-8; ministerial status, 51-2; Aboriginal demands, 53; end of land rights initiative, 53-4, 72-3, 76, 80-1, 95, 99, 102; preferred model, 103, 112, 114, 116, 124-6; opposition to Hawke-Burke position, 110; concern about AMIC campaign, 134; amending N.T. Act, 135, 140, 143; Aboriginal boycott of steering committee, 139; cabinet strategy, 144-5; political success, 144

Idea-based interest groups, xxi; U.S. and Australia, xxi
Ideology defined, 157
Indigenous population, xxiii
Interest group theory, xx-xxi; insider status, 148-9

Jennett, Christine, xx, 60, 156

Kakadu National Park, 42
Keating, Paul, 6, 37, 110
Keon-Cohen, Bryan, 23
Kerin, John, 50
Kickett, Daryl, 36
Kimberley Land Council, 19
Koogarra uranium project, 42

Labour Unity faction of ALP, 6
Land rights ideology, 8-18; symbolic unification function, 8; instrumental function, 9; ideological consensus, 9-12; ideological conflict, 12-16; moral responsibility, 12-15; socialist doctrine, 15-16; return to consensus, 17-18
Lands rights policy, xxii; political context, xxii; mining industry position, xxv; Aboriginal position, xxv; tokenism, 16; welfare approach, 32; secure title versus inalienable title, 33, 42; mining veto rights, 38-9; Aborigines as an interest group, 40; removal of veto, 41-2; Aboriginal support for government policy, 49, 51-4; Aborigines' minimum expectations, 52; Aboriginal campaign against government legislation, 53; W.A.-federal compromise, 111, 135; pro-land rights advertising, 130; Aboriginal delay of legislation, 130
Lawler, John, 142, 163
Left wing of the ALP, 110, 143
Liberal-National Country Party, 3, 11; Western Australia, 87; federal, 98
Liberal-National Party government, 9
Liberal Party, xxi, 3; federal, 33, 73; W.A. Liberal Party, 84; refusal to participate on land rights committee, 101,

109; federalism policy, 73
Lindblom, Charles, xx, 149
Lunch, William, xxi

Mallard, Margaret, 36
Malley, Stephen, 102
Manners, Jack, 83, 102
Mansell, Michael, 27-8
Marketing Centre Research Pty Ltd, 65
McDonald, Graham, 72, 101
McMullan, Bob, 3, 95, 114
Mills, Charles Wright, xx
Mining industry, political influence on land rights, 7-8; Aboriginal access to royalties, 26, 33, 89; Roxby Downs and Argyle diamond project, 31, 50; Aboriginal consent, 35, 38, 43; Aboriginal negotiating power, 45; veto versus control, 48; awakening to political problems, 55; threat of land rights, 56; land 'locked away', 56; trendy debate, 56; new style of public advocacy, 56-60; government criticism, 57; tax concessions, 57; importance of public opinion, 58, 63; religious basis of mining, 59; Western Australian campaign, 60-84; rationale for the W.A. campaign, 62-4; importance of consensus, 63; image problem, 63-4; strategy of W.A. campaign, 64-6; survey research, 65, 82-4; policy promotion program, 67-9; Aboriginal veto, 81, 120; importance to the economy, 117, 156; exploration applications, 142
Moore, Norman, 98, 100
Morgan, Hugh, 38, 56-9, 160; leadership of AMIC, 59-60; anti-land rights ideology, 59-60; Manichean doctrine, 60; criticism of Holding, 125
Munns, Neville, 102

National Aboriginal Conference (NAC), 52, 80, 101, 108, 158-9; origins, 9, 19-20; black parliament, 21; veto power, 21; sixth principle 21-4, 26-7, 32; position on land rights legislation, 29; land rights sub-committee, 29, 33-4; general principles of land rights, 29-32; opposition to ALP platform, 32; veto over land rights legislation, 40, 43, 48; federal 'sell out', 51; sabotaging W.A. legislation, 161
National Aboriginal and Islander Legal Services, 19
National Federation of Aboriginal Land Councils, 19
National Farmers Federation (NFF), xxi, 39-41, 46, 48
National Party, 39
Neate, Graham, 53, 101, 158
Nettheim, Garth, xx, 60, 156
Noonkanbah, xxv, 46

Northern Land Council (NLC), 11, 19, 21, 23, 53; pro-uranium mining, 24; rejection of exploration licences, 128
Northen Queensland Land Council, 19
Northern Territory, 10-11, 16, 20, 24, 27-8, 32, 36, 42, 45-6; mining exploration, 45; exploration licences, 45, 66, 108
Northern Territory Chamber of Mines, 142
Northern Territory Government, 20, 45, 118
Northern Territory land councils, 22, 45, 54, 87; amendment of N.T. Act, 116-17; veto provisions, 133, 139; videos of Aboriginal consultations, 140; protest at Parliament House, 140; restoration of the mining veto, 140; support groups, 142; successful campaign, 144
Northern Territory Land Rights Act (1976), 8, 11, 14, 16, 19, 32, 36, 38-9, 46, 48-9, 51-4, 56, 65-7, 69, 72, 86, 98-100; review of the Act, 20; removing the mining veto, 39, 41-2, 151; model for Western Australia, 106; W.A.-federal compromise, 114; removal of veto, 115; amendment, 115-16, 135; EL 'log jam', 116-17; AMIC's criticism, 117-24; paralysis of exploration and mining, 118; decline in exploration, 118-19, 128; veto power, 121-2, 127; counter-offensive against N.T. amendments, 139-46
Northern Territory Land Rights Bill (1975), 10-11, 56

O'Connor, Ray, 87, 96-8
Ownership of minerals, xxiii

Parbo, Sir Arvi, 58-9
Parkinson, C. Northcote, 63
Parry, Keith, 58-9, 63, 81
Pastoralists and Graziers Association (PGA), 86, 100-2; conflict with Liberal Party, 102
Peacock, Andrew, 33, 109
Pearce, Bob, 108, 110
Perkins, Charles, 19
Peterson, Nicolas, 156
Phillips, G. Paul, 57, 59
Pitjantjatjara Land Rights Act of 1981, 36, 41; AMIC's criticism, 119, 159
Pressure Groups, xxi
Primary Industry Association (PIA), 100-2, 109

Queensland, 20, 49
Queensland Mines Ltd, 142

Robinson, Ray, 28
Ray, Robert, 5

Richardson, Graham, 6
Right wing of ALP, 157
Riley, Rob, 36, 52, 159
Rowland, Barry, 160
Ryan, Susan, 7, 37, 110, 157

Sacred Aboriginal land, xxv
Scrutton, Stan, 36
Sculthorpe, Heather, 32
Seaman Inquiry, 20, 27, 34-5, 40, 56, 64, 69, 72-3, 75, 77, 80, 95, 99, 101, 106, 108; confrontation, 64-7; threat to miners, 150; nature of, 160-1
Snowdon, Warren, 140
Socialist Left (SL) of Victorian ALP, 1-2, 4-6, 12, 37, 86, 140, 151, 157
South Australia, 20; Maralinga Bill, 20; land rights arbitration system, 41
South Australian land rights legislation, 36
State land rights legislation, 44
States' rights, 13, 17, 62; W.A. versus federal government, 86, 92, 100, 103-5; constitutional basis of federal intervention, 104; Burke's position, 113, 131
Stephens, Tom, 106
Stokes, Geoff, 60
Strong, James, 38, 59, 117; objection to preferred model, 117-24; unworkability of N.T. Act, 117, 125; W.A. model for federal legislation, 125; electoral backlash, 126, 162

Tasmanian Government, 31
Thomas, Bill, 16
Thompson, H. M., xix-xx
Title to minerals, xxiii
Tiwi Land Couincil, 139
Toohey Report, 20, 32; pastoral leases, 32; excisions of pastoral properties, 33, 48
Toyne, Philip, 162
Traditional owners (T.O's), 10-11, 16, 42, 117-18, 135
Tsokhas, Kosmas, 156, 160

Uranerz Australia Pty Ltd, 142

Vincent, Philip, 161
Victoria Aboriginal land rights bill, 19, 27
Victoria ALP, 4-7; factions, 7, 14
Victoria Centre Unity or 'right wing' of ALP, 5

Victoria Socialist Left of ALP—see Socialist Left (SL)
Viner, Ian, 98
Vogel, David, 153

Walsh, Peter, 36-7, 50, 59, 110, 156
Watson, Sir Bruce, 126, 132; letter to P.M., 127
Western Australian ALP, 2-4, 6, 14, 39, 72, 87, 89; pressure on Holding, 23; 1983 election, 89, 96; opinion surveys, 90-6; marginal electorates, 92-6; land rights platform, 99-100, 105; removal of veto from platform, 106; factions, 156-7
Western Australia Government, 48, 52, 73
Western Australia land rights legislation, 72, 74, 81-2, 85; defeat, 93, 101-3; parliamentary debate, 110, 115
Western Australia, 3; public opposition to land rights, 18, 38; TV ads, 40, 45, 50, 61, 66, 71, 77; mining campaign, 59; 'mortgage belt', 90; federal-state rivalry, 91; 1986 state elections, 97, 102; importance of mining, 105-6; electoral zones, 161
Western Australia Liberal Party, 80, 85, 91, 95-6, 151; opposition to Burke, 96-105; anti-land rights campaign, 97, 99-105; position on land rights, 97-8; argument against land rights, 99; loss of support, 101; alienation of political constituents, 101-3, 106, 109; federal factionalism, 111; federal stalemate, 111-13; 1986 election campaign, 112-13; opinion survey, 113
Western Australia Liberal-coalition parties, 100
Western Australia National Party, 98; dispute with Liberal Party, 102
Western Mining Corporation (WMC), 38, 56; political leadership, 58-60; activism, 59, 160
Wheelwright, Ted, xix
Whitlam, Gough, 9-10, 55-6; conflict with miners, 56-7
Wilson, Keith, 106
Woodward Commission, 10, 32, 64, 99, 106
Woodward Report, 10-13, 20

Young, Mick, 42-3

www.ingramcontent.com/pod-product-compliance
Lightning Source LLC
Chambersburg PA
CBHW031551300426
44111CB00006BA/265